# Great Storms
## *of the Jersey Shore*

Larry Savadove
Margaret Thomas Buchholz

*Foreword by Senator Bill Bradley*

*Book design by Ray Fisk*
*Marion Figley, editor*
*Archival picture research by Ray Fisk and Margaret Thomas Buchholz.*

DOWN THE SHORE / **S**and**P**aper
PUBLISHING

*For information, address:*
Down The Shore Publishing, Box 3100, Harvey Cedars, NJ 08008
Down The Shore and The SandPaper, and the respective logos, are registered U.S. Trademarks.
*Production by The SandPaper, Inc., Surf City, NJ*
*Printed in Hong Kong.*
10 9 8 7 6 5 4 3 2

**Library of Congress Cataloging-in-Publication Data**
Savadove, Larry, 1941-
   Great storms of the Jersey shore / by Larry Savadove and Margaret
Thomas Buchholz ; foreword by Bill Bradley.
      p.     cm. — (A Cormorant book)
   Includes bibliographical references and index.
   ISBN 0-945582-14-5 : $42.00
   1. Storms — Atlantic Coast (N.J.) — History.   2. Hurricanes —
Atlantic Coast (N.J.) — History.   I. Buchholz, Margaret Thomas,
date-  .  II. Title.   III. Series.
QC943.5.U6S26  1993
551.55′09749—dc20                       92-41477
                                  CIP

**Front cover photograph:** Harvey Cedars, during the Great Atlantic Storm of 1962, by Dorothy Oldham.
**Back cover photograph:** The Hallowe'en storm, October 30, 1991, as seen from a NOAA weather satellite.
**Endpapers photograph:** Beach Haven boardwalk during a storm, circa 1925, courtesy Joan K. Simonin.

THE RECENT TERRIBLE STORM ON THE NEW JERSEY COAST.—SCENE NEAR HIGHLAND STATION, ON THE NEW JERSEY SOUTHERN RAILROAD.—GIGANTIC WAVES SWEEPING ACROSS THE PENINSULA.

# Tables, Charts & Maps

# Contents

Beach Haven, after the 1944 hurricane.

# Foreword

JUST BEFORE THIS BOOK went to press, New Jerseyans were reminded once again that we are only visitors on this earth. Suddenly, with little warning, a vicious storm strikes. Boardwalks become so much firewood; beaches evaporate; roofs and docks disappear. Anyone who has since visited the shore cannot help but be awed by the great power of nature.

The 127 miles where New Jersey dips into the Atlantic Ocean are at once the glory of our state and its responsibility. The shore's beauty and variety draw vacationers from the whole northeast region of the country and even the midwest. It contributes greatly to our economy, our recreation, and our sense of place in nature.

It is a result of the last ice age, which retreated some 10,000 years ago, but its present shape is due as much to the storms and, of course, the people who have visited since. It is a vulnerable, malleable, changeable 127 miles, and we must be aware of what can influence it, and how and what we can and cannot do about it.

Nothing demonstrates the shore's vulnerability more than storms — not only the great hurricanes that occasionally rip up the coast, but also the more frequent northeasters, the offshore squalls that pump up the waves or turn currents skidding now one way, now the other, the flooding tides. These are forces of nature that are to be not conquered, but understood.

Storms give us a respect for nature, and joy in it. As W. S. Gilbert wrote, "There is beauty in the bellow of the blast." But there is something beyond science and poetry. Their appeal is visceral, at once exhilarating and humbling.

We must also learn from storms. Until the December 1992 storm, most of those who come to the Jersey shore had never known a major storm. While our eyes may now be open, what we all need is the content, the benefit, of a larger perspective.

This book tells the stories of storms and of those who stood in their paths. It is evocative and provocative, gritty, beautiful, a rare historical record of some of nature's greatest moments, and a thoughtful look at what we have done and are doing to New Jersey's most precious resource.

Read it for the grandeur, the fun and, not least, the lesson.

*Senator Bill Bradley*
*Washington, D.C.*
*January 1993*

**Aerial view of the southern end of Harvey Cedars, March 8, 1962: A section of Long Beach Island is washed away by the Great Atlantic Storm.**

# *Preface*

THE JERSEY SHORE forms a neat dividing line between three thousand miles of land to the west and three thousand miles of sea to the east. It also lies almost halfway between the equator and the North Pole.

Being in the middle of such great influences on the weather, it is subject to a great many of its varieties, particularly out on the barrier beaches that make up most of the shoreline. Some of these islands are more like ships at sea than pieces of land. Standing on the beach, one can watch gales sweep across the horizon like grey brooms tidying up the wilderness. Clouds tumble through the open sky like puppies at play, or march in serried ranks like an army on parade, or spread darkly over the face of the sea carrying other oceans in their bellies. Waves rush in from distant and unimaginable sources to fizz out quietly at our feet, or rise frighteningly above our heads. Winds are redolent with the mystery of the sea, or fill the sky with the flavor of pines.

It is the heavyweight acts of nature that get the most attention, the hurricanes and northeasters with their imperious winds and punishing rains, their overreaching tides and biblical floods. These are massive forces that bend us to their will and break us on a whim. We respect them even when we try to outface them, and only the very stupid or the very wise ignore them.

But in the play and clash and flow of elements, other performers strut and bellow, too, shake their sequins and dance upon the beach. Thunderstorms rip across the sky in zigs and jags and make the air opaque with their tumult. Waterspouts wriggle like liquid snakes to pipes only they can hear, and occasionally their terrible cousins, the tornadoes, drop out of the sky in giant rants of ruin. Pellets of cold heaven fall as hail in the midst of summer swelters. And in winter there is the fairy tale sight of snowflakes settling on the muffled waves, sifting silently through the dune grasses, blurring all boundaries between land, sea and sky.

To be at the Jersey shore during the hurricane of 1944 or the northeaster of 1962 was to be witness to forces that boggle the mind, bend the imagination and beggar description, the kind that had our ancestors huddled in the backs of caves and continue to instill in us an awe approaching reverence. Only a few people get to experience the great storms and they tend to remember every detail of every moment. And while most hope they never have to go through one again, only a few wish they'd missed it in the first place.

In this book we have collected memories and images of the great storms of the Jersey shore. We drew on newspaper accounts taken from the front lines by reporters who struggled to convey the spectacle on the backs of ordinary adjectives. We mined official records of the United States Weather Service, the Coast Guard, the New Jersey State Police, and Civil Defense and other emergency agencies. We searched library files up and down the coast. We investigated the history of storms, their causes as well as their effects.

But it is the personal stories of people caught up in the outbursts of the elements that bring us close to the events, and we are indebted to all those who opened up their memories and their scrapbooks. Far more people answered our call than we expected, as if they had only been waiting for somebody to ask them, and we sifted and culled their stories to present what we hope is a coherent document, as moving for readers as it was for survivors.

Inevitably we had to leave out some stories, not because they were any less pointed or poignant than those we included but simply because we had to limit the size of the book. We tried to pick those individual accounts that best illuminate the whole. An encounter with one of these storms is an intensely personal affair, no matter how many other people are foundering together in the boat or taking refuge in the firehouse. Together, though, the experiences fuse into the realization that we share our place in nature's world and depend on one another to maintain it, and so our thanks to all who helped us make this book.

*Larry Savadove and Margaret Thomas Buchholz*
*Long Beach Island, New Jersey*
*January 1993*

9

# Acknowledgements

THE IDEA FOR A BOOK about storms along the Jersey shore came about at different times and in different ways to the people involved in this project. One inspiration for the book occurred about 1977, after a long-time resident of Ship Bottom dropped off a scrapbook at the *Beachcomber* office. Glued into the small, black, three-ring binder were yellowed newspaper clippings about storms from 1918 to 1939. Unfortunately, the donor was anonymous.

This project, with its scope and complexity, was possible only with the help, cooperation and enthusiasm of a great number of people, and the authors would like to express their deep appreciation for everyone's effort and generosity. Special thanks must go to David Ludlum and William E. Minsinger, M.D. for their encouragement and help early in this project; to Phyllis Gee, Dana Roberts and Yvonne Bleecker at the Long Beach Island branch of the Ocean County Library for their friendly patience with all requests; and to Philadelphia research assistants Barbara and Ed Johnson.

This book is based on extensive interviews up and down the coast, and we are, above all, grateful to those who answered the many questions we put to them and gave graciously of their time and memories, both those quoted in the text and the following:

Scott Abbott, Jean Alven, Carl Berger, Phyllis Berkheiser, Rebecca Blitz, Patty Bloom, Sophie and Adolphe Berdick, Phyllis Bur, Sally Calhoun, Wendy Clarke, Evelyn Colvin, Anna Cox, Cathy Cranmer, Marion Cranmer, Walter Curran, George Damminger, Ed Davis, Marguerite Decker, Dottie DiPietro, Mary Dodd, Richard Doremus, Robert Engle, Patty and David Foster, Edith Fritsch, Harold Gale, Linda Gargiulo, Jane Gates, Richard Gibbons, John Gideons, Mrs. Richard Gove, Joan Grant, Ed Grubb, Tess Harnick, Margaret Hawke, Barbara Heck, Marge Hendrickson, Dolores Hibbert, Arnold Hill, Jane and Joe Inman, Rudy Kirchgassner, Geraldine and Ernie Koschineg, Ron Kreh, Hilda Kugler, Mrs. J. Spicer Leaming, Anna Leadham, Jim Lindemuth, Dave Linglebach, Ethlyn Luby, Robert Lupp, Gay Marvin, Glenn McBeth, Roger McDonough, Claire McHale, Mary and Adele Meehan, George H. Moss, Elizabeth Neale, Nancy Nixon, Barbara Oler, Joan O'Neill, Nancy Osterhaut, Betty Panunto, Lois Pittas, Betty Rathblatt, Howard W. Reeve, Eleanor Reiger, Ed Richards, Leon Rider, Tom Rider, Dan Rodman, Marion Rossell, John Scott, Paula Scully, Mary Shockley, Gloria Shannon, Eleanor Smith, Penny Skier, Althea Sorenson, Anna Mae Sprague, Chris Swensen, Georgia Volpin, Jean Wallace, Lillian Walters, Robin Weber, Larry Weerheim and Ruth Yearly.

Access to documents and information otherwise unavilable was made possible by the following persons and institutions:

Carolyn Miller at the American Red Cross, Washington, D.C.; Joanne Sencindiver, Gini Molino, Lois Connor, Alice Messler, Rita Penrod Ebrecht, and Marge Potosnak at the Long Beach Island Historical Association Museum; Mike Cohen at the Longport Historical Society; Richard Leavitt at the March of Dimes Birth Defects Foundation, Washington, D.C.; Carmen Miguel at McCall's magazine; Bethany Theilman at the National Oceanic and Atmospheric Administration, Rockville, Maryland; Ray Smith at the National Ocean Service, Washington, D.C.; Martin Ross at the National Weather Service office, Philadelphia; Steve Kokkinakes and Sharon McKenna in the office of the Honorable H. James Saxton, Washington, D.C.; and R. M. Browning, Jr., historian, United States Coast Guard, Public Affairs.

Organizations which provided archival material include the Atlantic County Historical Society; Blue Hill Observatory, Blue Hill, Massachusetts; Board of Engineers for Rivers and Harbors, Fort Belvoir, Virginia; Cape May County Civil Defense; Cape May Historical Society; Historical Society of Riverton; Monmouth County Historical Society; National Hurricane Center, Coral Gables, Florida; National Weather Service, Rockville, Maryland; National Climatic Data Center, Ashville, North Carolina; Ocean County Historical Society; and Ocean County Review.

Assistance and guidance from the following libraries was invaluable. The courtesy and helpfulness of the following reference librarians made research a pleasure:

Robert Stewart at the Asbury Park Public Library; Marie Boyd, Heston Room Collection, Atlantic City Free Public Library; Anne Gurka, John Bailey Lloyd and Lois Brown at the Bishop Collection, Ocean County Library; Lenny Szymanski and Andrew Martin at the Cape May County Public Library; Muriel Scoles at the Long Branch Free Public Library; Free Library of Philadelphia; Library of Congress, Washington, D.C.; Monmouth County Library; National Archives, Washington, D.C. and Suitland, Virginia; Stockton State College Library; and Trenton Public Library.

By its very nature, a book like this, with its extensive layouts and use of pictures and other graphics, is a collaborative effort. So, finally, we would like to acknowledge those who took the raw materials for this book — a manuscript in pieces large and small, old scrapbooks and other collected items, leads for more photographs and ideas for graphics and charts — and, with much dedicated work, turned it into the book you are now holding.

Their efforts were made even more challenging by learning on the job a variety of new computer-based editing and design programs. These people behind the scenes — our friends and colleagues — whose work we gratefully acknowledge here, are:

Marion Figley, whom we thank for a finely honed editing job. She took the writings of two very individual authors and made them into one seamless manuscript.

Anita Josephson, for her yearlong struggle with that manuscript, and for the tedious and time-consuming job of fine-tuning the final layouts. Barbara Michallis for a careful job of transcribing interview tapes. Leslee Ganss, for so quickly learning how to do on computer what she does so well by hand: graphic design. Gail Travers, for careful proofreading.

And Ray Fisk, for long hours spent thoughtfully crafting the page layouts; for picture research from Toms River to Trenton to Washington; and for a compulsion in seeing that all the details of this complicated book met his high standards for accuracy, completeness and quality.

*Charles T. Higgens*/Philadelphia Evening Bulletin/*Temple University Urban Archives*

**March 7, 1962: The ocean cuts across Ocean City as homes burn to the ground, unreachable by firefighters.**

## Acknowledgements from the Picture Researchers:

Documenting a history of storms with pictures is a herculean task in a state with as much history as New Jersey.

In our searches we found, perhaps not suprisingly, many of the old photographs wrongly identified and dated. Even in public collections and archives we found errors, and we tried to verify the correct date wherever possible. With storm after storm hitting the same vulnerable places on the shore — and as memories fade — it's understandable that the dates get confused. Also, after development changes the landscape, it's understandable that some places are not recognizable today.

We have tried our best to cross reference pictures from different collections to ascertain with some degree of certainty the locations and dates of the pictures we present here. However, we won't be surprised if some readers correct us.

Under each picture, we have credited the individuals and institutions who were kind enough to provide us with access to — or actual pictures from — their collections. For all those who lent us pictures, and then waited patiently for the return of their materials through the many production delays, we are very grateful. We are particularly grateful to the following for their assistance and patience as we searched and copied images from their collections:

Stuart Farrell of the Coastal Research Center at Stockton State College for allowing us access to his collection of 1962 storm photographs made by W. Earle Hawkins. Mr Hawkins' dramatic pictures, originally shot simply for damage assessment for the Atlantic City Electric Company, not only provide an invaluable historical record of the 1962 storm, but have the aesthetics of great photojournalism.

The same can be said of the work of the unnamed state police photographers whose 1944 hurricane damage photographs appear here. We are grateful to Lt. Thomas DeFeo at the New Jersey State Police Museum, Trenton, for his persistence in tracking down this file of photographs, and to Det. Sgt. Bill Kryscnski at state police headquarters for his assistance.

Also, our thanks to: Dr. Robert Browning and Pete Milnes at the Historian's Office, U.S. Coast Guard Headquarters, Washington, D.C.; Helen A. Kehoe at the New Jersey State Library; Brian Mulvenna, Tony Bley, and Joe Gavin at the U.S. Army Corps of Engineers, Philadelphia; Tom Williams at the Ocean County Historical Society Museum; Dave Squier at NOAA's Satellite Data Services Division; Carl Van Thulin at Lynn Photo Service, Ship Bottom; Intera Service Corporation, Houston, Texas; Library of Congress; National Archives, Washington, D.C. and Alexandria, Virginia.

Also, Edward Brown, Evelyn Letts Brown, Peter Calabro, Peter Carey, Hank Crane, Rolf Engelsen, Stan Fayer, Rick Glascock, Jeanette and Con Hogan, M.S. Korfhage, Dorothy and Jonathan Oldham and the Harvey Cedars Bible Conference, Irene Panunto, Doreen and Robert Spreat, Carol Stewart, and Deb Whitcraft.

And for their work printing historical negatives, thanks to Patti Kelly, Tracy Mack and Tim Moersh of the *SandPaper*.

## Storm Warnings

**Small Craft Warning** — Conditions of wind and/or sea considered dangerous to most cabin cruisers, all sailboats. Winds up to 38 miles per hour.

**Gale Warning** — Winds between 39 miles per hour and 54 miles per hour, rolling seas, blown spray. Dangerous to all but the largest of ocean-going vessels. Head for harbor.

**Whole Gale Warning** — Winds to 73 miles per hour. Heavy to mountainous seas. Visibility impaired. Do not head for harbor as conditions make near-shore navigation difficult; ride it out.

**Hurricane Watch** — Set if the hurricane threatens a specified area for a specified time. It means a hurricane is possible, not imminent. Listen for further advisories to be issued. Prepare to leave.

**Hurricane Warning** — Where hurricane conditions are expected within twenty-four hours — winds of 74 miles per hour or more or high water even without hurricane-force winds. Get out now.

*U.S. Life Saving Service lantern slide, circa 1880/National Archives*

## Storm Definitions

**Hurricane Seedling** — A migratory disturbance that maintains its identity for 48 hours, whereupon it is given a number. Some one hundred of these formed each year in the Atlantic in the thirty years between 1960 and 1990, of which an average twenty-four per year attained the status of tropical depression, eight graduated to the rank of tropical storm and four made hurricane.

**Cyclone** — A low-pressure, closed atmospheric circulation rotating counterclockwise toward the center in the northern hemisphere, clockwise in the southern. Commonly referred to as a LOW.

**Tropical Cyclone** — A warm-core (inside warmer than outside), nonfrontal (not connected to a weather front), near-circular cyclone of synoptic scale (big) developing over tropical or subtropical waters and having a definite organized circulation. Distinguished by torrential rains and damaging winds that increase toward the center.

**Tropical Disturbance** — The weakest recognizable stage of a tropical cyclone. Rotary wind circulation may be absent at the surface but apparent at higher elevations. Maintains identity for twenty-four hours. From one hundred to three hundred miles in diameter. It creates a disruption in the normal flow of air and is usually associated with cloudiness and/or precipitation.

**Tropical Depression** — A still-weak state of a tropical cyclone whose sustained winds (more than one minute duration) are up to 39 miles per hour. Often used for the decaying stages of a Tropical Cyclone as well as the growing phase.

**Tropical Storm** — Just this side of a hurricane, with circular winds up to 73 miles per hour, distinct rain bands. At this point it gets a name.

**Hurricane** — Winds over 74 miles per hour around a distinguishing eye in the center. Generally circular, but can be elongated or elliptical. Dramatically low pressure within the eye. Several rain bands. Can be five hundred miles in diameter and involve one million cubic miles of atmosphere.

**Extra-Tropical Cyclone** — One that forms outside the tropics over colder waters (below 82 degrees). It usually affects a much wider area than a hurricane but, unlike hurricanes, the greater damage is not near the center, but farther out. The term is sometimes used for decaying hurricanes, abbreviated to E.T.

**Anticyclone** — An area of high pressure, often so vast it covers whole seas or continents. Winds circulate outward, clockwise in the northern hemisphere, counterclockwise in the southern. Commonly referred to as a HIGH.

# The Beaufort Wind Force Scale

**Force 0** — Calm — 0-0.9 miles per hour, 0-0.9 knots. Sea: Like a mirror. Land: Smoke rises vertically.

**Force 1** — Light air — 1-3 miles per hour, 1-3 knots. Sea: Scale-like ripples form but without foam crests. Land: Direction of wind shown by smoke drift but not by weather vanes.

**Force 2** — Light breeze — 4-7 miles per hour, 4-6 knots. Sea: Small wavelets, short but more pronounced. Crests have a glassy appearance and do not break. Land: Wind felt on face. Leaves rustle. Ordinary weather vane moves.

**Force 3** — Gentle breeze — 8-12 miles per hour, 7-10 knots. Sea: Large wavelets. Crests begin to break. Foam has glassy appearance. Scattered white caps. Land: Leaves and small twigs in constant motion. Wind extends light flag.

**Force 4** — Moderate breeze — 13-18 miles per hour, 11-16 knots. Sea: Small waves becoming larger. Fairly frequent white horses. Land: Raises dust and loose paper. Small branches move.

**Force 5** — Fresh breeze — 19-24 miles per hour, 17-21 knots. Sea: Moderate waves, taking a more pronounced long form. Many white horses.

Chance of some spray. Land: Small trees in leaf begin to sway. Crested waves form on inland waters.

**Force 6** — Strong breeze — 25-31 miles per hour, 22-27 knots. Sea: Large waves begin to form. White foam crests are more extensive everywhere. Some spray. Land: Large branches in motion. Whistling heard in utility wires. Umbrellas used with difficulty.

**Force 7** — High wind, moderate gale — 32-38 miles per hour, 28-33 knots. Sea: Heaps up, and white foam from breaking waves begins to be blown in streaks along the direction of the wind. Spindrift begins. Land: Whole trees in motion. Some difficulty walking against the wind.

**Force 8** — Gale, fresh gale — 39-46 miles per hour, 34-40 knots. Sea: Moderately high waves of greater length. Edges of crests break into spindrift. Foam is blown in well-marked streaks. Land: Breaks twigs off trees. Generally impedes progress.

**Force 9** — Strong gale — 47-54 miles per hour, 41-47 knots. Sea: High waves. Dense streaks of foam. Sea begins to roll. Spray may affect visibility. Land: Slight structural damage occurs (roof tiles, rain gutters, signs).

**Force 10** — Whole gale, storm — 55-63 miles per hour, 48-55 knots. Sea: Very high waves with long, overhanging crests. Resulting foam blown off in great patches into dense white streaks. On the whole, the surface of the sea takes on a whitish appearance. The rolling of the sea becomes heavy and shocklike. Visibility is affected. Land: Seldom experienced inland. Trees uprooted. Considerable structural damage (walls knocked down, chimneys toppled, roofs torn off).

**Force 11** — Storm, violent storm — 64-73 miles per hour, 56-63 knots. Sea: Exceptionally high waves. Small- and medium-sized vessels might be lost to view for long periods in the troughs. The sea is completely covered with long, white patches of foam. Everywhere the edges of wave crests are blown into froth. Visibility seriously affected. Land: Very rarely experienced. Widespread damage.

**Force 12** — Hurricane — 74 miles per hour and up, 64 knots and up. Sea: The air is filled with foam and spray. Sea is completely white with driving spray. Seas can hide large vessels. Visibility is very seriously affected. Land: Mounting to complete destruction.

*Ray Fisk/United Press International*

# How to Rate a Hurricane

The Saffir/Simpson Damage Potential Scale was devised to provide public safety officials, civil defense coordinators, emergency management authorities and others concerned with the effects of hurricanes with a quick fix on the severity of the storm as it moves. Developed by Herbert Saffir, a consulting engineer, and Robert Simpson, former director of the National Hurricane Center, it rates hurricanes on a rising scale from one to five.

**Category 1 — Winds 74 to 95 miles per hour.** Damage primarily to shrubbery, trees, foliage and unanchored mobile homes. No real damage to structures. Some damage to poorly constructed signs. Storm surge four to five feet. Low-lying coastal roads inundated, minor pier damage, some small craft torn from moorings in exposed anchorage.

**Category 2 — Winds 96 to 110 miles per hour.** Considerable damage to shrubbery and tree foliage; some trees blown down. Major damage to exposed mobile homes. Extensive damage to poorly constructed signs. Some damage to roofing materials of buildings. Some window and door damage. No major damage to buildings. Storm surge six to eight feet. Coastal roads and low-lying escape routes inland cut by rising water two to four hours before arrival of hurricane center. Considerable damage to piers. Marinas flooded. Small craft torn from moorings in unprotected anchorages. Evacuation of some shoreline residences and low-lying island areas required.

**Category 3 — Winds 111 to 130 miles per hour.** Foliage torn from trees. Large trees blown down. All poorly constructed signs blown down. Some structural damage to small buildings. Mobile homes destroyed. Storm surge nine to twelve feet. Serious flooding along coast. Many smaller structures near coast destroyed. Larger structures near coast damaged by battering waves and floating debris. Low-lying escape routes inland cut by rising water three to five hours before hurricane center arrives. Flat terrain five feet or less above sea level flooded inland to eight miles. Evacuation of low-lying residences within several blocks of shoreline required.

**Category 4 — Winds 131 to 155 miles per hour.** Shrubs and trees blown down. Signs blown down. Complete failure of roofs on many residences. Storm surge 13 to 18 feet. Flat terrain ten feet or less above sea level flooded inland to to six miles. Major damage to lower floors of structures near shore. Storm surge greater than 18 feet. Major erosion of beaches. Massive evacuation of all residences within 500 yards of shore required, plus evacuation of single-story structures on low ground within two miles.

**Category 5 — Winds over 155 miles per hour.** Severe damage to most structures, including complete roof failure on industrial buildings. Some complete building failures. Small buildings overturned and blown away. Major damage to lower levels of all structures within 500 yards of shore. Massive evacuation of residential areas on low ground within five to ten miles of shore.

The 1944 Hurricane was a Category 3 on this scale when it rounded Cape Hatteras, a Category 2 when it got to New Jersey.

# Hurricane Names

Below is the six-year rotating list of names for tropical storms. The first column is to be used in 1993 and will be repeated in 1999.

| | | | | | |
|---|---|---|---|---|---|
| Arlene | Alberto | Allison | Arthur | Ana | Andrew |
| Bret | Beryl | Barry | Bertha | Bill | Bonnie |
| Cindy | Chris | Chantal | Cesar | Claudette | Charlie |
| Dennis | Debby | Dean | Diana | Danny | Danielle |
| Emily | Ernesto | Erin | Edouard | Erika | Earl |
| Floyd | Florence | Felix | Fran | Fabian | Frances |
| Gert | Gordon | Gabrielle | Gustav | Grace | Georges |
| Harvey | Helene | Humberto | Hortense | Henri | Hermine |
| Irene | Isaac | Iris | Isadore | Isabel | Ivan |
| Jose | Joyce | Jerry | Josephine | Juan | Jeanne |
| Katrina | Keith | Karen | Klaus | Kate | Karl |
| Lenny | Leslie | Luis | Lily | Larry | Lisa |
| Maria | Michael | Marilyn | Marco | Mindy | Mitch |
| Nate | Nadine | Noel | Nana | Nicholas | Nicole |
| Ophelia | Oscar | Opal | Omar | Odette | Otto |
| Philippe | Patty | Pablo | Paloma | Peter | Paula |
| Rita | Rafael | Roxanne | Rene | Rose | Richard |
| Stan | Sandy | Sebastien | Sally | Sam | Shary |
| Tammy | Tony | Tanya | Teddy | Teresa | Tomas |
| Vince | Valerie | Van | Vicky | Victor | Virginie |
| Wilma | William | Wendy | Wilfred | Wanda | Walter |

If your name is Queenie, Umlaut, Xerxes, Yolanda or Zoltan you may be unique, but you'll have to be immortalized some other way. They don't use Q, U, X, Y or Z because of the scarcity of names that begin with those letters. In fact, if your name starts with any letter past G your chances are slim, and past J they're all but nonexistent. There are separate lists for Pacific cyclones, a season of which can run through one alphabet and start chewing up a second as well.

Some names are retired when it is deemed their hurricanes did enough damage to merit a place in the history books, and to keep them from being confused with a later storm, according to Miles Lawrence of the National Hurricane Center in Coral Gables. Or maybe it's superstition. Those whose time has come and gone since the naming game started in 1953:

| | | | |
|---|---|---|---|
| Carol, 1954 | Betsy, 1965 | Anita, 1977 | Elena, 1985 |
| Hazel, 1954 | Inez, 1966 | David, 1979 | Gloria, 1985 |
| Diane, 1955 | Camille, 1969 | Frederick, 1979 | Hugo, 1989 |
| Audrey, 1957 | Agnes, 1972 | Allen, 1980 | Bob, 1991 |
| Donna, 1960 | Eloise, 1975 | Gilbert, 1980 | |
| Cleo, 1964 | Belle, 1976 | Alicia, 1983 | |

**Hurricane Bob skirts the New Jersey coast, August 19, 1991.**

Ship Abner I Benyon. Cap.ᵗ C.B. Watts. in a hurricane. April 16.ᵗʰ '61.

# CHAPTER ONE

# The Hurricanes of History

*Blow winds and crack your cheeks! rage! blow!*
*Your cataracts and hurricanoes spout*
*Till you have drenched our steeples, drowned the cocks.*
— Shakespeare, "King Lear"

THERE IS SOME QUESTION as to whether or not Columbus discovered America. There is no doubt that he discovered hurricanes.

There are no hurricanes in Europe. Occasionally, the bottom of the British Isles or Portugal might get whiplashed with wind and rain from the tail end of a storm that is flattening itself out over the Atlantic, but nothing like the real thing ever hits.

The Admiral of the Ocean Sea, whatever his shortcomings as prophet, leader, businessman or nice guy, was a canny sailor and a sound navigator who could read the message in the winds and knew the sea by its colors as well as its currents:

> *Eyes never beheld the seas so high, angry and covered with foam. The wind not only prevented our progress but offered no opportunity to run behind any headland for shelter; hence we were forced to keep out in this bloody ocean seething like a pot on a hot fire. Never did the sky look more terrible; for one whole day and night it blazed like a furnace. All this time the water never ceased to fall from the sky; I don't say it rained because it was like another deluge.*

As stirring as his exploits seem now, they counted for little in his day. The Spanish who financed his vision were interested only in the golden part of it. His mismanagement of the settlements that were established, his cruelty to the natives, his inability, finally, to deliver a decent return on investment led not only to his being replaced as Spain's point man in the New World but also to his being barred from having anything to do with its affairs there.

But the gods of the sea still seemed to be on his side. During his last voyage in 1502, he saw the now-familiar signs: high mare's tail clouds, low, oily swells, a copper-colored sunset. He sent word to the governor of Santo Domingo — the man who had replaced him — warning of the coming storm, advising a delay in sending a waiting convoy of ships off to Spain and requesting shelter. The governor brushed off the warnings, ignored the advice and denied the old admiral access to the harbor.

The convoy — some records say twenty ships, others ninety — left for Spain. The hurricane hit. All the vessels were lost but one. The only survivor, by one of those ironies that argues for the existence of fate, turned out to be the small caravel that carried the scant remainder of Columbus' own assets, just enough to provide for his unwilling retirement. He lived out his years in ignored obscurity, watching as others swarmed over the path he had blazed in the sea.

Other early explorers encountered hurricanes in their search for the treasures that supposedly lay at the fringes of the world — gold, a passage to the East, even immortality. Ponce de Leon, seeking the fountain of youth, ran into two hurricanes within two weeks of one another. Each beached his vessel briefly; neither deterred him. Hernando Cortes, who eventually discovered the gold, lost the first ship he sent to Mexico in a devastating hurricane in 1525.

Storms took their toll over the years, but they were an accepted risk for the rewards offered the bold or foolhardy. Traffic flowed over on the trade winds, which blew steadily from the Azores to the Caribbean, and back on the prevailing westerlies in the higher latitudes. Spain had the largest fleet, but it was a big ocean and a long coastline: Other countries followed Columbus' road, and his lead — exploiting and enslaving the natives, taking whatever they could find and keep, and raiding one another whenever they could get away with it. Settlements turned into colonies which crept ever northward.

The English put one in Jamestown, Virginia, under Captain John Smith, the fellow Pocahontas saved. Whatever she saw in him was, apparently, lost on the rest of the colony. He was regarded almost as badly as Columbus had been — a swaggering bully, a loudmouth, an incompetent administrator and a womanizer.

The colony had not fared well. Its sponsors in England sent out an expedition with fresh supplies and fresh people, including three officers of varying rank who not only disagreed on who was in charge but also had differing views of the mission. They nonetheless found their way into history, via literature.

The expedition was overcome by a hurricane which sent one vessel to the bottom and scattered the rest. Some made it to Virginia where the colonists, desperately short of food and expecting to be saved, were instead visited with battered ships full of hungry people and ruined supplies. All starved through a bitter winter, eating dogs, rats, the leather in their shoes.

One ship that did not show up in the colony was the *Sea Venture*, the one carrying the three officers. It had almost foundered in the swamping seas. Everyone pumped until their arms wouldn't work anymore. Then they decided to get drunk, all but one, an old sea dog named George Somers. Sixty years old, rich from raids he had made against the Spaniards, semi-retired but still up for adventure, he stayed at the helm in that "hell of darkness" and found Bermuda, which had been characterized as "that dreadful coast of the Bermoothes, inchanted and inhabited by witches and devils and wondrous dangerous rockes and unspeakable hazard of ship wrack." The sea lifted the ship and wedged it high among the wondrous rockes, safely out of reach of the waves. After the storm, everyone waded ashore.

From death's door to the gates of heaven — instead of witches and devils they found berries and fish and wild hogs. They had not only been saved but blessed. Somers later wrote, "All the fairies of the rockes were but flocks of birds, and all the devils of the woods were but herds of swine."

He wanted to stay, but another of the officers, Thomas Gates, a soldier, not a sailor, ordered two small vessels built from the wreck of the *Sea Venture* and ten months later they, too, showed up in Virginia — more empty boats and empty stomachs. Somers volunteered to return to Bermuda, his "happy place," and bring back some of those wild pigs for the colony. But within a week he was dead "of a surfeit in eating of a pig," according to Gates.

His account of the island and of the wreck of the *Sea Venture* was published in England where it attracted the attention of William Shakespeare. Fascinated by the tale of such an island and the idea of "well-born and learned men" shipwrecked, he did further research, buying drinks for sailors on the London docks and listening to their stories, then transformed it all into the setting for *The Tempest*.

> *The sky, it seems, would pour down stinking pitch*
> *But that the sea, mounting to the welkin's cheek*
> *Dashes the fire out... A brave vessel,*
> *Which had, no doubt, some noble creature in her,*
> *Dashed all to pieces.*

More direct accounts by well-born and learned men include this report of a hurricane that hit the Plymouth Bay Colony in Massachusetts in August 1635, by its governor William Bradford:

> *About midnight it came up at N.E. and blew with such violence with abundance of rain, that it blew down many hundreds of trees, overthrew some houses and drove the ships from their anchors....The tide rose at Naragansett fourteen feet higher than ordinary, and drowned eight Indians flying from their wigwams.*

That hurricane followed a path that would be retraced with uncanny fidelity more than three centuries later by the Great Atlantic Hurricane of 1944 which so devastated the New Jersey coast.

Other reports of these shiveringly fascinating storms came from the

**Shipwreck painting for the US Lifesaving Service, circa 1880.**

letters and journals of eyewitnesses or from publications like this *Strange News* from Virginia:

> *The trees were torn up by the roots, and in many places whole woods blown down. The Sea (by the violence of the winds) swelled twelve foot above its usual height, drowning the whole country before it... accompanied with a very violent rain that continued twelve days and nights together without ceasing, with that fury that none were able to stray from their shelters, though almost famished for want of Provisions.*

This was the "Dreadful Hurry Cane of August 1667," of which another eyewitness related:

> *The night of it was the most dismal time I ever knew or heard of, for the wind and rain raised so confused a noise, mixed with the continual cracks of falling houses. The waves were impetuously beaten against the shores and by that violence forced and, as it were, crowded into all creeks, rivers and bay to such prodigious height that it hazarded the drownding of many people who lived not in sight of the rivers yet were then forced to climb to the top of their houses to keep themselves above water. They had been stormed by such an enemy as no power but God's can restrain.*

It continued up the coast, hugging it in a crushing embrace that encompassed what is now Delaware, New Jersey and New York.

Another hurricane night brought one of America's founding fathers on stage. It occurred in 1772 and ravaged the island of St. Croix in the Virgin Islands.

> *Good God! What horror and destruction! It is impossible for me to describe it or for you to form any idea of it. It seemed as if a total dissolution of nature was taking place. The roaring of the sea and wind, fiery meteors flying about in the air, the prodigious glare of almost perpetual lightning, the crash of falling houses, and the ear-piercing shrieks of the distressed were sufficient to strike astonishment into Angels... whole families roaming about the streets, the sick exposed to the keenness of water and air... In a word, misery, in its most hideous shapes.*

That was in a letter written by a young Alexander Hamilton to his father, who showed it around to his friends. Some felt "it might prove not uninteresting to the public," and it was published, so impressing other planters on the island that they raised a fund to send the boy to New York for proper schooling. There he continued writing, but about the political storms that were shaking the colonies, and in 1777 George Washington chose Hamilton as his confidential aide. He was twenty years old.

Hurricanes played a part in the American Revolution, too, mangling British and French warships off Rhode Island in August 1778. Two years later, a British fleet was struck by one near Daytona Beach, Florida, and, two weeks after that, by another near Bermuda. It was claimed that the British surrendered at Yorktown in 1781 because they did not want to risk losing the better part of their navy trying to run the French blockade during hurricane season.

That caution was no doubt prompted by The Grate Hurrycano of 1780, which was actually three hurricanes in one week in early October. The accounts came so quickly that it was difficult to know which storm was being treated, so they were lumped into one.

> The strongest buildings and the whole of the houses, most of which were of stone and remarkable for their solidity, gave way to the fury of the wind and were torn up from their foundation. Had I not been an eye-witness nothing could have induced me to have believed it.

> The sea swelled as it had never before; of a sudden bursting through all bounds and surmounting all obstacles, it overwhelmed the town and swept everything away so completely as not to leave the smallest vestige of man, beast or habitation behind.

> The most terrible cyclone of modern times ... the wind was unchained with such fury that the inhabitants hiding in their cellars did not hear their houses falling above their heads.

*Picture Collection, New Jersey State Library*

His new mansion, which had been built upon pillars, was lifted by the tempest and removed some distance, but being well made did not go to pieces. His wife, two ladies and five children were in the house and suffered little or no harm. Being absent from home, he knew not what had happened, but returning in the night, which was excessively dark, and groping for his door, he fell over the rubbish left on the spot and so hurt himself that he was confined for a week.

Hurricanes played only a small part in the Civil War. In 1861 the largest American fleet ever floated emerged from Chesapeake Bay and headed south. Rounding Cape Hatteras it was hit by a hurricane which scattered the ships, sinking two, but the rest soon recovered and regrouped.

The dread reputation of hurricanes led to the establishment of U.S. weather stations in the Caribbean in 1898 at the time of the Spanish-American War. Up until then, the United States Weather Bureau had to rely on reports of ships at sea for information on the course of the storms. Here is how William L. Moore, then chief of the Weather Bureau, recalled the decision:

> It was the beginning of the hurricane season. I knew that many armadas in olden days had been defeated not by the enemy but by the weather, and that probably as many ships had been sent to the bottom of the sea by storms as had been destroyed by the fire of enemy fleets.
>
> I reported the facts to President William McKinley. I can see him now as he stood with one leg carelessly thrown across his desk, chin in hand and elbow on knee.
>
> Suddenly he turned and said, "I am more afraid of a hurricane than I am of the entire Spanish Navy. Get this service inaugurated at the earliest possible moment."

Stations were quickly set up at various locations, emergency drills held, notices sent to all necessary parties, all for naught: The Spanish fleet was trapped at anchor in the harbor of Santiago, Cuba, and destroyed without the loss of a single U.S. vessel. No hurricanes appeared; they were late that year and the war was over too quickly. But the Weather Bureau now had the means of getting a handle on these storms, so fearsome that they could make a Republican president spend money.

## Hunting The Hurricanes

FOR ALL THE REGULARITY with which hurricanes visited the East Coast, the realization of what they were and how they worked was a long time coming. It was, not surprisingly, Benjamin Franklin who got the first clue.

He wasn't looking for hurricanes. It was late in the season, November 2, 1743, and Franklin had his instruments set to view a total eclipse of the moon. But a storm, described by a Philadelphia newspaper as "a violent Gust of Wind and Rain attended with Thunder and Lightning," eclipsed the eclipse. Since the weather had come in from the northeast, Franklin assumed that his brother in Boston had been disappointed as well but was surprised to learn that his brother got a good look at the eclipse before the storm arrived.

It didn't take long for the man who had tracked lightning down a kite string to figure out that a storm that moved toward the northeast when its

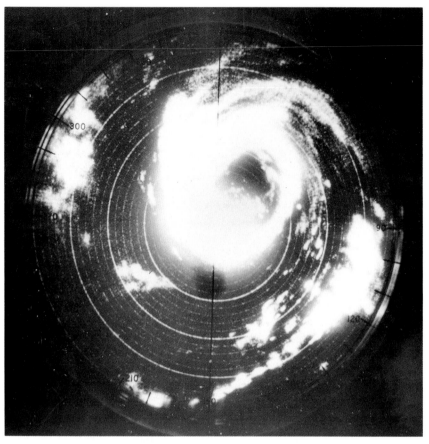

U.S. Navy/National Archives

**Dawn of the new technology, September 21, 1948: "Hurricane As Seen on Radar Scope, 3:04 P.M., U.S. Naval Air Station, Key West, Fla." Below: at the U.S. Weather Bureau office at Suitland, Md., 1967.**

west, while on his way back through the western parts of those states the trees had been flattened to the southeast. He then began looking at reports of the storm's passage and, applying compass to map, figured out what he called "rotatory storms."

Still, the whole subject remained little more than a scientific curiosity for most people. Mariners refused to believe any theories not molded before the mast. Redfield also demonstrated the relationship between the movement of the mercury column in a barometer to changes in weather but could not teach old sea dogs new tricks. The very idea of being able to forecast the weather was considered quackery. Proponents such as James Pollard Espy of Philadelphia argued with everyone in Washington. Here's how John Quincy Adams, former president but then congressman, put it:

> *Mr. Espy, the storm-breeder, is methodically mono-maniacal and the dimensions of his organ of self-esteem have been swollen to the size of a goiter by a report of a committee of the Franklin Institute endorsing all his crack-brained discoveries in meteorology.*

It was not until 1870 that a weather service was established as part of the Army Signal Service. The Weather Bureau was set up on its own in 1891.

The biggest advance in hurricane studies was made in 1943 by another man driven by curiosity and acting on his own, Maj. Joseph Duckworth of the U.S. Army Air Corps.

A pioneer in instrument flight, Duckworth was convinced he could fly a plane "blind," whatever the weather. (It was the rule then to fly around weather.) In late July a hurricane was headed toward Galveston, Texas. Duckworth jumped into a light plane and talked a navigator, Lt. Ralph O'Hair, into joining him "for some fun." At the time, the winds were already 80 to 100 miles per hour. Duckworth was sure that the plane could handle it, and that the instruments could handle the plane. It was a single-engine plane, a mouse on the flanks of that Everest of clouds. Winds tossed it about, rains dragged at it, clouds blinded it. Duckworth had trouble holding onto the controls. O'Hair noted:

> *As we broke into the eye of the storm we could see the sun and the ground. Apparently the eye was like a leaning cone as observation of the*

U.S. News and World Report/National Archives

winds were coming from the northeast was not a normal northeaster. He was not as interested in describing it as ascribing it, and began looking for reasons. He confirmed his original observation by tracing another storm from North Carolina to New England, but soon he was swept into the vortex of revolution and his weather studies halted, leaving it to another to discover that hurricanes have two movements, spin and linear. It wasn't until the mighty hurricane of 1821 that a New England saddle maker named William Redfield put it together.

This hurricane came bellowing out of the Atlantic in September, stirring up the Bahamas, tossing ships about off Cape Fear in North Carolina, swamping the tidelands of Virginia. Cape Henlopen in Delaware reported "furious" winds coming from the northeast, then twenty minutes later, from the southeast.

The eye passed over Cape May while the winds raged against Philadelphia, then Trenton, then New York, where it raised the incoming tide by a reported thirteen feet, submerging wharves and pushing ships into the streets. From there it went on up through New England and passed out to sea.

Worse storms had struck New England, but this was one of the best reported storms, with accounts from every point along its long path.

Enter Redfield, on a business trip. Traveling by coach through the eastern parts of Connecticut and Massachusetts, he noticed that the trees that were flattened by the storm lay with their tops pointing to the north-

*ground showed a considerable ground wind. As a whole the flight was not as uncomfortable as a good rough thunderstorm. The only embarrassing episode that could have occurred would have been engine failure which, with the strong ground winds, would probably have prevented a landing and certainly would have made descent via parachute highly inconvenient.*

On their return, Duckworth and O'Hair reported in to the weather officer, Lt. William Jones-Burdick. His only reaction was disappointment that he hadn't been along, so Duckworth took him aboard and went back. Jones-Burdick's more formal report concluded that the biggest dangers were from the static generated by the tremendous rain, from the engine overcooling and, of course, from the battering about of the crew inside.

Lt. Victor Klobucher was weather officer aboard a flight the following year and reported winds of 140 miles per hour and turbulence so jarring that even with both the pilot and copilot wrestling the controls the plane kept jerking out of control. When they returned to base, they discovered that 150 rivets had been sheared off one wing.

Specially designed planes overcame the technical problems, but the battering continues. Here's part of reporter John Eliot's account of flying into Hurricane David in 1979:

*The wind hits 183 mph. Something seems to seize the plane and jerk it wildly in all directions at once. "Some of our cockpit's coming apart! The radio console's out of its well!" someone on the intercom yells. Lockers in the galley bang open, spewing salt and sugar packets.*

*Suddenly my tape recorder, its handle looped around my wrist, jumps three feet into the air. It hangs there for a few seconds, then tries to dive down an opening next to the bulkhead. I glance across at the photographer. One of his cameras is floating around his eyebrows. His eyes look like ping-pong balls. The computer calculates the downdraft, a stomach-twisting 650 feet.*

*An updraft hurls us skyward, and our bodies feel twice the pull of gravity. "Hang on," barks the pilot.*

Bill Smith, a meteorologist who used to do this regularly before he retired to Beach Haven Gardens, explained some of the technique, and some of the mystique.

**Hurricane as seen from a hurricane hunter flight.**

*Since the wind spins around the center counterclockwise, you keep the wind on the left rear of the airplane at an angle of about fifteen degrees to the direction of the airplane and spiral in.*

*As the plane enters the eye, two welcome events occur — the plane stops bouncing and it's much brighter.*

*The eye is awesome. Frequently it is populated by birds that have been trapped in the storm. The wind is calm. The ocean is made up of huge swells moving in different directions. These swells only moments before had their crests blown off by the high winds surrounding the eye, but here the wind is calm and they are not flattened and wander about like lost behemoths.*

*As the airplane climbs up inside the eye, the cloud walls are visible through the haze and the flight is smooth and eerily comfortable.*

*Getting out of the eye is a challenge. You cannot fly out perpendicular to the cloud wall, of course; the wind shear on the plane would be catastrophic. You must start spiraling, counterclockwise, within the eye, and spiral out with the wind about twenty degrees on the right rear of the plane until you reach the fringes of the hurricane.*

*How do you know the wind direction? Simple: the wind blows the foam which makes streaks on the water. At about 100 knots of wind velocity, the ocean looks like a black table across which a solid band of buttermilk has been thrown.*

During a hurricane, flight crews do this several times a day. Only one plane has ever been lost.

A SCENE OF DESTRUCTION AT LOW MOOR, NEAR LONG BRANCH, DURING THE STORM.—Drawn by Schell and Hogan.—[See Page 762.]

Harper's Weekly, *September 21, 1889/New Jersey State Museum*

# CHAPTER TWO

# *New Jersey Storms*
# 1769-1889

*Lord how the ponds and rivers boiled*
*And how the shingles rattled*
*And oaks were scattered on the ground*
*As if the titans battled*
*And all above was in a howl*
*And all below a clatter*
*— The earth was like a frying pan*
*Or some such hissing matter.*

—Oliver Wendell Holmes

ANDY HOOK, AT THE NORTHERN END of the New Jersey coast, has been at various times an island, a sand bar, a peninsula, a shoal, a piece of the continent, a part of the whole. Now joined to Navesink Highlands, it was transformed so often that no charts could be trusted. Sandy Hook Inlet disappeared and reappeared like Houdini's hat, and a determined storm could straighten the hook itself into a needle. Cape May, stuck rather more firmly at the other end, is stable enough so that flocks of migrating birds use it as a rest stop, but nonetheless it changes profiles with the regularity of the seasons.

There isn't a spot on the 127 miles of beach that stretch between them that hasn't been under water. Hurricanes come close enough every ten years or so to mock the term "barrier beach" as they send waves up over the dunes and into the bays. And a freak storm in the fall of 1991 put enough wind behind two high tides to build waves into three- and four-story structures, eating whole beaches and sending meteorologists to their record books. A Noah-sized rainfall earlier the same year managed to dump a foot of water on Long Beach Island inside an hour and a half.

Some of the storms that visited New Jersey early in its history might have been hurricanes or not. In those days it was not known that the tropical storms of the Caribbean carried so far up the coast. There also was no clear definition of what constituted a hurricane, thus this entry in the 1769 diary of Jacob Hiltzheimer, "the wind increasing until it became a mere hurricane."

The *Virgina Gazette* had no hesitation in calling that storm "a most dreadful hurricane." It blew a sloop ashore at Barnegat City before proceeding on up the coast to cut a second inlet across Sandy Hook. But the Jersey shore has known northeasters that did more than that. "A Letter from Monmouth County" in the *New Jersey Gazette* describes one that struck in March 1778.

> The storm has destroyed many of the small saltworks on our shore, with all the salt in them. The night tide was several feet higher than has ever been known before — a considerable number of horned cattle were drowned on Long Beach and other places.
>
> The Long Beach is almost wholly leveled, and with little more than a sandbar left. The furniture has floated out of some houses. The inhabitants never saw so distressing a time.

October of 1783 brought a clutch of storms, one of which blew steadily for twenty-four hours. At Cape Henlopen, across Delaware Bay from Cape May, nine square-rigged, oceangoing ships were driven onto the beach by northeast gales, and on Long Beach Island two brigs came ashore. The winds pushed river waters back on themselves, lifting boats on the Raritan into New Brunswick back yards.

What Gerard Rutgers termed a coastal hurricane — "Its reach did not extend 100 miles inland" — knocked down his Belleville peach orchard in 1806. It also "upset" the *Rose in Bloom* off Barnegat Inlet with the loss of twenty-one of the forty-nine people aboard.

Wind provided energy in the days before electricity. The landscape of nineteenth century New Jersey was pegged with windmills. Two on Long Beach Island were used to pump water for the railroad. A huge one on

Windmill Island in the Delaware River was used to grind grain. Before the Statue of Liberty took up residence just off Jersey City, the most prominent landmark was the windmill on Paulus Hook, a graceful affair whose whirling sails of cloth gave it an aspect somewhere between a swooping bird and a swaying flower. But its sails were ripped to ribbons by a mighty storm in 1821 that was recorded variously as gale, hurricane, and hurricane gale. According to David Ludlum in the *New Jersey Weather Book*, it was not only a "full-fledged hurricane," but also the only one on record whose eye passed over "a New Jersey land area," that area being Cape May.

Cape May is particularly prey to the procedures of nature aroused, being all but surrounded by large bodies of excitable water. The storm approached with the speed of a yet-to-be-invented express train, overwhelming North Carolina's Outer Banks before dawn, heaving into Norfolk, Virginia, at noon, and rounding Cape Henlopen across Delaware Bay by midafternoon. It severed the town of Cape May from the rest of the peninsula. It flattened the cedar trees on Long Beach Island, some of which had stood for more than three hundred years.

Some claimed to have sensed its coming well in advance of the first winds. The *Cape May County Gazette* quoted "a man noted for his reticence but when he did speak it was mostly to the purpose."

*This summer is very hot, sultry, dry and calm; I think the devil is mending his bellows and will give us a blast before winter.*

He was proved right on September 3. The paper gathered eyewitness accounts from all across the stormscape.

*One vessel was found bottom upwards. A hole was cut, a woman taken out.... One chimney blew over against an adjoining store and when the wind shifted blew back again and stood erect as usual.... The force of the wind was so great that the spray of the salt water was carried 12 to 14 miles inland. Leaves of orchard trees on the side toward the ocean were turned brown and appeared as if scorched and dead, while on the other side the leaves were green and beautiful.*

Charles Ludlam of South Dennis in Cape May County wrote:

*At 11 o'clock it might be called a gale; at 12 it was blowing a hurricane. No clouds were to be seen but in their place was a universal haze like a thick fog. The writer of this had a favorite weeping willow that was blown down by the southeast wind and when it came around northwest, blew it over to the opposite.*

*On our bay shore the tide was higher than on the seaside; it came like a perpendicular wall some five feet high driven by the wind in an overwhelming surge. Drift was lodged in the tree tops at the Cedar Hammocks [hummocks] nine feet high.*

STORM AT LONG BRANCH.

Harper's New Monthly Magazine, *September 1876*

*In the pasture of Mr. Hugh Hand is a depression or basin of peat soil, at the time six feet deep, overgrown with alder, maple and other swamp growth; when the overwhelming surge struck and overtopped the hill that intervened between the marsh and the swamp, it tore up the peat soil to the hard pan and rolled it up the side of the basin like a sheepskin and left a clean pond where before was a peat swamp.*

People wrote in about their neighbors as well.

*Ishmael Armor had occasion to go to the barn and found the tide from the ocean running under it. Soon the tide crossed the farm, crossed its field, then on to Siggtown, hence to Mape's Mill, thence on down Nancy Creek till it met the water of old Delaware Bay. Ishmael was a truthful, reliable old trustworthy African, one of the last of Cape May county slaves.*

*Furman Ericson with his seven-year-old son William was on the meadows near Delmont seeing the rush of waters approaching, put his son on his back and before they reached the upland the water was nearly to his armpits and he was a tall man.*

*Elijah Miller lived in the southern end of Dias Creek. The elements were so threatening that he walked to the school house and asked for his children. The teacher replied, "Can't you stay a little while for we all will be going soon?" But Mr. M. replied, "No, I wish my children immediately and advise you to dismiss all the pupils at once and not wait until the regular closing hour."*

*This advice was heeded. One of Mr. M.'s children started to take a short cut through the woods but as the limbs and tree tops were breaking off, fearing they might be killed thereby, he hustled them homeward by the main road as fast as their feet would carry them. Looking back as they went up the hill they saw great waves capped with foam where they had walked but a few minutes before.*

Although the *Sussex Register* depicted the storm as a "very severe gale of wind, prostrating fences to the ground, uprooting and twisting from their trunks the largest trees, and leveling the corn and buckwheat with the earth," reports of a calm eye passing over Cape May and the shift of winds noted by the *Newark Sentinel of Freedom* seem to confirm its status as a hurricane.

Meteorologists assessing the various reports some 150 years later figured the storm moved along what is now the Garden State Parkway at a speed of about 50 miles per hour. When road crews cut the parkway through the Pine Barrens in 1954, they uncovered a section of the ancient cedar forest that had been knocked down by the 1821 hurricane, including trees buried in the marshlands and preserved whole in the oxygen-poor mud.

LITH. & PUB. BY N. CURRIER,    *Entered according to Act of Congress in the year 1846 by N. Currier, in the Clerk's office of the District Court of the Southern District of N.Y.*    2 SPRUCE ST. N.Y.

## WRECK OF THE SHIP JOHN MINTURN,

(CAPT STARK ) ON THE COAST OF NEW JERSEY IN THE TERRIBLE GALE OF FEBY. 15 TH 1846,  3 O'CLOCK A.M. WITH 51 PERSONS ON BOARD.

*By this melancholy disaster 38 persons were drowned or frozen to death.__ Among the lost were Capt. Stark , wife, and two children,__ the Mate , Pilot, and all the cabin passengers, 5 in number.*

*Library of Congress*

# 1846

The direction of the wind has a great deal to do with the damage it does. The winds on the starboard side of a hurricane — the right as it moves along — blow in the same direction the storm is moving, thereby adding to the speed of the counterclockwise winds circulating within it. Winds on the port side move in the opposite direction, and the cumulative force of the storm is thereby diminished.

If a waterway such as Delaware Bay is open to the southeast winds in the upper right quadrant of the whirling mass, the water will back upriver. During the hurricane of 1846 — also referred to as "The Great" — the Delaware River as far upstream as Camden "was lashed into a perfect fury and its roar would have drowned the thunder of Niagara itself," according to the *Daily Advertiser*.

But it was a midwinter northeaster, not a hurricane, that put 1846 in the record books when ten ships came to grief on the Jersey coast in a single frigid February day. They were the *Alabama*, the *Antares*, the *Arkansas*, the *John Minturn*, the *Lotty*, the *Mary Ellen*, the *New Jersey*, the *Pioneer*, the *Register* and the *Van Zandt*.

The grimmest story was that of the *John Minturn*, a 100-foot packet boat built only four years earlier, one of about 150 packets that operated up and down the coast. They were considered to be among the most solid vessels ever built and were rarely lost to the elements.

The *Minturn* was commanded by a Captain Stark, who had brought along his wife and two children on the run from New Orleans to New York. It carried a varied cargo including cotton, sugar, molasses, corn, lard and hides, as well as five passengers and a crew of twenty-two. Coming up the coast, the weather was fine, the sailing smooth, spirits high. Then an ominous encounter occurred. The packet came upon the wreck of the *Cherokee* and pulled twenty shivering seamen from its shattered timbers. There were now fifty-one aboard the *Minturn*.

The fine weather was blown away as the ship entered New Jersey waters. About four miles off Barnegat Light, a storm fell on them like a jungle cat might fall on its dinner.

From the testimony of some of the survivors and some of the rescuers at a hearing held a month later to investigate charges that the rescuers had not done all they could to save more of the ship's complement:

> *When I went to the shore that morning it was blowing a tremendous gale, the wind about E.N.E., dead on shore. It was very cold and raw. The gale was the worst one that I ever knew. —Joseph Borden, volunteer.*

> *The pilot ordered the topsails to be double-reefed, which the captain would not do, saying he did not think they needed double-reefing. The foresail was hauled up but the running gear being rotten, the sail blew to pieces. The pilot then held a consultation with the officers, passengers and more experienced part of the crew about what was best to be done and they decided to head before the wind and run her on the beach. —Stephen Mitchell, crew.*

But she hit a sand bar about three hundred yards out and foundered and cracked in two. The breakers pounded over the decks and the winds tore the rigging apart. The masts were cut away in an attempt to keep the ship together, but the effect was to create a jumble of spars and yards tethered to the ship where the sea jammed them repeatedly against her sides.

Two of the crew tried to launch the ship's small jolly boat, but it was quickly smashed to bits. Six others managed to get the long boat into the water with a line attached, but the current was so strong the boat was swept away and driven down-beach where rescuers pulled it out.

> *As many as could get hold of her ran in to seize her, and we took hold of hands, making a line in that way to the shore so as to prevent those of us furthest in the surf from being washed away. I was one of the first who seized the boat with my right hand. If my left hand had slipped its hold at the time a sea had come in I should, in all probability, have been drowned. —Lewis Johnson, volunteer.*

Johnson was the son of Hugh Johnson, wreck master of this stretch of the shore. He had been busy with the *Alabama* when the *Minturn* grounded but arrived in time to see the long boat make it to shore. Some of the rescued seamen testified they wanted to turn the long boat around and carry a line back to the stricken ship. Johnson thought the surf was too dangerous, but put it to the volunteers:

> *There were no thwarts or seats in the boat when she came ashore and we had no means of putting any in her. We got her ready for launching and tried to get a crew to go in her but no one would go although I offered ten and twenty dollars and finally any money. Their answer was that they would not risk their lives for money — they would go as quick without money as with it.*

Mitchell told the investigating commissioners that Johnson had not done all he could:

> *I told him that if he would get two brave men for a crew I would go, but could get no answer from him. It is my belief had the wreck-master been a persevering man nearly, if not all, that were on board of the ship would have been saved.*

Johnson's statement countered Mitchell's contention:

> *I applied to the sailors several times to go but they refused, some saying they were sick. They did not appear to be disabled or exhausted and were as able to go as any of our men had they been so disposed.*

*National Archives*

**Turn-of-the-century paintings for the U.S. Life Saving Service of a life car in operation, and a lifeboat under sail, left. The life car was developed by a Toms River boat builder and considered an advance over the breeches buoy, invented by a Manahawkin doctor who, as a congressman, established the Life Saving Service.**

But Borden, who had been doing this kind of rescue for twenty years, advised against it. "I never in my life experienced so bad a surf at any wreck," he said. Johnson even asked his son to make the attempt, but the young man refused, saying that Borden was "as good a judge as can be found on the coast as to when a boat can and cannot be put off through the surf. I would trust my life with him as soon as any man I know." Eventually, the elder Johnson agreed. "If we had succeeded in launching the long boat I think it had been as likely to be lost as any other."

All the while, unrelenting waves battered the *Minturn*. Those on shore could see people clinging to the icy shrouds, though any cries were carried away by the wind. Night finally hid the scene, but around ten o'clock, some eighteen hours after the ship had run aground, the watchers heard a terrible, crunching roar as the vessel gave under the pressure of wind and water. All aboard her were thrown into the sea. Thirty-nine persons, including the captain, his wife and his two children, were lost, their bodies washing up for days, some as far as eight miles away. There were thirteen survivors, most of them fierce in recriminations against the volunteers. One, Hugh Morrison, told the commissioners: "I felt that very little effort was made to rescue the crew of this vessel. Had there been a reasonable effort made there is not a doubt in my mind that it would have been successful."

Two others, Samson King and Isaac S. Davis, agreed.

*From the moment we struck, about half past 9 am, until sundown, the movements of the people on shore were perfectly visible to us and we saw nothing manifesting a desire to come to our relief. But everything that floated ashore from the wreck was seized with the utmost avidity by them, impressing us strongly with a belief that their anxiety for plunder was the predominant feeling.*

In their report, however, the commissioners exonerated the rescuers of all charges, adding:

*The records of the surf can show few more persevering, enduring and courageous efforts to save the perishing passengers and seamen than were shown by Monmouth surfmen on that occasion.*

One rescue was made by David Brower of West Mantoloking, who saved a young woman named Rebecca Jane. They were married a year later.

Wreck of the Ship "AYRSHIRE," on the coast of New Jersey, in a terrific snow storm, Jan. 1850. The Goverment Life Car saving 201 persons—see page 25 and 43.

# 1850

In 1850 three tropical storms climbed the coast to unload on New Jersey, a feat that would not be repeated for over a hundred years when Carol, Edna and Hazel in 1954 caused more trouble than the three witches of Macbeth could have conjured in a thousand bubbling pots.

It was also in 1850 that the determination and inventiveness of two men combined to revolutionize lifesaving.

Eleven years earlier, in 1839, Dr. William A. Newell of Manahawkin watched a stormy sea pound the Austrian brig *Terasto* into splinters and drown its captain and crew as they tried to swim ashore while rescuers on the beach watched helplessly. He became convinced there had to be a way to save such victims. He devised a way to shoot a line to a foundering ship with an open bucket, like a pair of breeches, that could be pulled back and forth. It was, of course, immediately dubbed the breeches buoy. That same year, Joseph Francis, a boat builder in Toms River, designed a watertight "life car"

to replace the breeches. Newell went on to take a seat in Congress and managed to get an appropriation of $10,000 to set up the U.S. Life Saving Service. Eight stations were established between Sandy Hook and Little Egg Harbor by 1849.

In January of 1850 the immigrant ship *Ayrshire* was driven aground off Squan Beach in high winds, heavy rain and thick fog. Lifelines were shot out to the ship as waves broke over it. The life car carried back two to four people at a time, a slow operation that took one afternoon and the following morning. All but one of the 202 people aboard were saved.

Four years later, however, storms crushed two ships that had grounded within sight of the shore while helpless rescuers could only watch. The most tragic was the wreck of the *Powhatan*, another immigrant ship, which struck a sand bar off Long Beach Island in the middle of an April northeaster that had been blowing strongly for two days and already wrecked twenty other vessels along the Jersey coast.

A Captain Jennings was the wreck master of the new life saving station at Barnegat City:

*On Sunday morning I observed a ship of about 900 tons thumping on the bar about 100 yards from shore. Her foremast was gone. The ship then keeled over to windward. The sea then, of course, made a clean breach over her, and passengers began to be washed over.*

*The main and mizzen masts soon went by the board and bodies appeared floating in the surf in great numbers. About dark, the sea rose to a great height and one large wave, fully a hundred feet high, struck the unfortunate vessel, and in one moment the hull was scattered into fragments which tossed wildly through the surf.*

*The shrieks of the drowning creatures were melancholy indeed, but I could render them no aid as the sea ran so high I could not get near. In a few moments all disappeared beneath the surface of the water.*

No one aboard survived; over three hundred bodies were found but it was believed there were more.

That same year, in November, yet another immigrant ship, the *New Era*, hit a sand bar just north of Asbury Park. She had sailed from Germany with 426 people, Captain Thomas J. Henry in command:

*Our passage from Bremen was very rough. I do not know that I ever made a voyage when the weather for so long a time was more severe. I supposed the ship to be on the coast of Long Island, and I carried a heavy press of sail to keep her off.*

*The first mate was on the deck. I was in the cabin when all at once I heard him ask the forward watch, "What is it that looks so light forward?" On hearing this I immediately jumped on deck, and then heard them cry out, "Breakers!"*

*I at once ordered the wheel up and in the same moment the ship struck. I at once caused the yards to be braced back, to get her off, but we only thumped further on. She went head on, made two or three thumps, and swung broadside to, and she was hopelessly aground. The sea at once commenced breaking over her side, breaking up everything on deck.*

Elias Smith, a reporter sent out on the news yacht *Achilles* to cover the wreck, described the scene.

*As we approached the wreck a most harrowing spectacle met our eyes. The jib boom, rigging and top of the ship, fore and aft, were filled with human beings closely packed together and clinging to each other and to the ropes while the ship surged to and fro with each returning wave, which broke in wild sprays far up the rigging and over the ship, drenching and suffocating the passengers, while the poor creatures filled the air with the most soul-*

*harrowing and pitiful outcries for assistance. On the beach were some 200 persons, gathered in groups, apparently consulting how to act, while others sat leisurely upon the gunwales of the boats, which the heavy surf rendered it certain destruction to launch.*

By morning the sea had calmed enough to launch the boats and rescue all who had managed to survive the night; 240 did not.

The wreck of the *May Smith* during "a howling nor'easter" in the middle of winter at Shark River was witnessed by Nelson Lillagore.

*Father and I heard the usual cry, "Ship ashore, ship ashore." We ploughed our way down thru the biting snow and stinging sand. The schooner was breaking up rapidly. My father, who had been the only ship carver in Philadelphia, turned to me and said, "Dory, I believe I carved the figurehead on that ship." And such was the fact.*

## 1869

The image of a ship suddenly small against a storm; the feeling of utter futility; the realization of powers of such magnitude that human challenges are mocked by its merest surge — these almost beggar the telling. But sometimes through the words of survivors can pour the awful experience itself, reaching the reader more vividly than pictures. Here is the account given by John Eliot of the passage of his ship, the *Idaho*, through the center of a storm in 1869.

*'Til then the sea had been beaten down by the wind, but now the waters, relieved from all restraint in the calm center, rose in their own might. Ghastly gleams of lightning revealed them piled up on every side in rough, pyramidal masses, mountain high — the revolving circle of the wind which everywhere enclosed them causing them to boil and tumble as though they were being stirred in some mighty cauldron. The ship, no longer blown over on her side, rolled and pitched and was tossed about like a cork. The seas rose, toppled over, and fell with crushing force upon her decks. Once she shipped immense bodies of water over her bow, both quarters and the starboard gangway at the same moment. Her seams opened fore and aft. Both above and below the men were pitched about the decks and many of them injured.*

Same year, different storm, on land, from an account in the *Evening Traveller*:

*Massive buildings rocked like toys, roofs of tons of weight were lifted and carried rods away or torn into minute pieces. Huge strips of tin and metal were torn from places where they had been securely nailed and blown*

National Archives

**"Grounded Schooner," from a U.S. Life Saving Service lantern slide, circa 1880.**

*like sheets of paper for long distances. Steeples rocked and fell, huge buildings were crushed in like egg shells, vessels were swept like chips upon the shore. The rise of the water was at the rate of a foot every ten minutes. Verily it seemed as if "Hell were empty and all the devils were here."*

After the blow, one witness recounted, "You can walk ten miles at a time on trees that are down without stepping on the ground."

# 1889

Storms that swept in from the sea, generally from the northeast and often backed by bimonthly, moon-driven spring tides, held the coast in thrall, treating human constructions as if they were just so many more sand piles, filling in channels here, carving new inlets there. This account from the *Jersey Journal* in 1889 could well have been written of the Great Atlantic Storm of 1962:

*From Sandy Hook to Cape May, the ruin wrought on this coast will make a permanent change in the shoreline. The tremendous hammering of the waves opposite the foot of the Navesink Highlands forced a reopening by the ocean through the peninsula into the Shrewsbury River. The giant waves destroyed everything in their path, tearing out bulkheads, ruining lawns and sweeping away beautiful summer villas. The swollen waters of the Shrewsbury River cooperated with the raging ocean to inundate the peninsula. All the pretty villages so popular for seaside summering — Sea Bright, Low Moor, Monmouth Beach, etc. — were woefully devastated by the great waves.*

*For three days terror reigned from Sea Bright to Long Branch and no one felt secure within 500 feet of the mad rage of the ocean. Ocean Drive was knee-deep in mud and strewn with countless tons of seaweed and sea wrack. The tracks of the New Jersey Central Railroad were in large measure destroyed or covered in hillocks of sand. The great ocean pier was badly shaken and damaged; the waves dashed in mountains to the very top of the frame-work, 65 feet above the low-water mark.*

*Heston Collection/Atlantic City Free Public Library*

**The northeaster of 1889 leaves beachfront damage in Atlantic City, above. At right, damage at Sea Bright after a severe winter storm in 1885.**

Harper's Weekly, *December 5, 1885/Moss Archives*

In 1889, Atlantic City did not yet have the Miss America Pageant to stretch the season, so "the worst storm ever," according to the *Journal*, affected mostly the permanent population.

> *With no trains arriving, the supply of meats, vegetables and other esculents has been cut short, and at this writing the butchers and greengrocers have exhausted their supplies. The milkmen went out of business yesterday. Fish and oysters are in great demand and mudhens have been killed by the hundreds with clubs. If the supply of fish, oysters and mudhens will hold out the people of Atlantic City may not have to go to bed hungry.*
>
> *Just what the outside world is thinking about us now we know not, as the telegraph and telephone have lost their connection. If the people who founded Atlantic City could have foreseen its greatness, they would doubtless have builded better than they did.*

The storm became known as the "Mudhen Hurricane," and on Long Beach Island, Margaret Wills from North Beach Haven wrote to her husband, George, to reassure him.

> *When you receive this you are not to worry for we have plenty to eat and are all well and comfortable. When you left us I took a walk down to the pavilion to see the tide come in. We had not been there long when the tide washed through the pavilion floor and the wind rose to a perfect gale. We made our way home with difficulty and when I reached there I found Miss Mathis, who had become frightened. Bessie came in to say that Mr. Hewitt was going to bring his family over; the ocean tide had climbed the hill and their porch was under water.*
>
> *I ran out and found the tide rushing down, or rather up, Beach Avenue. There was an open sea between us and Mathis' store and at once I thought*

> *the boys had not come back. Walter, who had just come, said he passed them at Walsh's but they never could come home alone.*
>
> *I was almost crazy for it was as dark as midnight by that time, but he bravely said he would go back for them. I waited in fear until he brought them home. They would have been drowned for they were in water up to their armpits and the tide rushing in.*
>
> *By that time the Lipps, Stiles and Hewitts were here, all waiting till the tide ran down, but the wind exceeded all that had ever been known on this island. We all went to bed but not to sleep; the storm was so furious and the water around us added to the driving rain made rest impossible, so Aunt Mary, Retta and I dressed ourselves and laid down no more that night. The younger children, Bessie and Kate, rested very well.*
>
> *Very early we prepared breakfast, and as the tide was then coming up and worse than the night before, I was not surprised to find Mr. Hewitt and all his family over before we had time to eat, and when we had scarcely finished, in came Mr. Harkinson to say he was going to transfer the Dolphin (guesthouse) to this house as the supports on the front porch had given away and the breakers were dashing against the house, so over they came, right out of bed, servants and all, who went to work and prepared breakfast. There were 24 people here all day.*
>
> *When the tide reached its height the scene baffled description. You can form an idea when I tell you the bulwark opposite the store gave way and the ocean tide dashed against our house, over the grading and around to the door. From the fence in between Stiles's and Crosta's was an open sea covered with white caps.*
>
> *All made the best of the situation. I was not a bit afraid. I do not know when we will meet but I never wanted you so much, but I will keep up a brave heart and everything will soon be right.*

**Sea Bright wreckage after the hurricane of 1914.**

# 1903-1937

*And behold I, even I, do bring a flood of waters upon the earth...and the windows of heaven were opened...
and the waters prevailed and were increased greatly upon the earth.*

— *Genesis, Chapters 6 and 7*

FOR THE FIRST THIRD OF THIS CENTURY, the waters decreased upon New Jersey. Few hurricanes made it this far, and none, except 1903, did appreciable damage. In 1901 or 1902 (records vary) a southeaster blew the belfry off Holy Innocents' Episcopal Church in Beach Haven and deposited it in the Cox Hardware Store across the street. Then the church itself was lifted from its foundations and set across the tracks of the horse-drawn trolley.

The hurricane of September 1903 caused almost as much of a furor in the newspapers as it did along the shore. The *Atlantic City Press* dubbed it the "Vagabond Hurricane," claiming it was largely a creation of other newspapers that had heard of a "blow" at the shore and were eager to spill ink all over it.

*A Philadelphia newspaperman came on the afternoon train, all excited and wanting to get a list of the killed and wounded. Another newspaperman from New York came down in a hurry and said, "Well, our paper will offer to raise a fund of $200,000 to aid the sufferers. Let's get a look at the hotels and piers that have been washed away."*

*When they investigated and found that the only damage done was the blowing down of a number of pavilions on the Boardwalk, many of which should have been torn down some years ago, the correspondents quietly kicked themselves, as the saying goes, and took the first train home.*

Apparently not to write corrections, however, for the story continued:

*...thousands of visitors spent yesterday taking in the sights. Many carried newspapers in their hands and used them as guides to where any damage was reported. The curious visitor was disappointed to find only a few scattered boards and a pile of tin. They were looking for houses toppled over and excited inmates running about.*

It was, in fact, not a hurricane but a tropical storm, the first to make landfall on the Jersey coast in a hundred years. The *New York Times* reported its top winds along the shore at 70 miles per hour, just four short of hurricane strength.

*In the four hours from 11 o'clock in the morning to 3 in the afternoon the wind shifted from east to southwest, thereby succeeding in reaching nearly all sides of various objects blown upon in the course of its peregrinations.*

*These objects were no less varied than the storm itself. The wind had its best amusement with the Flatiron Building and is said to have beaten all records of variegated misbehavior in its prancing about the freak structure. When not occupied there it turned its attention to the spire of St. Bartholomew's Church, which waved in circles and ellipses but held together.*

*The large plate-glass window in a Broad Street department store was smashed by the pressure of the wind and a large stock of women's hosiery and other garments went sailing down the street like a vision of a ballet corps gone mad. The fleet stockings escaped, except half a dozen pairs that wrapped themselves around a man's neck after kicking off his hat and spectacles.*

*In Jersey City, a dwelling house which stood on supports six feet high was lifted by the wind and deposited on an adjoining lot. Mrs. Frank Kennedy and Mrs. John Ryan, who were in the house at the time, were amazed at the behavior of their home as it sailed through the air, but were unhurt.*

If the *Times* couldn't resist the slapstick aspects of the storm, it also noted its damage and its carnage.

*The City Hospital building is an old one and the rain poured onto patients on the top floor who had to be covered with rubber blankets. Warden Roberts bored holes through the side walls at floor level so that the water might pour outside rather than dripping into the wards below.*

*At Bayonne, 47 yachts, ranging from the big schooner Ansonia down to catboats, were wrecked. James Cooley, twelve years old, was caught in a flood of water and carried into a culvert. He managed to get hold of the bars and to hold his head above water until he was rescued. A twelve-year-old boy in Plainfield saw an electric wire hanging from the limb of a tree by his home, jumped for it, caught hold, and dropped back dead. In Paterson, city of disasters, a team of horses belonging to the Manchester Company were killed by a live wire blown down as they were passing. The driver escaped by ducking the wire, though he was severely shocked by the electricity running up the reins he held.*

And under the headline "Castaways' Awful Tale," the paper ran this story, related by Captain Sorrenson of the steamer *Vidar* which had picked up six shipwrecked crewmen from the British steamer *Mexicano.*

*I was sitting in my cabin about 9 o'clock when I heard a cry. Thinking someone was fooling about I went to investigate. When I reached the bridge I heard it again. The sound seemed to be coming from the ocean, but I couldn't see anyone.*

*I ordered a boat to be gotten ready and when I heard the cry a third time I saw something in the water, like a small log about half a mile off. With the aid of my glass I found it to be small hatch with a man in oilskins stretched full length on it.*

*He was completely exhausted and had to be hauled aboard the boat. He was unable to say a word and, thinking there were no more, as I could see no wreckage about, I started on my way. I had proceeded about a mile when I found five more men clinging to pieces of wreckage. They, too, were exhausted, and one was nearly crazy. My men had to hold him in the lifeboat for he was determined to jump into the sea.*

One of the survivors, August Osterlind of Finland, told how they had been shipwrecked:

*About 4 o'clock we encountered a severe hurricane blowing from the south. About 12 o'clock it shifted to northwest and blew with tremendous force. A heavy sea swept the steamer from stem to stern, carrying away the lifeboats and ventilators, flooding the engine rooms and putting out the fires. The steamer then became unmanageable and was soon in the trough of the sea.*

*She rolled about for little over an hour, when she sank stern first. The men in the forecastle were called out and told to be ready to save themselves the best way possible when the steamer went down. The boatswain refused to leave his bunk saying if he had to die he would rather die in his bunk than in the sea.*

*We were on the bridge with the officers and jumped overboard just as the steamer went down. I heard two pistol shots and I think some of the officers shot themselves, preferring that kind of death to drowning.*

*We drifted about for several hours doing our best to keep together but when daylight came there were but seven of us together. The second mate was about exhausted. He took off his lifebuoy, handed it to one of the sailors, said goodbye to all of us, and went down. We had about given up hope when we sighted the steamer.*

*U.S. Coast Guard*

**The barque *Pero d'Aleniques* out of Lisbon stranded near the Mantoloking Coast Guard station, December 1915.**

One other survivor, Domingo Reyarberay of Spain, was picked up by another passing ship. He said he had been pulled under when the *Mexicano* went down but gotten entangled with some rigging attached to spars which floated up to the surface. He bound himself to a spar and then rode the turbulent seas for seven hours.

The *Mexicano* had carried a crew of twenty-three men. Two fishing schooners, the *Beatrice* and the *Swan*, had been heading for the Delaware breakwater with thirty men aboard each when the storm broke. Neither was heard from again. The fishing smack *Red Dragon*, out of Atlantic City, went down with all aboard. The hull washed ashore at Harvey Cedars a week later, the body of Capt. DeWitt Clark lashed to the mast.

While the storm apparently gave Atlantic City little trouble, it did leave scars on the rest of the shore. In some areas the barometer dropped a half-inch in just three hours. In Toms River the porch in front of Ernst's Cigar Store and Williams Restaurant was blown away and the tin roof rolled up. A freight car of the Central Railroad had its roof blown "clean off." On the river a fast tide came up, "waves combing like surf." In Barnegat the tall spire of the Methodist church blew over and crashed down through Morris Lazeroff's furniture store. "It cut through the store as with a sharp knife almost to the foundation." In Waretown only three boats were left at anchorage. Of the forty yachts moored at the Seaside Park Yacht Club, only six remained.

The storm, though not a hurricane, deserved more the name "Vandal" than "Vagabond."

A northeaster on Christmas night in 1913 set Sea Bright up for a near-fatal one-two punch, breaching bulkheads on that tentative whiff of land so that an even worse blow less than two weeks later "ended, for all practical purposes, a way of life." From the account of one witness:

*You gasped as each storm wave peeled at the beach houses, sending porches, trim, shutters flying in a bleach of sea foam. The real prize was to be in view when one of those grand old ladies went out to sea. The waves would roar beneath the house, building a pressure with each surge until the roof would explode with a geyser of salt water, and all the sides would fall in upon themselves. At its leisure, the ocean would lap up the rubble and pull it out into the surf.*

In Longport, what became known as the "big one of 1916" not only claimed its share of houses but also streets, effectively slicing off a mile and a half of the town. Chris Frye saw the destruction.

**Longport, looking west from Oregon Avenue in January 1914, after a northeaster.**

*I'll not forget that storm. The drive of the ocean was terrific on the Point. I saw houses drifting away, tumbling about in the cauldron of waters, boiling and foaming around the shore and the land disappearing from sight! One or two houses drifted back afterwards and we saved the timbers. What was left of First Avenue, Second, Third, Fourth, Fifth, Sixth, Seventh, Eighth, Ninth and Tenth all went. Also part of Eleventh. All gone now.*

The storm carried one-third of Longport's land south and deposited it in Ocean City. The loss prompted Longport to build a $1,100,000 concrete sea wall and stone jetty. Local taxpayers picked up the construction tab through levies on their homes and businesses, bills that ran into several thousand dollars for some homeowners.

In October 1923, one hurricane brought 82 mile-per-hour winds, with attendant waves, to the Jersey coast. Decades later, Manahawkin bayman Tom Nickerson remembered being on a barge under tow from Atlantic City to Beach Haven:

*I was about seven years old. The Nassau was pulling us, and we were the only barge in tow. The storm hit and I could tell by the angle — the wind was southeast — that the tug was going right in on the coast.*
*My father always said that of all the rough spots on the East Coast, Hatteras is a pussycat compared to Cape May and Barnegat. The movement of the bars, they change; they move back and forth. He got all hands up in the pilot house — it was two deck hands, my mother, myself — all ready to evacuate. The barge was pitching and heaving and rolling, and all of a sudden that barge went down and shuddered and hit and stopped. There was no motion whatsoever. It was just like it was nailed there. The water came in*

Storm damage
#128

U S LIFE-SAVING STATION

Oceanfront bulkheading proves futile against the battering from storms at Corson's Inlet Coast Guard Station in Strathmere in the early 1920s, left and below. Looking toward the inlet, a canyon carved by the sea lines Central Avenue behind the station at the corner of 58th St., February 1920, below, far left.

*U.S. Coast Guard (all)*

**Looking north toward Barnegat Lighthouse, at the site of an earlier Coast Guard station, December, 1921, after storms have cut away beachfront buildings.**

*over both sides, just like that. I was looking out and the waves were breaking on the pilot house and all you could see were the three masts sticking out of the water. The barge hit the sand bar and the suction of the bottom held it; the ocean just poured right in.*

*And that tug kept pulling, pulling — picture your dog shaking himself, and that's the way that barge felt. And I looked and the water was pouring off the sides of the barge and up she came.*

Five years later Nickerson's father was on another barge, one of three that were wrecked off Barnegat Inlet. He came ashore lashed to the steering wheel, covered with ice and unconscious, the sole survivor. Later he could not remember anything about the incident. In 1933, a barge on which Nickerson himself was working "went to pieces in the same place."

The shipwreck of the *Cecil B. Stewart* in 1927 spilled its load of railroad ties all over the beaches of Long Beach Island. As a local newspaper account of the incident later related:

*One of Surf City's more prominent matrons was then younger and sturdier than she is today. Although she had no special need for railroad ties,*

*when she saw all that salvage washed ashore she felt an obligation to island tradition and went out onto the beach and lugged a tremendous number up into her yard, almost killing herself in the process.*

*A few days later a local man came around, said he had been deputized officially to get all the ties back and sternly demanded her haul. Argument was of no avail. She had to give them back, and added a broken heart to an already broken back.*

*Well, your editor heard the Pennsylvania Railroad hired this guy to get them back at so much a tie. Nothing official about it. We don't know who he is but hope he is not around today to fall afoul of the lady we've been speaking of.*

What the *New York Times* called "the fringe of a Florida hurricane" sent gales of 50 to 75 miles per hour against the Jersey coast in September of 1928, catching the schooner *Blackman*, loaded with oysters and headed for Bivalve on Delaware Bay, scuttling her "somewhere in the raging Atlantic" with six men aboard. Five patrol boats went out from the Coast Guard station in Cape May to search for the vessel with no luck.

A Somers Point man left his cabin cruiser under the buffeting of the storm but drowned when the tender he boarded overturned. A Cape May man reportedly died of a heart attack when the wind blew down two 100-year-old buttonwood trees in his yard. In Atlantic Highlands, a man was electrocuted by a fallen high voltage wire in his yard.

On Long Beach Island, "...hardly a yacht or small boat moored along the bayside escaped being sunk or smashed. The Pennsylvania Railroad bridge across the bay served as a barrier to many drifting yachts which piled up against the timbers and hung there, bent, twisted and strained." The tracks were under eighteen inches of water from the mainland to the island, and the trains "proceeded very slowly, with men on the cowcatchers watching for debris which might derail the trains."

Point Pleasant's largest hotel, The Leighton, was undermined as "high seas, 1,000 feet in length, rolled through the inlet and back for two blocks." At Hammonton, "thousands of apples were blown from the trees and in many cases limbs were torn off by the gale." Crop loss was put at $20,000.

But it was in the 1930s that the entire Northeast was to be reminded forcefully of its vulnerability, of the toll nature takes for living on or by its seas, of the power that moving air and fluid water can bring to bear on less flexible objects like beaches and buildings and bones.

As a curtain raiser to this Great Weather Show, a northeaster with sustained winds of 60 miles per hour held the coast, asea and ashore, at its mercy for four days in 1932, getting this review in a local paper:

*Water! Water!! Water!!!—Fresh and Salt! Wind and Rain! A coastwise storm that broke all previous records. The tide came in until it ran down our streets in torrents, carrying an offering to the bay of New York's choicest garbage, discarded powderpuffs, electric light bulbs, bottles and radio tubes. The bay, not to be outdone, crept into the first floors of our homes until Dad's carpet slippers were replaced by his hip boots. Sneak boxes sneaked afloat into door yards, accompanied by skiffs, garveys, boardwalks, etc., that were all*

*A.W.O.L. Some of our neighbors on the bayside have gotten better acquainted with the second floors of their homes since the bay has taken charge of their first floors. Ocean-going craft hugged the safety of harbors. At its peak the tide was hurled far into the shore by heaving, thundering seas beyond. Breakers threatened to pound the two-story Coast Guard station to pieces.*

The station, on Tucker's Island, was finally abandoned. Five years earlier, on October 12, 1927, the Little Egg Harbor Lighthouse had collapsed into the encroaching sea.

In August 1933, another northeaster hit New Jersey, followed within days by what a Philadelphia newspaper characterized as the tail end of a tropical hurricane, "wreaking such monstrous damage as to exceed any similar catastrophe in the last half century."

*At least 100 craft — many of them carrying amateur fishermen — were off the Jersey coast yesterday when the storm struck suddenly. With the violence almost of a hurricane but without a drop of rain, it sent gigantic combers crashing to shore.*

*Never before in the history of the Atlantic Coast have so many boats been capsized, veteran fishermen declared.*

*Lewis Ressler and Edward Bartels, both of Wildwood Crest, were saved in a spectacular rescue off Cape May after battling for 52 hours to keep their frail fishing boat afloat.*

*About 500 persons congregated on the beach and boardwalk cheered as the Coast Guard patrol boat landed a lifeline across the fishing boat* Francis *after both boats were tossed about by huge billows for two hours.*

*Ressler and Bartels, benumbed by cold after having been drenched since Sunday and without food or water for two and a half days, were unable to reach for the lifeline with an oar when it was shot near them. After each failure the patrol boat was maneuvered into a "shooting" position again.*

*courtesy Dave Wood*

**The remains of the *Cecil B. Stewart*, wrecked on Long Beach Island in 1927. The Harvey Cedars Coast Guard station can be seen to the left.**

A rising billow removed the boat from sight and the rope dropped into the water as the boats were tossed farther apart. On account of the sharp breaking of the waves it was with difficulty the patrol boat was kept alongside the fishing smack.

There was a gasp from the crowd as the powerful beams of the searchlight showed the rope drop across the bow and a man groped his way over the slippery fishing boat. Ressler and Bartels almost collapsed after the Francis was towed ashore and had to be assisted from the boat.

Bartels recovered enough by the next day to tell his story.

We thought our time was up. It seemed days that the patrol boat was darting in and out, trying to shoot that line across. Ed and I were so weak we couldn't move fast enough to catch it. We started out from Two-Mile Beach at 5 a.m. Sunday. We only took a few sandwiches and a little water, heading for the old fishing grounds about 28 miles out. We started back at 4 o'clock p.m. just after the sea started to rise. We made about ten miles before our motor failed. We were battered about and all our fish and supplies were washed overboard. All Sunday night, with the storm raging, we worked on the motor trying to get it dried out. Monday morning we decided our number was up and we would never see shore again. The waves were running mountain high and there was nothing we could do to keep from rolling with them. Monday night it quieted a little and we tried our engine again. We kept working against hope and Tuesday morning we got it started again. We limped toward home but in the afternoon it failed again and by that time we were too far gone to do anything. We hoped we would drift ashore when the guards saw us and started shooting the line.

Ressler's first question on reaching shore was, "What day is it?"

The Coast Guard sent out more than a hundred patrol boats, cutters and destroyers during the four days to search,

U.S. Coast Guard (both)

rescue, tow. The storm had come up so suddenly the press called it a "sneak attack," a "freak," a "bombshell."

The ocean and the bays were full of Sunday fishermen. Three boats capsized in the shallow waters of Barnegat Bay. Coast Guard Captain Christopher Bentham warned all boats to stay out to sea until the storm blew over, but it only got worse. Dr. Charles McArthur was strapped in the fighting chair of a 38-foot charter boat when a sea pulled up the chair and carried both over the rail.

Owners of the fishing boat *Emma* asked the Coast Guard to find their boat, last heard from off Sea Girt with nine men aboard. The twenty-one boats of the Ocean City fishing fleet were also at sea.

*Capt. J.H. Allen, who owned five of them, hired a seaplane. He gave the pilot a life preserver to which he attached a bottle with a note in it instructing his five boats to head for Cold Spring Harbor. The pilot circled over the distressed fleet, singled out one of Capt. Allen's boats and dropped his note. The skipper retrieved it and headed south at once, followed by the entire fleet. They arrived safely some hours later.*

A 36-foot sloop captained by Harvey Benner and with four people aboard was unable to make headway off Barnegat Light and was towed three and a half miles by the Coast Guard. Mantoloking guards reported that five life preservers bearing the name *San Jacinto* washed up on the beach. Capt. Theodore VanSant was lost in an attempt to rescue the 30-foot sloop *Ella* which had foundered off Atlantic City. In the narrow Longport Inlet, the storm tide clogged the channel with wrecks.

*Harold Lichten, his wife and his two sons, Robert, 12, and Richard, 9, were aboard the* Goldie R., *the first boat to capsize in Longport Inlet. Mrs. Lichten was rescued by the crew of the* Polly S, *which also capsized a short time later. The two boys were picked up by the E.R.C., owned by Charles Curran, a past commodore of the Ocean City Yacht Club. In the vicinity of Longport Inlet the Coast Guard rescued more than 50 persons. Besides these, ten persons were rescued on the open ocean outside Longport Inlet and fifty others were transferred to Coast Guard vessels.*

Harold Lichten was not among them. The rescuer of the *Goldie R.* was Capt. Bentham who, during the operation, got his leg entangled in a line and twisted to the point he could not stand on it. He stayed on the job, however, putting out to sea again after the *Emma* to search for others. His leg was later found to be broken.

The *Madison*, a coastal liner with ninety people aboard, became disabled and sent out an SOS, reporting that its entire forward housing had been knocked off. The cutter *Carabasset* set out for her and got smashed in herself, but continued to guide the disabled ship to port, pouring oil on the waters before it to calm the seas, a practice dating back to biblical times.

Two of the *Madison's* crew had been lost. First Mate Lycurgus Lawrence and Quartermaster Edward Corbett had gone up on deck to assess the damage after the first wave and were taken by a second.

Three days after the storm, the Coast Guard was still picking up wrecked boats. The four-masted schooner *Kohler* washed ashore. Fish pounds were pulled up and the pilings, buoys and nets distributed along the coast. Waves snatched away the 300-foot pier at Cape May, and winds toppled the 90-foot radio mast atop the Coast Guard station there. The raging waters marooned the men inside the building. The city was without electricity and armed Marines patrolled the streets.

Street lights in Wildwood snapped off. One radio station in At-

*Ocean County Historical Society*

**1929 storm damage to beachfront homes at Bay Head.**

**In August, 1933 it is feared the Barnegat Lighthouse might finally fall as the sea cuts away its base on three sides.**

lantic City reported "gigantic waves marching toward the beach." At Lake Denmark in Morris County, Marines and townspeople threw up sandbags to buttress the dam as the water rose behind it. Ten tons of sand were used to reinforce the concrete structure which had burst twenty-five years earlier and inundated towns as far away as Denville, fifteen miles downstream. This time it held. The wholesale destruction of trees, bushes and even grass was reported from Toms River to Atlantic City and as far inland as Hammonton as the leaves were "literally whipped to death" by what one paper called the "baby hurricane."

A heavy, new-moon tide added to the assault. The Delaware River at Camden "went on a rampage" and the Schuylkill rose twenty feet above normal. Another paper commented, "Suburban Philadelphia was flooded and beaten by the wind and brought to its knees." And 125 homeless living in cardboard shacks on a sandspit in the river were marooned, their shelters rendered into papier-mâché.

After the usual storm-tossed statistics and ravage reports and tales of tragedies visited and tragedies averted, news items like these piled up on editors' desks and overflowed into newsprint:

Miss Liberty's torch was extinguished last night when lightning struck the power plant at Ft. Wood. The plant was repaired and the light functioning again before dawn.

Benjamin Bryant was a passenger yesterday in the ill-fated Anna M., a 30-foot cabin cruiser that capsized with six aboard in Longport Inlet. Four passengers were picked up by the Coast Guard and one was drowned. The overturned boat drifted about until a flood tide carried it through Great Egg Inlet, where it struck the Ocean City bridge, righted itself, and —lo! there was Bryant under the boat. He had been there for 45 minutes and none the worse for his experience.

In the Military Training Camp at Ft. Dix 800 students, stripped of uniforms and wearing bathing suits, accepted the storm as one of the highlights of their camp experiences. They matched wits against the gale in their efforts to keep their tents from blowing away and every company street has a wager that it will have the most tents left standing by morning.

A motor boat was washed ashore at Corson's Inlet yesterday afternoon. The crew of four were picked up by an unknown rumrunner.

From 9 p.m. until after midnight, police barred admittance to the Recreation Pier in Long Branch where a dance marathon was in progress. Earlier in the evening the dance was stopped when light service was temporarily disrupted. The storm did not end the dance, however, and marathoners were still competing today.

On Baltic Avenue, Atlantic City, the rain caused the wooden paving blocks to float away. Residents donned bathing suits and worked in the storm to lay in next winter's fuel supply. It will cost $10,000 to replace the street.

Given the opportunity to write up one of nature's greatest shows, who can blame them?

Wind-whipped torrents shrieked out of gray heavens, across which darker gray scuds fled like stampeded herds, swelling meek runlets and mild, meadow-flanked creeks to devastating flood.

The ocean was heaving and tossing as though tormented by demons.

At sea, shipping shuddered in the grip of the clawing waves.

But it was the prospect of seeing Barnegat Lighthouse finally topple into the sea that really uncorked one reporter's adjectival juices. The venerable tower was fairly well protected on its sea side by a jetty, but there was nothing but a sandbank on the bay side where the wind-driven water could easily undermine it. When the wind shifted from northeast during the northeaster to northwest during the tail-end hurricane, the Coast Guard warned that the lighthouse might go.

Assaulted on all sides by storm-maddened tides, Barnegat Light defies the ravages of the pounding ocean whose treachery it has been its mission for 75 years to warn mariners against.

Its original place in the lives of those who dare the sea usurped by a floating beacon off the dangerous coast, the old lighthouse still remains, primarily a cherished landmark, a memento of the days when it flashed warnings of peril to the storm beset. Year after year the furious gods of wind and tide have stretched their greedy maws toward the tower. But each time when the gales subsided the tower stood erect.

Scores of visitors, anxious to see the death throes of the monument, came to Barnegat City certain that the high winds which had developed in the last 24 hours would give the surging waters sufficient reinforcement to eat away the fifteen feet of sand which is all that remains to fight back the currents. Slowly but surely the sand bank is crumbling into the furious waterway. Danger lurks today.

Weeks later, engineers closed the lighthouse and warned that unless a protecting wall were built at once "the beacon will, in all probability, fall into the sea."

Joseph F. Yearly, courtesy Lester Yearly

**Long Beach Boulevard in Loveladies at flood tide, August, 1934.**

*Ocean County Historical Society (all)*

**A northeaster in November, 1935 cuts the Beach Haven fishing pier in half, above, and takes out a seawall in Harvey Cedars erected in the twenties, below. Carol Stratton copes with the high tide on Bay Avenue in Beach Haven, right.**

But the 1930s were just getting their wind. Nineteen thirty-four brought in a tropical storm the day the ill-fated *Morro Castle* caught fire and beached at Asbury Park. (The two incidents were not related.) Although 1935 was not visited by Huracan, the Carib Indians' mighty storm god, the Jersey coast was not ignored by his local cousins. A November northeaster made a call and ate its way through bridges, railroads, piers and whole sections of beach. It pulled up the Pennsylvania Railroad bridge that spanned Barnegat Bay, bent the tracks of the Jersey Central Railroad into curls, rolled ten-ton rocks out of the breakwater at the mouth of the Manasquan River, ripped away fishing piers in Ocean City, Ventnor, Beach Haven, Beach Arlington (Ship Bottom) and Sea Isle City, and caused the highest tides on record in Margate and Harvey Cedars.

In Atlantic City the sounds of howling wind and drumming rain were interspersed with the yips and yaps of animals at Joseph Paxson's zoo.

*Cries of distress were raised by the frightened creatures as the onrushing tide drove them from their shelters and into the deeper water beyond. The animals fought pluckily for their lives, but were unable to successfully battle the fury of the elements and were drowned. Among the victims were reindeer, coyotes and hyenas.*

It was the storm's taste for sand, however, that most upset its unwilling hosts. "A Storm Came Up from Out the Sea and Built a New Inlet for Barnegat Bay," one account put it, continuing:

*The ocean stormed on one side. On the other the bay grew swollen, heavy as the wind bore down upon it, crashing the sandy strips for room. The men of Barnegat peered through the storm and watched. The wind went screaming out to sea, and the gray clouds, like broncos, went galloping away, and a pale November sun shown down on an inlet where there had not been an inlet before.*

Island Beach broke about a mile north of Barnegat Inlet. The new inlet was about 250 feet wide and seven feet deep at low tide. Though big enough to navigate, the Coast Guard declared it "uncertain." Within a week, westerly winds began stitching it closed again. Owners of fishing shacks nearby helped by throwing old rubble and wreckage and "anything they could lift" into the gash. During the winter, heavy ice in the bay slowed the tides running through the new channel, and Seaside Park Mayor Francis Freeman experimented with barbed wire entanglements covered with catbrier and weighted down with sandbags to further slacken the currents, as slow-flowing water deposits its sand as it goes.

*Joseph F. Yearly, courtesy Lester Yearly*

**Remains of the Jersey Central Railroad bridge over Barnegat Bay after a northeaster, November 11, 1935. Below, the stretch of debris-covered trestles from Cedar Bonnet Island to Bonnet Island.**

What the mayor wrought by day, however, boat owners attempted to undo by night. Some people liked the idea of a new inlet since Barnegat Inlet was considered generally unsafe for navigation. The biggest channel churners turned out to be rumrunners, with the Coast Guard chasing their wakes.

In March, the channel narrowed enough to drive a beach buggy across. No one could remember the sea ever chewing its way through Island Beach before but old maps revealed that an inlet had once cut the narrow peninsula further north and that Barnegat Inlet itself had been formed the same way.

Mayors of towns up and down the coast, seeing their seats as uncertain as so many sandcastles, were appalled. They met hastily in Deal and sent a message to President Roosevelt warning that "ensuing storms will be calamitous" and insisting "the magnitude of interests involved merit substantial Federal allotment of moneys." With the nation still wallowing in the Depression, they added a clincher: "The resulting benefit to labor would be great and widespread and thus labor would be applied to work of greatest value."

A local editorial put it another way:

*We who live in a sector that receives periodic batterings from a storm-swept sea, who can realize the potential danger that is forever dogging this part of our coast, cannot understand why the Federal Government has not allocated funds for coastal erosion prevention already. The government has spent and continues to spend huge sums in boondoggling projects, making work where none exists, throwing money right and left for projects that will benefit but a few people, but when it comes to projects that would protect our natural assets for all of the people, there seems to be an endless ribbon of red tape to cut.*

*Ocean County Historical Society*

Joseph F. Yearly, courtesy Lester Yearly

**Residents help a neighbor escape through flood tide in a northeaster at 78th Street and the Boulevard in Harvey Cedars, November 17, 1935.**

In an odd turn, Long Beach Island grew fatter in the storm. The beach at Surf City was widened by 30 yards, at Beach Haven by a reported "several score." In many places, in fact, the beaches extended to cover the streets.

Seventeen tropical disturbances formed over the Atlantic in 1936, second only to the twenty-one that appeared in 1933. Only five of these managed to reach full hurricane status, and only one of these made it this far, in August. A reporter for the *Philadelphia Inquirer* found himself trapped on Long Beach Island.

> *This correspondent, crossing the Causeway at 7 p.m., saw the water close over behind him, sweeping stalled automobiles beneath its tide. As the storm renewed its ferocity, 3,000 persons were marooned on this strip of sandy beach, in the very teeth of the gale. High tide tonight was the ominous*

> *deadline for which the island waited. If the storm does not abate, the entire island may be plunged underwater.*

The scrapbook page on which this item was found also bore a neat, handwritten note: "Very much exaggerated, tho' it was bad enough at best." A new deathwatch was set on Barnegat Lighthouse:

> *Jetties have been built; a bulkhead has been made of derelict automobiles and kegs; prayers have gone up from the old salts who still steered by its flash, spurning the new-fangled ship to the East. But that has not been enough. In 1933, the unrelenting sea approached so close that the shaft was closed. Yesterday's storm, with gusts reaching hurricane force, all but completed the conquest. Two hundred feet of sand built up in front of the lighthouse was eaten away and the water splashed within six feet of the foundation. But, again, it survived.*

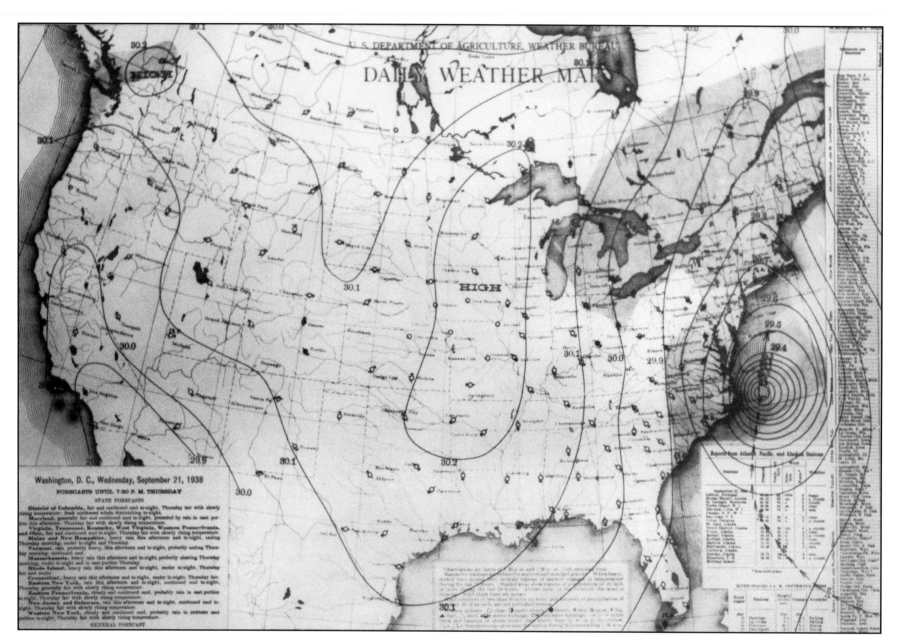

# 1938

SHORE PEOPLE KNOW that September is the blessing they get for tolerating crowds all summer. The water is warm, the breeze balmy, the beaches smooth and sweet. They also know September is high hurricane time. There have been hurricanes as early as June, but the concatenation of events that must take place to create a classic howler, the kind you can hang a name on, usually occurs in late August or September. Then they erupt in headlines, like these from the September hurricane of 1938.

Storm Curves North; Warnings Posted.... Bridge Falls; Scores Stranded.... Flood Waters Peril County Roads, Homes.

Plus the quotable quirks:

The Empire State Building swayed a little more than four inches at the height of the hurricane, the widest yet recorded. Officials said no one noticed. Engineers constructed the 1060-foot building to withstand a 12-inch sway....

A man on Long Island received an expensive barometer he had ordered on the morning of September 21. The needle seemed stuck on "Hurricane." He shook it a few times, then wrapped it up again and sent it back with an angry letter....

This gusty tramp from the tropics "picked" four million bushels of apples in 24 hours, crushed 26,000 automobiles, and whitened windows with ocean salt 120 miles from the sea.

The coastal forecast had been for "fresh southerly winds except fresh north or northeast near Sandy Hook, increasing this afternoon or tonight and overcast with rain." There was a hurricane that had worked its way up from the Caribbean to about Cape Hatteras, but it was supposed to turn east and sputter away over the ocean.

Instead it turned north, at an incredible forward speed of 60 miles an hour.

Forecasters still thought it would veer away and issued only gale warnings. A newspaper editor in New England said later that "in none of these warnings was the word hurricane used...it is doubtful if anyone considered anything really dangerous was at hand."

And so it was that a storm that was described by another journalist as "a roaring demon as big as Ohio" showed up unexpectedly on two doorsteps.

Josephine Thomas was never comfortable with the sea, a Midwesterner come to Long Beach Island to marry and raise a family by the bay. From a letter to her mother:

Everything began to happen just about noon. Within one hour the tide had risen from its ordinary mark to the edge of the road while the meadows between here and the lagoon were completely covered. I blithely announced that I would go over and get the mail, that "I liked to walk in the rain and wanted to see a newspaper." Tommy (her nickname for husband Reynold) wouldn't let me take his oilskins as he said he wanted to be ready to dash out at any minute if any of the anchors on his two craft started to go. So off I went in raincoat and sneakers.

Well, when I got from the lee of the house and that wind struck me I was somewhat staggered but it didn't seem any worse than plenty of blizzards I have walked in during the winter. It was only when I got past Gordon's and started down the exposed length of 80th Street that I realized how bad it was. I got about opposite Charlton's and decided I had best turn back — only I couldn't. The rain hit me in the face with the force of a fire hose, and instead of making any headway I just lifted one foot after another from the ground and stayed in the same place. So I headed for the post office again and ran all the way, afraid that if I slowed down to a walk the wind would turn me end over end. At the post office I got my paper and a letter from Dorothy, tucked them inside my raincoat, got my breath, heard the reassuring news that the barometer was lower than it had been in six years, and went outside to see if the wind had abated any.

As I stepped on Lear's porch, Andy (an employee) went by with the truck but although I hollered my loudest he neither heard nor saw me. The wind had NOT let up any and I knew I could never get down that unprotected length of 80th Street alone, so I stopped across the road at Hartman's to telephone home to have Andy come back in the truck and get me. Tommy greeted me over the phone with the first bawling out he has ever given me — evidently he had no idea I would keep on going and he had just let me go outdoors to see what I thought of it.

So I waited some more, dripping all over the Hartman's kitchen, which didn't make any difference as the water was coming under the back door so fast Mary Lou couldn't keep it mopped up. I tried to reassure her by saying I *had seen the tide much higher in other storms, but I saw no reason to tell her I had never seen the wind as bad.*

*Andy came along in a half hour and I got home to find Tommy drenched to the skin in spite of his oilskins and unable to get any hot coffee because the electricity was off. The house by this time was draped with wet clothes and Tommy was looking about for still another change. About this time the big front window started buckling, bending inward as though it were made of rubber, and while Tommy yelled at me to take Michael (the Thomas' son) and stay in the other end of the house, he and Andy got boards from the attic and nailed them across the window.*

*The whole west end of the house was cracking and shivering. I figured that if the west end of the house stove in, the best place for us to get out was through the east window in Pooch's (daughter) room. I got a hammer and knocked out the screen, carried my raincoat and hood in there and a heavy coat and boots for Michael, and sat on Pooch's bed with him, partly to keep him quiet and partly to see what was happening to Tommy. Between gusts of spray I could see him, now in the skiff, now in the dredge, and then making his way, half crawling, over that rickety little bridge of Boone Stewart's. Then the spray blotted him out again, and to keep from collapsing from anxiety about him I began to read Mother Goose to Michael, who didn't want to stay in Pooch's room.*

*Then I saw that Reynold was rescuing Stewart's birdbath and some other things they had left outside. "Blankety blank," I raged, "isn't that just like Reynold Thomas to get himself drowned trying to save a damned old birdbath" — "Yes, Michael, yes, Michael, storm go boom" — where, oh where is Tommy — oh, why did he go across that little bridge — "Michael, please be quiet just a minute" — now he's coming across the bridge — "MICHAEL BE QUIET — don't cry, honey, mother didn't mean it — here, mother will read all about Little Bo Peep — see, Little Bo Peep lost her sheep" — oh, there he comes across that bridge again — and so on and on and on. I was as close as I have ever been to just having a good dose of hysterics.*

*The wind was too hard now for Tommy to get across the bridge except on his hands and knees. He got over all right and ploughed through the water in the meadow which was almost to his hips, literally fighting every foot of the way. Back in the house he had once more to strip to the skin. By this time he was using my sweaters for undershirts and just forgetting about his wet pants. The water was sweeping over our bulkhead in a torrent, the spray pounding on that west window and the surf roaring even above the howl of the wind.*

*Suddenly I thought of Poochy. It was almost time for school to be out and I had so many other things on my mind I had practically forgotten her. Tommy telephoned to the wife of the bus driver who said he had gone down the road to make sure his bus could get through, and that he would take every child all the way home. She was still not here fully an hour after that and we could get no response from Barnegat City. Finally a telephone call came from Small's place. The bus driver had tried to come down our street but he couldn't see a thing driving into that rain and he would keep Poochy in the bus if Tommy would come and get her. But Andy had the truck and the car wouldn't start, it was so wet. While Tommy was trying to have Pooch left somewhere else, the yellow bus finally loomed out of the rain and Tommy carried her in.*

*She was shivering with fright because she heard somebody say the ocean was breaking through. She thought our house was going to be washed away, and especially after I explained why she and Michael must keep away from the big window. Tommy said later he also thought the house might go and that he had the skiff in readiness all afternoon, as our best bet would have*

*been to head straight across the bay to Manahawkin. About four o'clock the tide and wind began to slacken as quickly as they had come up, and in another hour the bay had dropped back to its usual level.*

*The Atlantic Ocean had not, however. From our kitchen window as far as we could see up to Loveladies we could see the surf dashing high into the air above the dunes. It was a magnificent sight, but I fear I didn't appreciate the magnificence — then. I would have preferred a nice, flat mill pond to look at.*

*And that was the famous hurricane of 1938. It did very little damage to us, although the yard looks very bedraggled; all the flowers are flat. I spent the whole day getting wet things on the line and thanking heaven for sunshine. Tell Dorothy her letter almost was among the casualties. As I came out of the post office, the wind took my newspaper and her letter out from under my raincoat and had them out in the meadows before I knew what happened. I crossed off the paper to profit and loss, but did go after the letter and finally tracked it down in a puddle, very soggy and ink-stained but still legible.*

The storm only skirted the Jersey coast. It banged head-on into Long Island and New England. There had been nothing like it there since the Great Hurricane of 1821. One of the most gripping accounts ever written of being in the heart of a hurricane was given by Helen Joy Lee who lived at the southern tip of Rhode Island.

*About four o'clock the wind burst from the south, much harder than before, at about 100 mph. It was all I could do to close the front door against it. Spray and sand came under the door so that I could not do anything to keep up with it. Debris that had gone to sea with the wind from the northeast began to come back and crash on the house. A piece of the roof went and water poured in over the door. In a few minutes I was ankle deep.*

*There was nothing to do now but wait for whatever was going to come to me, and to get where I thought would be the safest place. That, I figured, was the side porch. If the house collapsed I would be better able to get away. I took my waterproof wristwatch from the mantel and put it on. I took the dog and cat into the kitchen, tied the dog to the knob inside the door, put on Eunice's reversible raincoat, and put the kitten in my pocket. Then I went out on the side porch to look things over. I saw our three-car garage lifted up and dropped into the bay. I had to hold on with both hands against the force of the wind. I got soaked with each wave as it went over the house.*

*The kitchen door slammed shut behind me; the glass broke and hit my back and fell on the floor, but was quickly washed away by a wave. My coat whipped out and the kitten was blown out of my pocket and sailed away like a miniature rug. I tried to open the door but I could not, so I broke off the jagged glass and pulled the dog through.*

*There was a bottle of whiskey in the kitchen and I thought if I was going to have to sit outside for an hour or so it would be a good idea to have a drink. Taking a log of firewood, I used it as a battering ram and managed to get the door open and drop the log in the crack. Water cascaded out a foot deep. I could not push the door any wider.*

*It was 4:20. In my other pocket I found a bandanna and tied that on my head. I saw the porch roof on Kitty's house get folded back with the posts attached and torn off the house like a piece of tablet paper. I watched the squares of concrete sidewalk go out with each wave and skim into the bay. I turned to Tucky (the dog) and said, "Well, I wonder how much longer," when something hit the house a terrific thud — I think it was the concrete retaining wall — and brought the porch down on me, dislocating my left elbow. Tucky and I, in ten seconds, found ourselves 150 feet from where we started. I was sitting as if on a toboggan and was carried into the road and over the wall and into the bay. Near me were the pieces of sidewalk piled at an angle and sticking a foot out of the water.*

*Looking back where I had come from I saw more of the porch and a large piece of lattice work coming at me. I had to think fast so I doubled up next to the pieces of sidewalk and let the wave and lattice go over my head. When I came up for air, there was the kitten on a board ten feet away crying loudly. Tucky was southwest and next to me. I undid her leash and the last I saw of her was five minutes later when she was 50 feet away and northeast of me, standing on some debris.*

*I decided I had better get out of the churning, shallow water. Stumbling over concrete and hanging on with my right arm to a fallen pole, I got out into deep water. I tried to hang the injured arm over the pole but I couldn't raise it that high. Somehow I managed to get astride the pole. I saw a woman in a dark dress standing at the edge of the bay. I do not think she was being washed in. I did not see her or anyone else again. Up on the pole I was exposed to flying debris, so I got down into the water again. I felt something hitting me on the chest and back and found I was being wedged in between two green doors (perhaps our own garage). I could see the corner of one about an arm's length away, so I took a long breath, went down, kicked hard on the bottom, and luckily came up beyond the edge of the door.*

*All fear left me when I hit the water and had to do something to save myself. It was the half hour of total helplessness in the house that was the worst time for me. I began to talk to myself, aloud. "Well, this is really a hurricane and you are out in it. You have gotten this far okay so you might as well see how much farther you can get." Gray spray and rain made low visibility. Pieces of wood, shutters, doors and chairs were flying through the air. Some were hitting me. I saw a small porch roof, perhaps my own, so I pushed through wreckage for about ten feet and got on the leeward side and climbed up. I had to pick up the bad arm and lay it up ahead of me, hunch up, and repeat the process until I could reach the shingle edges over the peak. My feet were in the water. I just was settled when a wave capsized it and I went under. I put my right arm over my head for protection against the nails but I came up in open space — next to my pole.*

*The side of a house came along; there were two holes where windows had been. The edge was jagged and it buckled in the waves and I could not get on it. I was having a hard time getting my breath against the rain and I was about ready to give up when a piece of a house came by and I crawled on; it was like a surf board. This was pretty exposed and as I came up the side of a wave a board hit me across the left eye. The roof came back, upside down, so I crawled into that and lay in water at the bottom of the V. I stayed in this a long time. The flying debris struck the roof first and me only second.*

*There was a book lying open in the water, the pages turning back and forth, that kept circling my roof — or maybe I was spinning around. My bandanna was gone. It was getting darker. A mattress came along that seemed to be moving faster than I was, so I changed steeds, pushing through all manner of wreckage. The mattress was very comfortable for my bad arm. I would have stayed on the mattress but part of a boat came along faster so I changed again. I know the tide was low at noon, so would be going out again about 6:30 and if I did not get to land I might get washed out to sea.*

*Luck was with me. Shortly after I got into the boat I heard a different scratching. Looking, I saw I was going over some treetops; they are 20 feet above the usual water level. Soon my boat stopped. It was just 6:30 and black night. The wind was still strong, debris flying, and it was raining. Somehow I got up on a branch which was just at the water level, and winding my legs and one arm around the tree I must have dozed.*

Her ordeal was far from over. By the time she struggled through the night to astonish a family in a still-standing house, she was so raw and swollen and torn and bedraggled that finally, in the hospital, her own doctor did not recognize her. "My head and face were cut and bruised so that I could not stand to have my hair touched for four days."

Among the 680 who died during that hurricane were one hundred who were never found. Some observers commented it was fortunate the storm hit after the summer season was over, else the toll might have reached that of the current recordholder, the 1900 blast that claimed six thousand lives in Galveston, Texas. At one point, the wind was clocked at 182 miles per hour and downtown Providence was under thirteen feet of water. Freighters were overturned in Boston Harbor. Nearly seventeen thousand vacation cottages and two thousand permanent homes were destroyed. Also, twenty-six thousand automobiles were smashed, six thousand boats ruined, 275 million trees broken or torn out of the ground, and thousands of cattle killed, along with hundreds of thousands of chickens, geese, ducks and turkeys. One hundred bridges had to be replaced, and telephone repairmen were called in from as far away as Arkansas and Nevada to work on downed lines.

In New Jersey, the bridge over Absecon Inlet collapsed and marooned Brigantine for two months. Waves breaking on the beach at Sea Girt were visible at Bay Head, three miles away. The fall tomato crop was ruined as well as half the apple harvest as winds tore up trees and rains bore fruit-laden branches to the ground. All of Ocean Avenue in Manasquan lay under a three-foot layer of sand. In a North Haledon pheasant farm, the wind herded four thousand birds against a fence with such force that a thousand were squeezed to death.

Throughout the storm, five hundred beavers in Palisades Park tended their dams and were given credit for restraining the waters of rain-swollen rivers and streams which otherwise would have overflowed their banks. Rangers reported the beavers chewed down trees all night to reinforce the dams and thereby saved several highways from being cut off, prevented the destruction of at least one bridge, and preserved hundreds of acres of topsoil.

Still the 1930s had not vented all their weather upon the Jersey shore. The following year, the last of the decade, as if to insure its entry into some great meteorological record book, "the season's worst storm" came from a new quarter, the southeast. As one paper reported, "It was a versatile wind, shifting during the day and night to all directions and sometimes seemingly coming from everywhere." The gusts had enough force to blow Jersey Central Railroad's crack Blue Comet off its tracks in the middle of the pinelands. At the Little Egg Harbor Yacht Club, "only masts could be seen above water."

If the storm was daunting enough for veteran sailors, it was almost disastrous for garage attendant William Sherwood on Long Beach Island.

*An inexperienced sailor, Sherwood had gone out from the Spray Beach Yacht Club in a sneak box. Unable to return in the storm, he found refuge on a small island in the bay and remained there until morning. After being listed among the missing for almost 24 hours he returned to shore wet, hungry and apparently healthy.*

Another paper referred to the storm as the "Great Southeaster," but it didn't stick. It wasn't until September 14, 1944 that the elements whipped up another "Great" — the "Great Atlantic Hurricane of 1944," so powerful it pushed World War II off the front page and so overwhelming along the New Jersey coast that it still looms large in the memories of those who witnessed it.

**The 1944 hurricane which destroys twenty percent of the homes in Harvey Cedars leaves some blocks wiped clean, as this Navy blimp photo shows.**

# CHAPTER THREE

# 1944

*Who hath desired the sea? — the sight of salt water unbounded —*
*The heave and the halt and the haul and the crash of the comber wind-hounded?*
*The sleek-barrelled wave before storm, grey, foamless, enormous and growing --*
*Stark calm in the lap of the line or the crazy-eyed hurricane blowing.*

— Rudyard Kipling

LIFE AT THE SHORE DURING THE SUMMER OF 1944 flowed in a subdued rhythm marked by events of the Second World War. The Allied Forces invaded Europe in June and young men who in another summer might have guarded New Jersey's beaches fought their way across France; by Labor Day, battle-toughened veterans of the First Army penetrated the Siegfried Line. On September 14, troops captured Roetgen, the first German town to fall to American soldiers.

The Battle of the Atlantic had been declared officially over. U-boats no longer stalked shipping off the New Jersey coast. The last attack in nearby waters was in December, but local men still served in the Coast Guard Auxiliary, supporting the regulars, standing six-hour watches in station towers from Cape May to Long Branch. The end of the war was in sight that hot dry summer, and an optimism that sons and husbands would return soon was in the sea air.

Hundreds of thousands of visitors crowded the shore's dozens of boardwalks — any resort worth its salt air had one — and filled the hotels from late June, many extending summer into a warm September. Visitors streamed into Atlantic City for the Miss America Pageant and cheered on Janice Hansen, Miss New Jersey. At the nearby Steel Pier, dancers from the Coast Guard musical *Tars and Spars* modeled GI bathing suits for "girls of the Coast Guard."

The New Jersey Resort Association met in Asbury Park and reported a $220 million resort industry income. It announced that a one-mile-wide coastal strip between Sandy Hook and Cape May had an assessed value of more than $700 million, and proclaimed that it was time that tourism was recognized as a major industry.

But no one needed reminding there was still a war on. Gas and food rationing restricted travel and restaurant menus — the price of coffee was frozen at five cents a cup — and wounded servicemen convalesced at oceanfront hotels. What had to be done was made fun: Victory gardens, war bond sales, surgical dressing classes, scrap paper drives.

Some communities had more than the war effort on their minds. The remnants of a hurricane that had originated in the Caribbean passed offshore on August 1. It was still a hurricane when it slammed into North Carolina, but as it crossed Virginia, Maryland and Delaware its force diminished. By the time it hit the tip of Cape May it had been demoted to a tropical storm. Still, the high tide seriously eroded the beaches at Cape May Point, Harvey Cedars and Holgate.

Cape May City's commissioners were considering a unique postwar solution to their continuing beach erosion problem: a combination jetty and entertainment pier. The base would be a permeable jetty and the superstructure a revenue-producing mix of concessions, restaurant and theater. If the pier were erected at Madison Street, the theory went, sand would collect between it and Convention Hall Pier. Officials pointed out that beaches west of Convention Hall suffered less from eroding currents than those to the east. They reasoned that a long, solid jetty running toward Cape May Point would be a permanent solution but knew such a project couldn't be funded on a local, county or state level — the federal government would have to pay.

In Harvey Cedars, Mayor Joseph Yearly worried that the ocean was trying to force an inlet through his town. On August 1, Harvey Cedars resident Glenna Wilcox stood at the end of Seventy-eighth Street with borough officials and watched the ocean cut away the dunes.

*Most people think the water comes up over the dunes, but it doesn't. It cuts the dune right out from under, like a hot knife in butter. We watched a wave come up with this big swirling, swooping motion and cut out a chunk of sand, and the next wave would cut out some more. And the third wave would cut out so much the whole cliff of sand would collapse. Now you've got this great big pile of sand for the ocean to hit. And it would hit, and hit, and hit. Then it would wash that all away and then start cutting in again. After three or four more waves another big chunk would fall in. And while I stood there, about half an hour, I'll bet about six feet of that dune just vanished.*

At 11 P.M., the borough's High Point Volunteer Fire Company retrieved the household furnishings of the Lindauer and Kroberger cottages on Seventy-seventh Street when the wash from heavy breakers eroded the dunes and undermined oceanfront homes. The mayor remembered the April 1929 northeaster when he moved his Seventy-seventh Street home back from the sea to a bayfront location. He spoke at the Long Beach Island Board of Trade's late August meeting and made an impassioned

*courtesy Joe Krug*

**In early August, before the hurricane, the sea was already gnawing at the dunes in Harvey Cedars, threatening homes.**

appeal for help, telling the group that only "four feet of gravel levee" remained to protect the town. Residents of the other threatened towns crowded the meeting and island officials approved dispatching a delegation to the State Board of Commerce and Navigation's September 11 meeting.

Henry McLaughlin, Philadelphia attorney and pioneer developer of Brant Beach, urged concerted appeals to Congressman James Auchincloss for the installation of systematic barriers against the ocean. "The correction of beach erosion on this island is a Federal job, one too big for local, county or state units," he counseled. The Board of Trade invited a War Department engineer to inspect erosion on the island and Army Corps engineer Col. Clarence Renshaw pledged the cooperation of his agency and said he hoped to observe the conditions soon. Director Fran Holmes of Commerce and Navigation responded to the board's request for state aid: "The governor has stated that he will release money from the $1.25 million erosion appropriation only for emergency projects. Plans must be prepared by engineers and money raised on a fifty-fifty basis by such units as the Borough of Harvey Cedars."

Della Lonabough, a summer resident of Surf City, suggested that the board consider the historical success of the Dutch, who plant grass on their artificial dikes. She pointed out that the island had long stood the onslaught of the ocean because of the natural barrier of beachfront dunes: "When man tears down these dunes or destroys the rich growth of grasses which holds their shifting sands together, he invites damage from the cycle of the tides washing the loosened sand."

## September 14

First Lt. Ted Barber, a hurricane alert officer with an Army weather unit in Antigua in the Caribbean, started a long-awaited home leave to Barnegat City on September 9. At just about the same time, a tropical storm was spotted east of Puerto Rico; Barber's newly formed unit was credited with the storm's early detection. When he reached Miami, the storm had

gained hurricane force and moved northwest, placing its center northeast of Nassau in the Bahamas. Florida was put on full hurricane alert as the storm stalled for eight hours 650 miles east of Miami, leaving meteorologists scrambling to predict a course which would either endanger the coast or carry the storm out to sea. As Barber would later recall, the storm followed him right up the coast.

To emphasize the hurricane's power and ferocity, the Miami office of the Weather Bureau named it the Great Atlantic Hurricane. Now on the move, the storm recurved to the north at 9 P.M. on the twelfth, aimed directly at North Carolina's Cape Hatteras, and took off at 25 to 30 miles per hour. The following day, the *Philadelphia Inquirer* warned, "A great hurricane fraught with peril for life and property is bearing down on the North Carolina coast; only a last minute change of direction could save the coastline from a raking by winds of a force comparable to the New England Hurricane of 1938."

The U.S. Weather Bureau in Washington, D.C., advised residents of low-lying areas on the North Carolina and Virginia coasts to leave immediately for higher ground, and the Coast Guard issued an alert as far as Eastport, Maine. The emergency advisory read, "Winds will begin to increase and reach hurricane force north of Wilmington, N.C., to Cape Hatteras early Thursday forenoon. Indications are for continued north-northwest movement with slight increase in speed."

Spiraling out over a 500-mile radius in the Atlantic Ocean, the hurricane passed Hatteras at 9:20 A.M. Eastern War Time on September 14, turned slightly to the northeast and accelerated to 40 miles per hour. Barometric pressure dropped to 27.97 inches, and winds were clocked at 110 miles per hour. The tide crested at seven feet above normal as the storm hit Cape Henry, Virginia, at noon. Winds increased to 134 miles per hour and gusted to 150. By 3 P.M., the hurricane's center had reached ninety miles northeast of Norfolk and was moving at 50 miles per hour. The Weather Bureau requested alerts to be broadcast by all radio stations within the affected area.

Since the morning of the twelfth, frequent rain had saturated the 127-mile length of the New Jersey coast. In some areas, flood conditions from the rainstorms existed by late on the thirteenth. Jersey City police received more than 200 calls from homeowners whose cellars were flooded. In Newark, floodwaters swept over sidewalks, stranding homeward-bound pedestrians and motorists. At Pennsylvania Station, bus passengers removed their shoes and stockings and waded to higher levels, and police emergency trucks towed several stalled buses to drier sections where they were able to operate. State police up and down the coast kept a close watch on the weather, teletyping regular reports to Trenton headquarters on the condition of beaches, roads and communication lines. Meanwhile, winds swirling around the hurricane's center pushed surging swells 500 miles ahead of the storm, and a powerful surf hammered sea walls and scoured beaches.

At 2 P.M., the Seaside Heights Coast Guard station reported that the seas were "kicking up" and predicted the beginning of the blow by early evening. Local radio stations broadcast hurricane warnings. At Atlantic City radio station WFPG, program director Ed Davis issued reports every fifteen minutes. Red and black hurricane warning flags flew from Coast Guard stations and municipal buildings up and down the coast. By 5 p.m., the hurricane's center stood fifty to seventy-five miles off Delaware Bay. The fury of the wind was so great that roofs blew off dwellings near Cape Henlopen. The Red Cross evacuated thirty-five youngsters from the Children's Beach House near Lewes, Delaware, and hundreds of coastal residents left their homes for shelter inland.

## Cape May County

At the mouth of the Delaware Bay, waves were turbulent and confused, their height impossible to estimate as they crested and broke, spouting up fusillades of foam. Force 10 northwest winds lashed Cape May, where the barometer dropped to 28.83 inches. Commander Carl Gaskell of the Cape May Coast Guard Station canceled all drills and liberties. In Cape May City that morning, John Hewett received a call from the Red Cross asking him to prepare volunteer workers for the emergency. He enlisted Lena Hughes to phone the Columbia Hotel to reserve rooms for anticipated evacuees. Sue Leaming, Lena's daughter, got a kick out of these preparations and commented, "Oh, it's just another northeaster." Mother and daughter continued their work around the house, three blocks from the ocean, but a frightening wind began to blow and the Leamings' barometer fell rapidly, down and down, to 28.5 inches. A friend's father told Sue that should the mercury fall to 28.3, the town would simply blow apart.

Sue Leaming wrote a letter to her aunt late that night.

*I was upstairs and called down to tell mother that I could see lumber floating up Benton Avenue; the wind and rain were furious by then. I went to the basement and as I opened the door, I heard an awful gushing. I rushed to the preserve closet and moved the preserves up as fast as I could, yelling all*

*New Jersey State Police/Picture Collection, New Jersey State Library*

**Houses buckled by the storm at Townsends Inlet.**

the time for mother. We got the bikes up on top of the washtubs and most of the valuables up high. In fifteen minutes, the water was up to my knees and I heard my husband, Pic, on the front porch trying to get out the rowboat. The tide had come up so fast none of us could believe it.

At the height of the wind and rain, Roberta Corliss, who lives two houses down from me, tried to walk over here. She was pregnant and was scared to death. Midge Steger was following her, carrying her child. Last of all came her poor maid, Lucy. Mrs. Shubert, who lives in back of us, called over to say that Curtis' living room had eight inches of water, and later Pic rowed over and found two of the casement windows blown off. Water was about six inches above Aunt Elnora's door, and the Stegers had to move their furniture upstairs. They had sixteen inches inside and so did Spencers

Mr. Steger, who owns Lovell Beach Concession, was at the beach trying to save his tents. He had put them over on the porches of the beachfront houses, and then all of a sudden this terrific tide swept in and there weren't any porches on the homes. His tents were all over town. At one point, I heard a thunderous crash which seemed to come from Mecray's corner; we thought it must be the boardwalk crashing into the houses.

We had all these people at the house, so we baked potatoes, cooked some peas and fried the last of our Victory Garden tomatoes. The electricity had gone off but we still had gas and water, so we all enjoyed a cup of hot coffee and sat and ate by the light of the oil lamp. By the time we finished supper, we had no water to wash dishes and couldn't flush the toilet. We put a bucket in the bathroom and — it sounds terrible — but we had to throw it out from the back porch. Spicer, our son, had not been feeling any too well all day, and just before supper the poor child sat on the living room floor and vomited. That just about made the picture complete.

We sat out on the porch until midnight. The stars were out, and it was warm and lovely. Boats were going by all evening, taking residents back and forth. We thought we were in Venice.

*New Jersey State Police/Picture Collection, New Jersey State Library*

**The end of the road in Sea Isle City.**

Although tides had been running at about normal levels throughout the day, the arrival of hurricane-force northeast winds late in the afternoon pushed tidal levels from a few feet above normal to a record 9.6 feet. Just before five o'clock what was described as a "towering 40 foot tidal wave" smashed into Cape May. The term "storm surge" was not commonly used then but the storm-formed mound of moving water topped by cresting waves looked to those on shore like what they imagined a tidal wave to be.

The wave crashed into Cape May's boardwalk, Convention Hall, and Hunt and Pennyland piers, ripping and snapping the understructure, sending pilings and sections of boardwalk smashing into beachfront homes and hotels. It destroyed the entire two-mile boardwalk in a matter of minutes. Beach Drive washed out and was buried under thousands of tons of sand and wreckage to a depth of at least four feet.

At Convention Hall, the storm surge smashed in the rear of the ballroom, pushing before it musical instruments stored behind the stage. The water dumped the grand piano into the ocean and scattered pieces as far as Stockton Beach. The Coast Guard and Navy evacuated three hundred families — most from the area east of Perry Street — to the Columbia, Colonial and Lafayette hotels. Red Cross disaster workers maintained a 24-hour shelter and canteen service.

The next morning, Sue Leaming put on her husband's boots and walked around the corner.

*New Jersey State Police/Picture Collection, New Jersey State Library*

**Hurricane damage in Ocean City.**

*Blair's tree was blown over, and the sidewalk was sticking up several feet above the water, which was clear up to the top of the boots. Aunt Elnora's rugs were soaked, but I guess her wallpaper escaped unless seepage may ruin it, as Mrs. Ricker says her wallpaper is just beginning to get wet today. On my way back, Mrs. Ricker asked me to ride with her on one of the boats. We stopped and picked up my sons and went down to the foot of Jefferson Street. What a sight! I had no idea there had been such damage. There was no boardwalk at all east of Convention Pier. At Stockton, the boardwalk is clear over to Cliff's store. The Convention Hall is demolished. The stage and half the dance floor is gone, and there's no fishing pier at all.*

*Aunt Elnora found an icebox on her front lawn, and Aunt Gert has lots of water in her basement. The sand is halfway up Stockton Avenue. That lovely house with the stone wall on the corner is ruined. The worst of the tide came up Jefferson Street. There's a big piece of boardwalk with an upright lamppost floating in front of Ken Miller's around the corner, and the beanpoles are all leaning in our Victory Garden, which is no more.*

*The ducks that Shuberts got last Easter are swimming around their yard, and out in our backyard I watched a turtle swim in and around the seesaws, swings and slide. He finally climbed up on the slide to sun himself.*

*Now there's a terrible smell of sewer gas and fuel oil; Pic had to open the door under the porch to let in some fresh air. The fire whistle just blew. Pic started out in his hip boots, but it didn't amount to anything, and the fire engines got stuck in the sand, and we're all dead tired.*

Thirty-five miles north, Commander Charles Jennings of Ocean City Coast Guard, Group Strathmere, logged a barometer reading of 28.98 and Force 12 northeast winds at 4 P.M. The increasing forward speed of the storm now added to the force of the wind. An hour later, the ocean inundated the station, and Jennings called his men down from the tower.

The wind blew down nine homes, and the roof of one cottage was tossed one hundred yards to Reed's Beach on the bayside. Three cottages at Whale Beach washed into the sea. Strathmere was isolated for hours.

At the north end of Sea Isle City, almost the entire colony of homes washed away as the ocean met Ludlam's Bay. Some were carried across the old railroad bed and into the marshes. Private duty nurse Caroline Nick drowned after she left the beachfront home of her employer at the height of the storm. Her body was found 150 yards distant, covered by sand and debris.

The hurricane spared Wildwood's boardwalk, placed farther from the ocean than other towns' and separated by an exceptionally wide beach. However, Sea Isle City and Stone Harbor lost theirs. Stone Harbor Mayor John Biggs watched a portion of his town's boardwalk ride the crest of a monster wave over the top of a house and crash onto First Avenue.

Some residents tried to escape the engulfing waters, but too late: Jack Gibson got as far as Strathmere when his car stalled, and he took refuge in the Corson's Inlet Coast Guard Station. Public Service bus driver Bill Keyes was trying to reach Sea Isle City, but the water rose too quickly. He stayed with the bus for a while, then climbed out and hung on to a telephone pole until he could swim to a nearby retreat house where he was rescued by some priests. They dried his clothes and put him to bed.

## Ocean City

In the late afternoon — while the storm was sending tree limbs, broken glass and jagged wrecks of roofs tearing through the air, while buildings were collapsing under the battering impact of wind and water — the Cassells, an elderly Ocean City couple, climbed into their Chrysler in an attempt to escape the rising tide. They drove along Eighth Street, toward Bay Avenue. Just beyond Moore Avenue, a savage gust — winds were peaking at 93 miles an hour — pushed the car off the street and into an empty lot deep with water. They fought their way out of the car, but the surging water was too strong for them and they sank beneath the surface. At that moment, policeman William Sproule spotted their bobbing heads, swam in, grabbed each one under an arm and dragged them back to the refuge at Red Men Hall.

*New Jersey State Police (both)*

**The Ocean City boardwalk and beachfront buildings are severely battered by the hurricane.**

The hurricane tore into Ocean City several hours ahead of its predicted arrival, pushing the ocean into the bay, submerging the city to a depth of up to six feet by 8 P.M. Whole houses washed away in the northern section, from Fourth Street north to Atlantic Boulevard, and others broke up. The boardwalk was quickly destroyed, and the roof of the Breakers Hotel blew off. Ralph Clayton, an officer in the local Coast Guard Reserve Flotilla, was out on flooded Roosevelt Boulevard attempting to help stranded motorists. As he drove into the wind, the hood of his car lifted up and sailed into the air. Within a minute, waves swept his vehicle off the road and turned it over, stranding him until the water receded.

A family near Forty-eighth Street sat down to dinner before realizing they would have to flee. The force of the wind and water tore off a corner of their house, and the table leaf holding the meat, peas and potatoes was washed away. It was later seen floating, still neatly arranged, carefully

picking its way around larger, drifting obstructions.

The storm surge washed out the first two levels of Howard Frick's four-story Central Avenue home. The top two stories, practically intact and with only a few roof shingles missing, settled down to where the lower ones had been. At Twenty-seventh Street and Atlantic Avenue, police officer Frank Parker opened the door of his patrol car to help a woman; then the ocean poured in and swept away the car. Parker and the woman were left clinging to a pole.

A mast of the *Sindia*, a 329-foot barque beached in a December gale forty-three years earlier, had projected from the Seventeenth Street beach ever since, marking the grave of the four-masted steel hulk. The wind snapped off the top 30 feet, leaving only a rusting stump. Jim Macallister took a walk on the beach after the tide had subsided and saw that "the hurricane had knocked down the big mast, and the crow's nest was lying right there at my feet. Some old bolts were holding it together but I pulled them off. I took one board home with me and kept it in my basement for quite a few years. When the historical society was formed I gave it to them and it's hanging over the door of the museum today." The wreck of the *Sindia* was not exposed again until 1962.

High sand dunes behind the boardwalk north of First Street had been considered a guarantee of protection by residents who built homes in their lee, but even before the hurricane peaked, the boardwalk was gone and the dunes flattened. In the hard-hit Second Street beach section, the side of one house was smashed and the floor curled up, but a vase of artificial flowers remained upright. In another, the kitchen furniture was scattered about, but dishes rested undisturbed on the drainboard. Two crockery vases stood on pedestals at the entrance to one untouched home, yet half a block away whole buildings were twisted, tipped and lifted off their foundations.

In all, fifty homes were destroyed and more than a hundred damaged. Evacuees — shivering, shocked, some injured — were taken to city hall where volunteers went to work gathering blankets, hot coffee and food. Tillie's Sandwich Shop and the Chatterbox, handicapped by broken windows and several inches of water on the floor, ferried a continual supply of food across the alley to the tired, sodden group in the makeshift shelter. The Salvation Army sent a mobile kitchen to feed the Coast Guard reservists, and the Red Cross set up its canteen in the Methodist church.

The Cassells were moved from Red Men Hall and eventually taken in by Andrew Blizzard and his wife, who wondered why the couple waited so long to evacuate. "We intended to leave earlier," said Mr. Cassell, "but friends assured us the storm wouldn't amount to much."

Fisher, 63, stepped out the back of his house to close a banging screen door. The wind whipped off the door and blew him against an adjoining house. Electric lines whipped and snapped in the 91 mile-per-hour gusts, and fifty-four inches of water rose inside Police Chief Richard DePamphlis' Oberon Avenue home. As loud slaps of water sprayed up to her second story window, Margaret Stetzer watched the ocean and bay meet in the middle of Sixteenth Street.

## Atlantic City

Lt. Everett Allen's men at the Atlantic City Coast Guard Station attended chemical warfare class that morning but attention quickly turned to a war against the water and the station went on full emergency alert. By 4 P.M., the barometer read 28.73 and Force 11 northeast winds were howling around the Huron Street base. At the same time, the Weather Bureau's anemometer clocked 105 miles per hour. Everett ordered the lookout to abandon the station tower when the city's famed boardwalk started breaking up at 4:45 P.M., just fifteen minutes before the eye of the hurricane raced by.

Maurice Nathanson, a wholesale milk delivery man for Abbotts Dairy, heard a radio warning in midafternoon, saw the rising tide seeping into the streets and moved his car over to a garage on Delaware Avenue. The garageman gave him a lift home to Rhode Island Avenue, but they couldn't make it past Oriental, so Nathanson waded back to his apartment building.

## Longport

Longport, the southernmost town on Absecon Island, is a shifting finger of land pointing into Great Egg Harbor Inlet. Erosion had been chewing away the beach for fifty years, washing the sand across the inlet, creating Ocean City Gardens. Wooden bulkheads and jetties were already in place by 1915, and a stepped concrete sea wall, combined with iron and rock groins, was completed in 1919. The small community had tried everything in an effort to stabilize the beach.

The hurricane's blast hit the narrow town broadside. The boardwalk built inside the sea wall disintegrated. Boards washed all over town and smashed into oceanfront homes, but the sea wall held. The roof from the fishing pier blew across town, and furniture from the Canterbury Hotel's first floor ended up in the bay. David

*Longport Historical Society*

**The railroad along the bay in Longport, looking north from 17th Avenue.**

**Only the lifeguard tower remains on vigil where the Atlantic City boardwalk turns into Absecon Inlet.**

*U.S. Weather Bureau/National Archives (3)*

**Hurricane damage in Atlantic City, clockwise from far left: sections of the boardwalk and cars are washed into buildings on Rhode Island Avenue; a building on Seaside Avenue in the Inlet section loses its wall; the Heinz Pier split in two, causing the Coast Guard to rescue survivors with a breeches buoy.**

*My apartment was on the third floor, so I could see out over the surrounding two-story buildings. The wind had really picked up suddenly and the water was rising; the ramp to the boardwalk came whooshing down Rhode Island toward Pacific. Next, huge boardwalk sections came slamming down. I watched Heinz Pier get sliced in half, and pieces of that floating down; it all happened so fast. Then we began hearing a horn blowing. Over on the block between Massachusetts and Metropolitan, from Oriental to the boardwalk — at that time an open lot — a car was floating and the horn shorted out. It was blowing continuously as it got toward dusk. It's a very weird sound.*

Splintered remains of Heinz Pier, the city's oldest, mingled with hunks of boardwalk; some 50-foot sections ended up blocks away. Nathanson watched the debris smash into buildings, eventually carpeting the street from side to side. The building on the pier was an isolated island on pilings, the stormy sea boiling around it. The boardwalk approach to it was a pile of kindling.

The Coast Guard dispatched a crew to save three men stranded on the pier. A newspaper later reported that "a human chain of 25 men under Commander Thomas Husselton saved Walter Wallace, Burley Waters and Clarence Davis," but Nathanson remembers it differently.

*The Coast Guard set up a cannon on the lot between Rhode Island and Metropolitan — a nursing home's there now — and fired out a line to carry a cable to the stranded men. They were setting up a breeches buoy. The men on the pier pulled in the cable, block and tackle and attached it out there, then one by one, they were hauled back, dangling over the water, to safety. This was after the worst of the storm had passed, but the wind was still blowing strong and cinders were hitting my wife and me in the face, but we were so fascinated by the rescue operation that we didn't want to leave.*

*U.S. Weather Bureau/National Archives (3)*

**The hurricane-driven ocean smashes boardwalk and pavement alike. Above and right, the Atlantic City Boardwalk, with the severed Heinz Pier beyond; below, Seaside Avenue after the storm.**

The Inlet section took the worst of the storm, as the wind screamed and the nine-foot tide washed over the northeast corner of the resort city. Near Maine Avenue, Mae Allen was hanging clothes on the line outside her home.

*I noticed that the air was different, something strange about it. I put the radio on, and they were talking about the hurricane. We were about three blocks from the water, but I wasn't frightened or anything: I'd been through hurricanes.*

*My husband came home, and we nailed boards over the windows against the wind — we never expected water — and all of a sudden the water was going into the garage. It was so fast, we couldn't believe it. Our house is three feet up from the ground, and the next thing we knew, within fifteen minutes we had about six inches of water washing around on the first floor. I sent the children to the second floor and put on boots while I fixed supper. After dark, the water started to recede.*

Marie Boyd had better luck with her cooking. When the electricity went out she was getting ready to bake Christmas cookies for her husband overseas, and the next day was the deadline for mailing. "I had a gas stove so I baked five hundred cookies by candlelight. The post office was open and my husband got his Christmas present."

Businesses suffered the worst from the flooding. In most Inlet shops, stock floated around in waterlogged ruin or was completely submerged. The hurricane struck so swiftly that most people talked about it in a state of dazed wonder rather than despair.

At one point, what was described as a riptide surged up and down Massachusetts and Madison avenues. On Madison, eight teenage boys navigated a 40-foot section of boardwalk, railings intact, down the street, finally fetching up against the front of a barbershop. The current even propelled a Plymouth coupe into a sand-locked lot.

In another barbershop on Pacific Avenue, Lee Gordon and her parents waged a battle against the water.

*My father had a shop connected to our dining room. I was in high school. We didn't know there was going to be a hurricane. There was no TV,*

*no radar. We had a radio, but it wasn't on. When the hurricane came, we said, "Oh! My God, what's this!"*

*It was grey, dismal. Terrible, terrible. The ocean met the bay, the water was so high. We were close to the ocean. We bailed and bailed, pouring the water from the floor into the toilet, bailing into the sewers, then thinking it's going back into the street again. We were trying to keep the water away from the electrical outlets. We just kept bailing buckets of water into the toilet.*

*We didn't have any drinking water; we didn't even think about eating or nothing. We only thought that if that comes up one more inch, it'll hit the little electrical outlets in the wall.*

As she bailed, Lee Gordon saw men rowing outside. "Lifeguard boats were riding right up and down Pacific, right in front of our apartment," she said. But they didn't stop to check on the Gordons, safely back away from the beach. Shortly after the storm hit, the Red Cross had phoned for boats to evacuate people from the devastated boardwalk area. Beach Superintendent Dick Hughes supplied eleven lifeboats manned by two guards each. Dodging debris, they ferried flooded-out residents to the relative safety of Pacific Avenue.

Power and telephone service went out by 5:40 P.M. Ed Davis remembers that the 4:35 train from Atlantic City got about three miles out into the meadows and was stranded by fallen poles and debris blocking the track. The force of the 70 mile-per-hour winds actually bent the glass in the windows of the railroad car.

The Coast Guard sent crews in trucks to help where they could. One crew attempted to secure boats moored in Delta Basin, while another took injured seaman Wilkie Brimfield to the Coast Guard infirmary in Longport. Brimfield had been badly gashed when the windows of the radio shack where he'd been on duty blew in. Both trucks were abandoned

when the water rose over the engines. Fortunately for Brimfield, his truck didn't die until the return trip.

The seven hundred-man Coast Guard contingent patrolled all night in boats, trucks and, where possible, on foot, from Absecon Inlet to Longport, communicating with a hastily contrived shortwave system. Guardsmen transported hundreds of frightened refugees to shelters at Convention Hall, the Armory and the railroad station, and treated those suffering from shock and exposure in their station's sick bay.

Military and shore police were on emergency patrol, too, with strict orders to deal firmly with looters. They stopped all who ventured onto remaining sections of the boardwalk without business there. Jeeps negotiated the hazardous routes left open on remaining sections. Wave-smashed gas mains added to the danger, and a no-smoking zone was established and enforced.

About a thousand persons took refuge at Convention Hall, lit by candlelight and the beams from automobile headlights. Doctors treated evacuees with fractures and cuts, as well as hysteria. Many never made it to the shelter. Families rode out the storm in isolated boardwalk apartments with their valuables and emergency belongings packed up: The time between the threatened high tide and the storm surge that shattered the boardwalk and coursed down city streets had been too brief to allow escape.

At least two people at Convention Hall that night took away happy memories, however: First Lt. Thomas Murray, a thirty-mission B-24 bombardier, and Lucy Stetson were married at 9 P.M. Murray's parents held flashlights to illuminate the ceremony as bedraggled, barefoot guests who had been evacuated from the Ambassador Hotel looked on.

Five hundred Brigantine residents were marooned after the seas broke up the bridge that connected the island to Atlantic City and submerged town streets under four feet of water. The Coast Guard evacuated over a hundred persons to the Red Cross shelter in Central Junior High School on the other side of Absecon Inlet. The Navy-occupied Brigantine Hotel took in about seventy-five families whose homes were flooded or destroyed. The storm wrecked all buildings on Brigantine's north end and destroyed the Coast Guard station.

But Mr. and Mrs. Clayton Ely and their cat were saved. "The water was up to our waists," Mrs. Ely said, "and we'd gone up to the second floor when two Coast Guards with a line came and told us they would take us to safety. Halfway to a nearby grocery store, which we were trying to reach by pulling ourselves on the line through the water, I fainted, but they revived me and we reached higher ground. Then my husband came back and got our cat, Mitzi, because we couldn't just leave her to drown."

The Coast Guard also aided in the next-day evacuation of the Col. Thomas England General Hospital, after the storm wiped out its water and electricity. More than a thousand sick and wounded servicemen were loaded onto hospital trains and sent to Staten Island's Halloran Hospital. Soldiers and guardsmen carried 275 bedridden patients on litters down the winding stairways of the fourteen-story former hotel, now Resorts International. Flashlights and kerosene lamps were used to guide the last of the stretcher bearers.

Samuel Deitch, director of the Atlantic City Weather Bureau, said that this storm was not as bad as the one in 1933, but Joseph Leeds disagreed. Leeds, descendant of a pioneer South Jersey family and a resident of Atlantic City since 1899, said the city hadn't ever had a hurricane before: "They were all northeasters. In the old days, it took a northeaster two days to get the tide up. This thing got it up in a matter of minutes." His wife, born on Absecon Island during a northeaster and delivered by a doctor who arrived in a rowboat, agreed.

*New Jersey State Police (3)*

**Over 500 people are stranded in Brigantine when the bridge is taken out, opposite. Four feet of water wash the island clean, above.**

Deitch, who later assisted in establishing the national hurricane warning system, said that those who say no storm warning was issued were either not listening or chose not to listen. He had a tough time warning people of the hurricane, which he'd been tracking for five days. Atlantic City radio station WFPG began to broadcast his alerts, and his office was deluged with phone calls. Most natives, he recalled, had never experienced a hurricane on the Jersey coast and didn't believe a tropical-born storm could strike here. Some businessmen accused Deitch of destroying their late-season profits, and one caller even threatened his life. "I stuck to my guns," he said, and never again did he encounter disrespect for his weather forecasts.

Although the aftermath of the storm was dreadful to behold, the warm September weekend lured thousands of sightseers to the famous city. Among waist-high driftwood and drowned rats and mice, they stretched out for sunbathing on the tide-hardened sand.

## Long Beach Island

In spite of hurricane warnings Thursday morning, more than a hundred schoolchildren lined Long Beach Boulevard at their usual stops, waiting for the yellow buses to take them to schools in Barnegat on the mainland. A light breeze blew from the southeast, and the humidity was oppressive.

During the morning, the wind picked up and shifted to northeast; by noon, warm, humid breezes had increased to 25 miles an hour. An hour later it started raining, and winds were at full gale force. School officials put the beach kids — as the island students were known — back on the buses and sent them home. Pooch Thomas, a seventh-grader at the time, remembers the ride over the low, plank causeway across Barnegat Bay.

*As we came across the Manahawkin meadows, past Thompson's Bar, the wind caught the bus and it began to rock. The usual rhythmic rumble of the causeway's planks played a counterpoint to the whistle of the wind through the crack in the window that the kid in front of me insisted on keeping open.*

*The northeast wind churned the bay as white as I'd ever seen it. Spray and sheets of water slapped against the bus, buffeted by the winds. When I got off in Harvey Cedars, I noticed that the side of the bus had been coated white with dried salt.*

On the south end of the island at Bonds Coast Guard Station, Chief Petty Officer Fred Griffen, who had sent his wife and children to the mainland in the late morning, detailed men to nearby houses to ask residents to move to the station. His younger brother, BM 2/C Warren Griffen, went with Adrian King and Bill Johnson to Little Egg Harbor Yacht Club to secure all station boats moored there. After the storm passed, Griffen wrote about the experience.

*At 1:45 p.m. started up the beach, really raining very hard and wind 70-75 mph. King driving station wagon, hard to manage; it was all over the road. We made the boro line, then the motor drowned out. King tried to start it again, but no good. King said let's get out and turn it around rear to the wind. We did and after a few choice words and grinding on the starter, the engine started on one cylinder, and after a few minutes was running OK again.*

*By this time the wind was screaming through the power lines overhead, and the water was rising so fast we could actually see it rise around our feet.*

*Lynn Photo Service/Ocean County Historical Society*

**A fire hydrant barely breeches the flood in front of Lynn Photo Service on Fifth Street in Ship Bottom.**

Bill Kane, courtesy Dorothy Hayes Smith

**Two survivors head south on an eroded Bay Avenue to see what's left of Holgate.**

We got turned again and proceeded to the yacht club. When we arrived, the water was up to the floor of the station wagon. From this time, the fury of the storm was on.

We went out and checked the boats; everything was OK. We then went into the yacht club for shelter, going out often to check everything. About 2 p.m., the wind velocity indicator was registering between 100 and 110 mph. The wind was screeching so loud, it was necessary to shout to be heard only a few feet away.

The water had risen to be waist deep, and great difficulty to keep your footing, all kinds of debris floating by. It was getting a little risky now, all docks and catwalks were under water, only tops of piling showing between the seas.

This was a severe storm. I never saw one like it, and I was concerned about the men at the station, it surely must be worse there than here. Conditions were so bad, I decided to go out to the motor lifeboat and see if I could get the station on the radio. Had difficulty getting aboard. The boat was riding so high, I had to grab the gunwale and pull myself up. The lines, which were normally slack, were taut as banjo strings, at about a 35 degree pitch, holding the hull down in the water.

After getting aboard, I tried to get the station on the radio. I called several times, tried the marine operator in New York, but no answer. Later I found out that all power lines were down. So here I was out on the lifeboat, the seas were coming over everything, and I couldn't get off again.

Back at the Coast Guard station, Chief Griffen and Seaman Sam Kleva attempted to save a new car belonging to a woman who had taken refuge there with her baby. Gunners Mate Hank Biernat watched them go.

Neefy and Sammy Kleva left in the Coast Guard pickup truck. The chief must have gone too fast, cause the water was high and started to come over the road. They went halfways down that road when the motor stalled, so he waited for us to come push the truck back to high ground at the station.

They started walking toward the ocean where this new car was supposed to be. Four of us ran to bring the truck back, and a big gust of wind blew us off the road into a ditch. We were in water up to our chests. Then it really hit. We looked back to where the chief was but couldn't see him. I thought, "Well, they're gone."

By 4 P.M., the barometer had dropped to 28.80, and northeast winds were blowing Force 12. Biernat said it was easily gusting to 115. The wind was pushing the sea along the island, sucking it out of the bay, and a massive storm surge — some say thirty feet high — washed across the southern end of the island. Roofs popped off houses and walls collapsed. Some houses were floating whole; then they'd hit another building and jam up, forming islands of debris in the meadows.

Hank Biernat saw an attic section sail past with people in it screaming for help.

> We had to go out and get these people without a lifeboat. We didn't have much clothing on; we just had life jackets, a lot of rope and flashlights. If you stood next to me and I tried to talk to you, you wouldn't hear me, the wind howled so loudly. The only way I could speak — if I wanted more line for a rescue operation — was with the flashlight. I'd make a circle of light, and they'd play out more line. If I wanted them to hold it taut so I could come back with the person, I'd make a beckoning motion with the flashlight. We swam from island of debris to island of debris to get to these homes and pieces of homes. Rather dangerous because there was a lot of stuff flowing fast with the water, and things flying through the air.
>
> We pulled people out of the homes and took them one at a time back down the line. One young woman, we pulled her out of her attic window. There were some people that must have gone in the bay that we didn't see, and of course they perished. I think we lost six people, but we saved twenty-three the hard way — just by swimming and pulling them in. I was in the water for about two hours, and the water was very warm because the Gulf Stream was diverted from offshore. But in spite of the water being warm, because of the tension from being immersed so long, they had to pull me out because I got the shakes.

Kate and John Lovett did not evacuate soon enough to avoid the wall of water that hit their home. In fact, they'd already taken in two women and children who lived even farther from the Coast Guard station. Before they could get out, four feet of water came into the first floor; they grabbed life jackets and moved up to the attic. Whole cottages floated by; one crashed into their house, collapsed a wall and filled the attic with water.

Lovett kicked out a window and helped his wife and the others onto the roof. Two of the women and a child floated through fifteen feet of water to the station. Lovett, who didn't have a life jacket, swam into the attic of another house. His wife and one child disappeared in the raging surf. Her body was found the next day; the child was never found.

For Mariana Johnson, the loss of her grandparents' Holgate home was "like a death in the family." She and her cousins, Carol Mastran and Isabel Wickham, returned there the next day on an Army flatbed truck. "All the landmarks were gone, telephone poles were gone; we were all crying. The Whitmers' house next door had been washed onto our property and only the attic and a part of the second floor were left. There was nothing there from our house except an anchor that had been under the house, a few pieces of slate and a marble tabletop. I had nightmares for a year."

Chief Griffen and Sam Kleva had taken refuge in the Whitmer house and were trapped in the attic. "They watched the destruction of our house. They saw shingles spin off and around in a circle, then saw the slate come off," recalls Carol Mastran. "The house was well boarded with bolted shutters; it was airtight and the wind lifted it off the foundations. When it

*Bill Kane, courtesy Jane Smith (2); Charlene Paulsworth (bottom)*

70

sank back down, this gigantic wave took it into the bay and then it washed back, breaking up into pieces. Because they witnessed the wind pick up our house, we collected insurance."

Warren Griffen, stranded in a lifeboat at the yacht club, watched the seas coming over everything. Small boats, parts of houses, planks of the boardwalk, pieces of beach pavilions and sections of Nat Ewer's boardwalk gift shop were all pushed into the bay.

Just east of the yacht club, Mabel Reeve waited out the storm at Betsy Ross Rooms and Bath House on the southeast corner of Holyoke and Bay avenues. In a letter to her husband the next day, she wrote:

> While the streets were flooded, I saw flashlights going past, so I called to them. It was two Coast Guards. They came in and I asked them if they thought it was safe here for the night. They said the wind had gone down and changed S.W. and the tide was going out, so everything was all right. I couldn't have gotten out anyway for the water was nearly up to their hips. I told them I thought the Coast Guard might have boats to take people to safety; they said no boat could stand that wind. The water came up the porch, then the little house in back banged against the porch and it's about to collapse. The front steps are gone, and the bath houses are lying out in the lot. Menns' house is out in the middle of the sidewalk on Holyoke Avenue, and a lot of the furniture out of it is over in the lot in front of us. As far down as I can see toward the point [Holgate], houses are sitting out in the street.

Ellwood Barrett, about to enter the service, was spending two weeks with his mother, aunt and ten-year-old sister in a second-floor apartment near the ocean on Seventh Street in Beach Haven.

> We saw the wave come over the island and go across to the mainland. It took what it took. A single wave. Just one big wave. I think as the crest of the wave passed by our house, it was probably eight or nine feet high. You could see it coming from way out, and it came at one shot. The beach at that time was relatively steep and wide, and to come across the beach and pass by our house at eight or nine feet — that was a hell of a wave. When that wave got to the mainland, it turned around and came back. I think people at that time said that the return of the wave did more damage. It just sucked everything out. The boats from the bay were now on the beach.

Barbara Johnson stood looking out the window of the Baldwin Hotel lobby on Pearl Street and Atlantic Avenue. She'd been sent home from the Beach Haven Grade School in midmorning. Her father, Charles Yocum, owned the hotel. "I was looking at the boardwalk when the big wave struck.

**The Whitmer house in Holgate, where CPO Fred Griffen and Sam Kleva took refuge, manages to outlive the storm, opposite top. Other Holgate houses and the Inlet Inn do not fare so well. Coast Guardsmen and volunteers search the wreckage for bodies, above. In the distance, the tower of Bond's Coast Guard Station pokes up over the rubble.**

It was huge." The Baldwin beachfront bathhouses split in half, and the same wave hit Cassie's Japanese gift shop on the boardwalk. Johnson saw Cassie jump out of the window. "He had on a slicker and was carrying a bag of something, maybe valuables, and was running for the hotel. It was just before the wave broke. A big piece of boardwalk smashed into the hotel, and Nat Ewer's Sea Chest was picked right up and washed back over the dunes. Then what was left of the fishing pier crashed into it."

Jane Smith was at home with ten-year-old Jimmy Sheck and his parents at the other end of Pearl Street.

*About five o'clock, all hell broke loose. The boardwalk was the first thing to come down the street. Jimmy was out on the sun porch, real excited, hollering, "Here comes the boardwalk! Here comes the Jap shop!" Then we lost our electricity, and it got scary and we heard the water rushing into the cellar, and Jimmy waded down and turned off the gas. When it was calm — the eye must have passed by — Jimmy and his father went over to their laundry next door. The water was up to Jimmy's waist. When they came back, it wasn't such an adventure; Jimmy was really scared. Everything in the laundry was ruined.*

*Bill Kane, courtesy Jane Smith (top); U.S. Navy/Picture Collection, New Jersey State Library (above)*

*Lynn Photo Service*

**The pilings of Beach Haven's boardwalk march past the remains of the Playland Amusement arcade on Centre Street, opposite bottom, which has collapsed like a house of cards, opposite top and above.**

Joan Simonin was home on Centre Street, next to the Kynett Methodist Church, with her mother, Elisabeth Krause; an aunt; and five-year-old daughter, Ann. A neighbor had been monitoring the Coast Guard reports all day and advised the four women to leave. Elisabeth Krause said, "We've been here for sixty years. What's another blow?" and they stuck it out. The power went out, and they cooked supper on their Sears Roebuck coal stove, said Joan.

*We had just enough coal in the house for one meal and were eating to the tune of wind and rattles when a huge slab of wood crashed into the window. We had shuttered the windows but peeked out and saw waves in the street. The Skee-Ball machines floated by. The beachfront comfort stations were propelled by the wind and stayed afloat; iron benches from the boardwalk sailed by on top of the water as though they were leaves. The Centre Street boardwalk ramp landed at the telephone pole in front of our cottage. It stayed there and didn't budge.*

Young Ann was worried about that pole. "A piece of the boardwalk latched on to the pole, and it leaned toward our porch and kept leaning further and further. I kept wondering — will the pole hold or will it crash down on the house?"

Just down the street, Lea Marshall was at Green Gables, visiting with its owner, her friend Del Hoffner. The two women waded to the higher house next door and spent the night in the top floor of the quaking structure. Lea's daughter Liliane Reynolds remembers her mother telling how she prayed, clicking her rosary while the house shook. Her mother said, "I never thought I'd see Palmyra again." The next morning, the roof of the boardwalk pavilion rested in the middle of Centre Street. Among the debris, the women found ashtrays, post cards and other souvenirs imprinted with "The Sea Chest."

Beach Haven native Joe Sprague reported to the Ventnor Boat Works that morning — he was on a crew building a 110-foot submarine chaser — but as the hurricane approached the coast, his boss told him to go back home. About 5:30, his Sixth Street home was surrounded by water, so he carried daughters Audrey and Helen through waist-deep water to neighbor Helen Joorman's home, which was on higher ground. As he waded back across the street, he looked toward the ocean and saw two houses wash down and jam up at the intersection of Sixth Street and Atlantic Avenue.

Sprague's house weathered the storm without water damage, but the Joormans were not as lucky. Helen Joorman suddenly heard a big swish.

*The whole cellar cracked right down the middle, and the water gushed in like a fountain, that's the pressure there was outside. Everything down there was floating — washing machine, heater — it was a mess. The upstairs bathroom dormer window sprang a leak, and water ran between the floor and the ceiling and came down through the living room chandelier, but I caught it in the baby's bathtub. Every sheet and towel and pillowcase I had was stuffed in cracks and windows and under doors.*

Charles Yocum and Horace Johnson left the Baldwin and braved the high tide in the street to check on a neighbor. When they struggled back, Yocum was down to his undershorts. His pants had been ripped off by the force of the water — or something; he was never sure — while he held on to a telephone pole. He had fifty dollars in the pockets.

Another Beach Haven man who had driven from Camden to rescue his family had the day's business receipts, $1,200, in his pants. He waded down the street holding an infant over his head with both hands while his wife clung to one arm and the nursemaid to the other. When a spike in a whirling piece of lumber tore his belt loose and let his trousers drop down around his ankles, he miraculously managed to keep his footing but stepped out of the trousers. The pants and the $1,200 drifted off toward the bay.

The tidal nightmare wasn't riding only along the ocean. Water rose two feet inside police headquarters on Bay Avenue and relentlessly oozed into Pete Calabro's bayside rental unit.

*It got pretty bad — the thundering, shrieking wind, and then the bay rose up. We were in a heavy bungalow, maybe one or two cement blocks off the ground, and the water started coming up through the floor boards. My mother would have panicked and wanted to leave earlier if she had known how bad it would be.*

*Bill Kane, courtesy Jane Smith (top); courtesy Bea Stokes (above)*

**In Beach Haven: A car trapped under a beachfront house, top; part of Nat Ewer's Sea Chest on the boardwalk, above; and parts of the boardwalk on Centre Street by Paxton's Drug Store at Bay Avenue, opposite bottom.**

*It wasn't our furniture, but Mother was concerned, so we picked up anything on the floor we could and rolled up the rugs and put them on top. The house had only one story. It got dark, and we all huddled in one room. What could we do? I was sixteen, my brother and sister a little older. Mother told us to lay down, but we didn't.*

After the eye passed, the wind shifted to northwest and then west, and blew for an hour as hard as it had from the northeast. Warren Griffen watched the shift from the safety of the yacht club: "The boats that survived the northeast winds were sitting ducks for the backlash. The bay tide raised them up, then dropped them down, piercing the hulls on pilings, right through the cabins."

The size, power and solidity of the initial storm surge shocked and stunned most islanders accustomed to the gradual buildup of a northeaster. Most had no experience with the destructive power of the sea when it joins forces with hurricane-strength winds, no knowledge of how the wind can knock over a building, giving it to the waves to churn and crush, creating a battering ram of debris.

Bill Kane, courtesy Dorothy Hayes Smith

**A houseboat cruises Long Beach Boulevard in Beach Haven Crest.**

Bill Kane, courtesy Jane Smith

Vander Messick was building a house on Third Street and paid attention to the hurricane warnings. "We had a half-completed house and went to see if we could do anything about it, brace it or something, but it was getting worse and worse by the minute, so we backed out of the property in the truck and here's this wall of water coming down the street toward us."

Messick was driving but couldn't open the door against the gushing waters. His employee got out the passenger side and Messick followed, just before the truck tipped over and washed down the street.

That same wave was the beginning of the end for the 54-year-old Spray Beach Hotel. Mea Noonan remembers how viciously the ocean hit that spot on Twenty-third Street. "The hotel was very close to the beach, and one wave hit it. There was an enormous flow of water and sand even through the third floor windows. The piano on the ocean side of the ballroom washed right through to the dining room near the street. The hotel was patched up but eventually torn down."

Jack Lamping, a writer and county official, and his wife were at their home on the bay side of the boulevard in Beach Haven Gardens. Jack was in the Coast Guard Auxiliary, a cadre of men who relieved the regulars by standing watches at Coast Guard stations near their home.

"Jack was on duty at the Bonds Coast Guard Station," remembers Virginia Lamping. "At eight in the morning he called me about the weather, to keep some fishing friends from going to sea and so others could decide whether or not to leave the island. After the ten o'clock radio broadcast, Jack's mother and a neighbor packed up and went back to Philadelphia."

In a letter to friends, Virginia Lamping chronicled the storm:

*Jack and I tied the boardwalks to the steps, took the birdbath into the garage, stored garbage cans and other outside things, and tried to look out for absent neighbors in the same way. We even made a minor roof repair as the first drops of rain started to fall. The air was very still and the threat of hurricane wind seemed far off. I went to the store for some Crisco so I could entertain the storming hours by baking some cookies. As the rain began to beat heavily against the north windows, it matched the wind's increased momentum, and it was my responsibility to wipe up the rain as it blew through.*

*I couldn't keep up with the job upstairs and down, so I called Jack from his newspaper writing — he realized no more writing would get done that day; he had a full-time hurricane assignment. We mopped up buckets of water; every towel was in use. As the wind continued to increase, Jack said the garage was swaying, and I could see the flagpole giving way too.*

*At 5:45, a car came down our driveway with four people aboard. It might as well have been a boat for the ocean was following them. These four strangers had been occupying an oceanfront cottage for the week.*

**A flattened Holgate looking from ocean to bay, above. A beachfront bathhouse in Brant Beach, opposite top. A police car mired in the muck in Brighton Beach, opposite bottom.**

*They had finished a chicken dinner and gone out on the front porch to check the progress of the storm when a wave broke over the dune and rampaged down the street, threatening their house. They didn't know where they were going, but they were on their way to get as far from the ocean as they could. When I saw the ocean following them down the street and begin to surround our house, I knew we were becoming more and more helpless, for high tide was still two hours away and anything could happen.*

*Realizing that everything on the first floor would soon be a part of the Atlantic Ocean, the rush was on! In five minutes, the living room rug was upstairs, books off the lower shelves, photo albums, linens, mattresses, bedding — just about everything we could move went up. How we worked! I filled jugs of every description with water and set up candles and took out food for the emergency we were sure would exist. Along with this, Jack got flares from the garage, braving the storm to do it, and with innertubes and a tire pump made as many life preservers as he could for the six of us. We women were about exhausted with the work and excitement.*

*As the storm grew worse, our menfolk went out to get a boat in case something happened to the house; two braved the swirling water to get to the dock, one kept watch and we continued our upstairs vigil. The minutes seemed like hours.*

*At last! "The wind has changed," Jack called. With the ocean on one side of you and a wide stretch of bay on the other, the wind can change the course of your life as well as the waters. This wind switch saved the island from complete destruction for the ocean was blown out to sea.*

*Ten o'clock is a blessed hour in my memory for then the storm began to really subside and our weary men could feel that the struggle had ended. Such rejoicing I've never before heard in our house! We were hugging each other and wondering how we could thoroughly show our appreciation for God's goodness to us. The glory of this passing scene came when we looked from our living room window into the southern sky and saw the dark clouds lifting as if it were a great stage curtain, and the stars below were never as brilliant as we saw them that Thursday night of September 14, 1944.*

Bud Berdick and his brother, Robert, got permission from their grandmother, Anna Herz, to go sailing that morning but listened to her usual advice to keep an eye on the weather and return quickly if it grew threatening. When the sky became heavy and grey, recalled Bud, they sailed back to Harris Harbor, tied up their little sneakbox and walked home to Beach Haven Park.

*By the time we got back, Grandmom had heard the hurricane warnings on the radio and my father had called from Rydal, Pennsylvania, that he was coming to get us. Grandpop was down at Wida's Hotel in Brant Beach doing some work, so Grandmom filled the bathtub with water for washing, and pots and jars for cooking. I found out what a hurricane lamp was when she filled two with kerosene. We brought everything loose from the yard and stowed it in the garage. While all this was going on the wind was picking up and I tried to find our two pets, a Manx and an alley cat, but they never came home.*

*My father couldn't get on the island and we were on our own. Waves started breaking over Buddy Peck's house, next to us on the oceanfront. The water crashed through the windows on the ocean side and came out through the windows next to us. I was really scared. If my grandmother was, we never knew it. We heard a loud boom and crunch and saw the waves take our garage toward the boulevard. Next, a loud, strange, cracking noise made us look out the back; McDonalds' large oceanfront house had washed from Texas Avenue into our back yard.*

*Now we were all huddled on the couch with our dog, terrified. Grandmom was reading from the Bible and we were all praying — it seemed to go on for hours. Every time a wave would hit our house it would jiggle the couch a little, and we ended up on the other side of the room.*

*Lynn Photo Service/Ocean County Historical Society (top); courtesy Jane Smith (above)*

**Only the roof remains of the summer home of three Ship Bottom survivors, above. A survivor of the Victorian age in Surf City doesn't make it, either, opposite.**

*When the eye passed, we looked out the front window and saw Mr. and Mrs. Bachs motion to us, asking if they could come over. To help them back through the water, Robert and I made a chain with Grandmom. A piece of lumber hit her in the knee and she had a scar all her life. After the wind shifted to the west it was terrible again — shingles, glass, whole roofs flew through the air.*

*The next morning Grandpop walked the four miles back from Wida's. Grandmom asked him to fix something and he went out to get his tools from the garage. We laughed and cried: We forgot there was no more garage. I was only eleven then, but it's as vivid now as that day.*

Karl Held Sr., home on leave from the Pacific theater of war, watched the waves destroy an unoccupied house built close to the ocean on New Jersey Avenue.

*We had huge sand hills at the end of New Jersey in the thirties and forties; you really had to climb to get to the beach. The beach road went through nothing but dunes and bayberry bushes. Sometime before the war, a man put up a house on steel pilings about a hundred feet in from the dunes, with massive steel girders. Then he said, "Well, that'll stay put."*

*I saw those waves come over those dunes and hit his big slant-roofed porches — the waves just picked them up and tossed 'em. Then another wave bounced up over the dunes and hit the house; it shook a little, and the next thing I knew the house came floppin' down — all that was left was the pilings and girders, the house was on the ground.*

At Wida's Hotel, a testimonial dinner was planned that night for Ocean County School Superintendent Charles Morris. Waitress Irene Cummings Parker called from the mainland at 3 P.M. to see if the dinner had been canceled. It hadn't.

*We got over there by four, but it was really bad. Tubs of raw chicken were all over the kitchen. Mr. Wida said we should get off the island. At three, they said come, but by four, it was crazy. We went up and looked at the ocean, and it was wild, starting to foam and coming over the sand dunes. This was maybe 4:30. The waves were breaking right up close to the houses, but by the time we got to Ship Bottom, waves of solid water were coming down the street.*

*We got over the drawbridge, and when we got to the causeway, people were out of their stalled cars and were making human chains, hanging onto*

*Lynn Photo Service*

*the wire railing — the old causeway just had a wire railing on short posts. They were begging for us to stop, but we couldn't, we had to keep going and going, and they were hollering.*

*I felt terrible but knew if we stopped we'd be in the same situation. The water was coming in the door, it washed gravel and orange sand and mud right in, but the old Plymouth kept going. It took a long, long time to get across that causeway, slowly, with people making human chains to walk in the wind and begging for us to stop. The Good Lord was with us, I guess.*

Irene was struggling to drive off the island at about the same time Ronald McCormack was desperate to get on. His wife and two children were at their Ship Bottom cottage, and he had the family's car in Philadel-phia. He made it to Twenty-fifth Street before the car stalled in the rising water; then he waded five more blocks. Attracted by a candle in the attic window of the Roots' cottage next door, he found his family.

Three cottages between the McCormicks' and the ocean were ripped from their foundations. One wedged against a solid house, and the others broke up and went down the street. While the children slept, the adults prayed.

One block north, Carol Mather and her sister-in-law, Dottie Gannett, and Dottie's two children hunkered down in their house, second from the ocean. That morning, neighbors said the storm was passing out to sea, so the two women took the children on a planned trip to a Steel Pier matinee. When they came out of the theater, the gale had started and they ran for the car between gusts, the wind pushing them along. "All the way to the island, billboards dropped like dominoes," Carol remembered. The group made it back to the island before the causeway flooded.

*Dottie and I thought we'd better have something to eat because we didn't know what might happen next. Sitting at the dining room table, we saw this giant wave break cleanly over the seven-foot lattice running from the house next door back to a little guest cottage. I said softly to Dottie that we should have a picnic upstairs, and we moved the food and the children to the upstairs front bedroom. We got there just in time to look over and see houses on Thirtieth Street begin to collapse and wash down the street. The second floors seemed to stay intact, so we formed an emergency plan to use a sheet to tie a child to each of us and get out on the roof if the house began to float away.*

*Coast Guards from the nearby station checked on us and at one point, the storm was so intense and the noise of the wind and things breaking up and crashing so loud that when they hammered on our front door we couldn't hear them. They moved through the waist-deep water by tying each end of a long rope to one man so one could hold on to a building or tree or fence while the other moved ahead for another handhold.*

Mary Hendrick and her husband were painting the kitchen of her father's little house on the ocean side of Fourth Street in Ship Bottom. "The four children were outside playing," she recalls, "then the wind and the rain started and the children came inside. I had the radio on, playing music to amuse them. All day it was getting darker and darker.

"Then the children screamed that all their toys had washed away, and suddenly the water came down the street. There was no place to go; we had come down by bus because of the gas rationing. The wind was everywhere: It didn't seem to come from the east or north, just everywhere. I was petrified. We were there all the time with just one candle. We sang all night. We thought we were gonna die singing Frank Sinatra. About 10 o'clock, my ears started to hurt. I thought I was having ear trouble, but my husband said no, the noise has stopped. The roar was so loud all day, and it stopped suddenly."

Ethel Donnegan had been coming to her Surf City Victorian home since 1910. In June 1944 the train brought her to Barnegat where her Ninth Street neighbors, Wilhelmina and Frank Plunkett, met her. Richard Plunkett, a child then, remembers Ethel Donnegan's ordeal.

*Mrs. Donnegan lived perhaps a hundred yards from the ocean, the second house, and she'd weathered so many storms since 1910 that she saw no need to leave. She turned over her rocking chairs on the porch like she always did for a northeaster, but it got more and more blustery and the water was starting to breach the dunes when she watched the huge Victorian pavilion — one street away — wash down the street intact.*

*As the waves got higher, the pavement was dug up, then the garage behind the next-door house went, and the wind ripped her porches off. The dunes weren't very high there, and she thought the house would go next. The water was above the floorboards in the living room, which was about five feet off the ground. She decided she'd better get out and try to make it to the Surf City Hotel, so she jumped out of her front door into the water and swam to a telephone pole. Two men rescued her, and the three of them made it to the hotel.*

**The only Victorian turret to outface the hurricane overlooks the remains of its more modern cousins, opposite. A North Beach family scans the flattened dunes from their wrecked beachfront house toward the still-standing Troast house, above.**

The wife and two young children of Howard Sleeper from Mount Holly narrowly escaped, too, as they struggled through the water to the hotel. Mrs. Sleeper carried her three-year-old, but her eleven-year-old son was caught in the surge and swept under. He managed to maintain his footing until two men came from the hotel and pulled him in. At the height of the storm, scores of people took refuge at the hotel. Women prayed aloud as the water rose above the floorboards.

Josephine Thomas cooked nervously at her Harvey Cedars bayfront home, preparing for the blow. Her husband, Reynold, a borough commissioner, nailed boards over the bay window, rolled up the Oriental rugs and moved up everything that could go up. Josephine baked a cake. "I remember stirring up a cake and at the same time hurriedly trying to finish roasting a leg of lamb before the storm hit. My husband watched me put the wastebasket on the table and the cake pan on the floor and asked why I bothered when I was scared about the storm. `Me? Scared?' I scoffed, as I reached for the baking powder and carefully measured out two teaspoons of Old Dutch Cleanser."

Reynold packed his wife, young son and daughter into his Dodge pickup, deposited them at the National Hotel in Manahawkin and returned to tend his dredge, which had been towed into Harvest Cove to ride out the storm. His wife had left three changes of clothing for him, but they were soaked so quickly that he and his hired man spent four hours shifting lines and moving anchors bone-cold naked.

Reynold watched the first wave strike. "It lifted itself twenty-five feet above the dunes and advanced toward the boulevard in a solid wall of water, no foam. Lloyd Good's huge, oceanfront home broke in two, and the north and south wings rose up in the air like a vee."

Larry Lyons worked for his brother-in-law, Paul Troast, at Mahoney-Troast Construction Company in North Jersey. When Troast heard the hurricane warnings that morning, he sent Lyons and a crew to check the family's two large homes at the south end of Harvey Cedars. Everything was fine when they arrived, and by three o'clock they had secured the houses, one on the ocean and one on the bay.

*Even though the wind was picking up, we thought it would be a good idea to take down the steps over the dunes that went to the beach, but that was futile. We were wearing shorts, and the sand was like a blasting machine. We still wanted to get those steps off, in case they would blow into the house and break the windows.*

I started down to Walt Smith's garage in Surf City. About a half mile down the road, a mail truck was stalled. The mailman got out and waved us down. When we told him where we were going, he said, "You'll never make it; the ocean's broken through," so we came back to the bay where I wanted to pull out a couple of sailboats and a small outboard moored there.

We walked about seventy feet on a narrow walkway running over the marshes and mosquito ditches and picked up one of the boats: The wind grabbed that boat and threw it about thirty feet. I decided to forget the boats. We had to crawl back along the walkway on our hands and knees.

At this point, I decided I'd better get over to the ocean house and let the others know how serious this was, so I fought my way against the wind and got there and one of the guys was sweeping water out of the second floor. I said, "Come on, fellas, let's get outta here." As we went back down the steps, I heard a loud, rumbling crash, louder even than the

*courtesy Dave Wood (2)*

*wind, which was really howling now. It was the oceanside front wall collapsing, so we really moved.*

*The water was about two feet deep on the driveway. We got to the boulevard, and here was this woman and two children swimming and stumbling. I recognized Inez Galbraith, heading for the Coast Guard station a quarter mile north. I said, "You'll never make it. The ocean just broke through at Bergen Avenue. Come with us."*

*The water was up to my waist as we all got into the bay house. We stayed there, and I thought the roof was gonna blow off, the wind was so terrific.*

The Galbraith house, just over the borough line in North Beach, had been moved back from the ocean the year before. The first wave crashed through the first floor, carrying away two walls and the stairs and porch to the second floor living room. To escape the house, Inez jumped ten feet

*New Jersey State Police*

**Harvey Cedars takes a heavy hit. An Ocean County road grader moves sand off the boulevard, above. Little remains of the large oceanfront Van Nest house, left. The Remington house, opposite bottom, will be moved to the bayfront.**

into chest-deep water, then caught her five-year-old daughter Kit, tossed down by ten-year-old Ned.

The Harvey Cedars Coast Guard Station covered the block between Cumberland and Cape May avenues. Frederick Remington had a large oceanfront home nearby but was on duty with the Coast Guard Auxiliary Delaware River Patrol. He'd called and warned his family to evacuate. His wife tried to get the car out of the garage, but the northeast winds plastered the doors shut. She went to the station for help, leaving nine-year-old Bill with his four-year-old sister, Sally, who remembers it well.

*My brother and I were playing in the living room. I have very vivid memories of making card houses on one of those sisal rugs that had lines going through it that looked like roads, and we used to run our cars on them. We were happy as clams.*

*Suddenly, I saw water coming in under the front door. My brother yanked me out into the swirling current. We had a flagpole in the front yard, and as we crossed the yard, the flagpole crashed down. My brother pulled me out of the way just in time. I can still feel it going down my back, the whoosh of it as it went down.*

As the children traveled down the street in the water, they met up with two guardsmen from the station sent to rescue them.

Dave Wood's parents, Jane and Ellis, had a small cottage, The Woodpile, on the south side of the station, separated by one street and a field of bayberry bushes. Ellis's Aunt Eva's house was tucked behind a dune just to the east.

*My parents decided to stick it out. They're sitting there and hear a tremendous bang. The first wave hits and Aunt Eva's house is gone. They see water all around the house and say, "Let's get out of here."*

*They make it to the garage which has old-style barn doors that swing out, so Mom gets in the car to back it out and Dad's standing outside with his arms spread out, pressing against the door to keep it open. The garage faces south, so he's pressing hard against the door on the east, which is where the wind's coming from. A gust hits the garage door and he's shoved in against the car, but Mom keeps coming. Dad's pounding on the car, but she can't hear him and keeps coming and runs right over his feet, but the sand is so wet she doesn't break them, they just sink into the ground.*

*So she backs the car out, and the next wave hits and the car stalls. She climbs out, and in a minute the car is gone, brand new station wagon on its way to the bay. They make it to the Coast Guard station, swimming and wading and hanging on to the bayberry.*

*The station's steps were washed away, and there's a four-foot reach up to where other people are — apparently everyone went there because the place is built like a brick shithouse, big mudsills and pilings — so the Coast Guards pull them in, and then here comes another local woman, and they reach down to haul her up and she's screaming, "Don't touch me! Don't touch me!" My mother says this is no time for histrionics, but the woman's still yelling "Don't touch me!"*

*Well! She'd fallen into an open cesspool and was covered with — guess what? — but they dragged her up. Water comes into the first floor of the station, so they move up into the tower and have to lie down flat on the floor because the shingles are blowing off the station and another house and — whap! — shingles are flying, crashing through the windows, flying through the air, spraying glass all over. They spent most of the time lying flat.*

*The next day the Coast Guard guys helped them pull their car out of the bay — they got rid of it — but they found their aunt's refrigerator in the bay with the eggs still in it, whole.*

In the center of Harvey Cedars, the section that used to be called High Point, the storm surge carried away more homes than anywhere else on the Jersey coast. Between Seventy-third and Eighty-first streets, the ocean struggled to join the bay: Most of the town's destroyed homes disappeared from this eight-block area. The family in the sixth house from the ocean on Seventy-seventh Street watched the other five wash down the street. Two blocks away, four elderly persons were in a cottage that crossed the boulevard and fetched up against the pheasant house of the Frederick P. Small estate. Only up in the roosts could they stay dry, and there they perched until the water receded.

Stuart Gurney's real estate office on the boulevard started to give way under the pressure of the water. When he tried to escape, he was washed over to the bay on Lee Avenue where Bill Lange found him

*New Jersey State Police*

**Stuart Gurney's real estate office is deposited in the middle of the boulevard in Harvey Cedars.**

clinging to a telephone pole. His office was moved to the middle of the road.

The Hagers had two rental cottages on Seventy-seventh Street. The lower floor washed out of one; the other vanished, but the tenants had evacuated in time. One was baking a pie when she received a telegram from her husband to leave at once. "The pie was still in the oven when we found the stove way over there on the meadows," said Dudley Hager.

Earlier in the summer, James Flynn had tried to find men to move his home to his more secure bayside lot, but because of the war and lack of manpower, he couldn't. The hurricane did it for him, floating it along and dropping the house exactly where he wanted it.

Lt. Comdr. and Mrs. Harry Krug's new beachfront home on Seventy-fourth Street vanished without leaving a splinter to show where it had stood. A few years later, Benny Haines found one of their silver forks. In 1955, James Flynn was digging on his bayside property and found the other eleven, still in their protective flannel bag.

Bert Krank's parents had a side-by-side duplex on Seventy-fourth Street. Her father was concerned about continuing beach erosion, so when his real estate agent produced a buyer, he sold immediately. "I asked Elsie Canetti, the Realtor, if the new owners had seen the condition of the beach," remembers Mrs. Krank. "She told us, 'They didn't ask, and we didn't offer.' Two days after we closed, the house was gone — completely gone."

Glenna Wilcox was spending the season with her mother at her summer house on Seventy-eighth Street. Her husband had returned to duty, leaving his wife with a newborn baby and two toddlers. With her mother, Glenna had listened to the weather report first thing in the morning:

*The guy said the hurricane had come in at Hatteras and then veered out to sea, so mom thought everything was fine and said she was gonna can the peaches. My dad had gone home, so it was just mom and me and the three kids. She turned the radio off and got her bushel of peaches and started canning. The sun was shining, it was a lovely morning, sort of quiet and clear, but the sky just looked different. Chub was sixteen months old, Caroline was three, and baby Elaine was six weeks.*

*I took them to the beach, but it got greyer and greyer and kind of purply-looking so I came home and told mom, "It looks very threatening." She said, "Well, that hurricane is probably going past the coast right now." I didn't think too much about it and the wind kicked up a little more and it got steadily and increasingly worse. It got scary. But my mother was in the kitchen peeling and scalding and getting the jars ready and I was busy with the kids — when you have a new baby you're always busy. But I went to the porch a few times and looked up to the beach.*

*I could stand on the front porch and see water foaming over the dunes; you know, a little bit trickling over and dying off into the sand. I thought that can't be the ocean that high, and I walked up and it was. I came back and said, "Mom, the water is right up to the end of the street, right up to the top of the dune," and she said, "Well, it must be high tide." She wasn't gonna let anything interfere with the canning. I kept watching and more water came over and pretty soon it was washing down in steady streams and then it came on down the street and got higher and higher and higher. I said, "Mom, come on out here and look at this." She came out on the porch and said, "Aaaahhhhheeeeee." I mean it scared her half to death.*

*She sent me down to Robicek's corner store, to use their telephone to call my father and tell him to come down and get us and take us home. About a half-dozen men were standing around. They said, "Your father can't get you; the causeway's under water."*

*The water was between my ankles and knees when I walked down, but it got higher in just the few minutes I was out of the house. We had a little front porch, four steps up from the sidewalk. On the top my mother had two big heavy flower boxes, and the water got high enough to wash them right away, then it washed the steps away, then it washed away a five-car garage from across the street. My three-year-old was so excited. She said, "Oh, Mommy, there goes Jake's garage. Oh, Mommy, there goes Wilson's steps. Oh, Mommy, there goes..." Well, mommy was looking and didn't like it one bit. I was holding my little baby and was so scared.*

*Then two men came up from the store; they said it was higher there and we should come down with the other people. They both looked at Elaine and since she was six weeks old, neither one wanted any part of carrying her. I wrapped her in a blanket and then a rubber sheet. I was scared to death she wouldn't be able to breath, the wind was so strong.*

*One man took Caroline and one took Chub. My mother said, "Wait." She wasn't going without money because she never went anywhere without money and she wasn't gonna ruin her clothes and she wasn't gonna lose the money or get it wet, so she put on her "garment," her corset. She pinned her money inside and then put on her bathing suit. Well, a bathing suit over a corset is about the worst-looking thing you can imagine. The garters were dangling from under the bathing suit, her hair was wild and her garters were flapping — I can laugh now but then I hoped no one would know it was my mother.*

*One of the men went out carrying Caroline and another carried Chub. I wrapped him in a grey shawl with long fringe. The water was above my armpits and I was holding Elaine above my shoulders and bracing my heels in with every step and kind of feeling my way and also looking back because there were big pilings washing down. If one hit me, I knew I'd go down.*

*The man carrying Chub stepped in a hole where the sidewalk had washed away and went in over his head, and I guess he automatically threw up his arms...and he dropped Chub. I saw the man come up, feeling in the water for my baby and here I am holding one baby and can't do a thing about it and my other baby's gone. But Chub drifted into the cedar tree in front of Lippincott's house and we both saw him at the same time: He yelled and I yelled. The fringe had caught in the branches, and the man reached into the water under the shawl and scooped him up. He was hollering mad; he coughed and sputtered and started yelling right away. The water was warm and didn't bother him much.*

*It was late afternoon. I know because we went to the store without Elaine's six o'clock bottle and by six she was screeching. By ten we were still there and she was still screeching. Everyone in the store — a lot of people were there — was sick of screaming babies — there were two of them.*

*Slim Landerfield had a granddaughter there and these babies never stopped screaming.*

*When the eye passed, everything got deadly quiet. Everyone in the store walked out on the porch and listened but we couldn't hear a thing except running and dripping water. Nothing else.*

Glenna Wilcox never knew who rescued her family; Susan Richmond never knew the name of the people her husband, George, helped to the safety of the general store. The Richmonds were renting on Lee Avenue.

*That afternoon we were told the fire siren would blow if we had to leave the house. Well, it didn't blow until we had water under the house, and the ocean had already undermined the bulkhead at the end of our street. The pilings were all floating and acting just like ramrods, crashing into all the houses. We took our children and waded up to the general store.*

*My husband went up the street to help rescue some woman and her children. There were lots of children in the store and babies crying; we were wet and uncomfortable, but we slept there. The store man said take anything you need, and the next morning the Red Cross brought food. My kids had coffee and doughnuts for breakfast and thought that was magnificent; they'd never had coffee before.*

*courtesy Joe Krug*

**The sea snips off the dining room of Ethel and Victor Stephens' Harvey Cedars cottage but leaves the china stacked and intact.**

*We got back to our house the next morning. Nothing was on the lot but some little cement blocks on the lot. That's all. A pair of my slacks was wrapped around the telephone pole on the main road. One house was shredded by the big pilings; the bottom was gone, and the top was setting on the ground. It had floated from the ocean to the boulevard, and the beds and all the furniture were just like the family left them. Another house had three walls of the kitchen sliced away, but all the furniture was setting nicely and the cups were hanging in the cupboard.*

Doris Einselen Nocito sat out the storm with her family on Eighty-first Street. Her grandmother, immobilized with arthritis, looked out the window and joked, "I couldn't go to the ocean, so the ocean is coming to see me." They evacuated to the Harvey Cedars Tavern where Doris helped to serve soup to about thirty-five stranded homeowners.

Tom Houghton's family rented rowboats on Eighty-third Street and Kinsey Creek. "My dad, Al, could tell there was a northeaster coming. In those days we didn't get warnings like today, so he called the Barnegat City Coast Guard Station and they told him, `Batten down the hatches, it's just gonna be a severe northeaster,' " recalls Tom who was fourteen at the time.

*It was warm and we still had thirty boats in the water, so we secured them and then walked over to the Harvey Cedars Tavern — sometimes after*

*school I'd play checkers or pinochle in the back room with Libby McDermott, the owner's wife. Suddenly the water was coming down Eightieth Street and it was getting extremely windy. My grandmother and Aunt Rosie were renting Nancy Weiseisen's house at the corner of Eighty-fourth Street and the boulevard, so I walked down to see if they were all right. By the time I got to Eighty-first, the water was waist deep. When my father realized how quickly the water was rising he followed me, leaving my mother at the tavern.*

*By then the ocean had already come over the floorboards. A little while later we heard a pounding at the garage door: A woman and man and dog had made it from one of the other houses closer to the ocean. The garage was built into the first floor, and the water was so high they had to climb in on top of the car. Water shorted out the horn and we couldn't disconnect it, so it kept on blowing.*

*We climbed to the second floor as the water rose. We knew by then that it was a full-fledged hurricane. My dad's parents had owned a house on Long Island, one mile in from the ocean, and it was destroyed by a tidal wave during the 1938 hurricane, so he knew pretty much what to expect from a storm like this. The waves were crashing onto the windows of the second floor and we were up there praying. Then it started to get dark, then very calm, then came the shift-off from the bay as the hurricane passed.*

*The ocean receded very rapidly and water came up from the bay around our house. The boats were all tied together bow-to-stern so they just sank;*

**A house blocks the road near the Harvey Cedars-North Beach boundary.**

*they didn't go anywhere. We never knew what happened to my mother until the next day; she was at the bar all night not knowing whether we had made it safely or not.*

The next day Mayor Joseph Yearly and tax collector Josephine Thomas picked their way through Harvey Cedars' wreckage with a tax map in hand. The mayor said, "It's impossible to tell where many houses stood by just looking at this barren sand. The whole town will have to resurveyed before we can rebuild."

Out of 350 homes, 125 were severely damaged and 69 destroyed.

Lt. Barber ended his journey back to the family home near Barnegat Lighthouse on September 13 with the hurricane still breathing down his neck. He made it just in time to secure his property.

In the morning the Coast Guard had told Al Houghton to batten down and stay put, but by three o'clock Commander Walter Warren logged: "Advised all seeking information on the hurricane to go to higher ground." The increased forward speed of the storm had caught the Coast Guard off guard.

The power went out at 4:55 P.M. in Barnegat Light, and hurricane force winds continued until 7:50, when they shifted northwest. Warren detailed men to remove residents from unsafe homes: Twenty-two were quartered at the station and thirty-two at the Social Hotel on Fifth Street. At 6:30, the tide rose several feet in minutes. The ocean broke through the dunes near Sixth Street and quickly wiped out two homes and several sheds and garages. Former Mayor T. Jay France's snack bar and soda fountain was torn off its foundation and lodged in the sand at the intersection of Fourth Street and Central Avenue.

Young John Larson had been sent home from Barnegat Grade School on the mainland. His father came from the Coast Guard station and told the family, "It's gonna be a bad one." Now a commercial fisherman like his father, Larson remembers:

*My parents, Carl and myself got into our '39 Olds, and my sister Mary Ann and Uncle Louis in his '41 Olds, pretty new for the war years, and we all headed for the mainland. Uncle Louis got to Loveladies before the ocean broke through the high dunes there, but across from the Loveladies Coast Guard Station his Olds stalled out.*

*Mary Ann said she had new shoes and she wasn't gonna walk in the water, so Uncle Louis carried her to the station, and there was only one guy there, George Whitman, a caretaker. Already, all the little houses on the beach side of the station were pounded to kindling.*

*We were just a little while behind them, but a wall of water broke through the dunes, and our car just hit it and stopped. It would hardly run in rain, and nothing was ahead of us but salt water. It was blowing about 90 by now, or so it seemed to me, and we had to turn around and walk back to town, but my mother says we have to push the car off the road so no one will run into it.*

*The next morning, Georgie Svelling and I went with Ike Maxwell in a Jeep, riding through sand and holes and water to Harvey Cedars. Everything was all sand there, all mixed up, no more streets, pieces of houses. We saw our friend, Jimmy McClellan, and I yelled, "Hey, Jimmy, how ya doing?"*

*Jimmy said, "We lost our house. I don't know where it went."*

**The former Lavallette boardwalk at the foot of New Brunswick Avenue.**

## Northern Ocean and Monmouth Counties

Providence did not respond to the prayers of the editorial writer in the September 14 issue of the *Ocean Grove Times*. The weekly newspaper's headline proclaimed: "Storm-battered shore not prepared to withstand another assault of the elements" and the story continued:

*While the New Jersey coast has experienced heavy rains, we have escaped anything like wind of hurricane force, which is, indeed, fortunate. With the entire length of the shore made vulnerable to the ocean at storm tide by erosion, wind of high velocity would have done irreparable damage to our beaches. It is possible that we may get a northeaster this fall, but we certainly hope that Providence spares us because our weakened shore erosion defenses will not stand another hard battering by the elements.*

Ocean Grove and the whole of northern Ocean and Monmouth counties got a lot worse than merely the beach damage the *Times* had prayed they wouldn't. At the same time that Cape May residents were shaking their heads in disbelief at the quick flash of destruction, those in Monmouth County resorts were hit by what they, too, thought to be a tidal wave. In minutes, the boardwalks that lined the coast from Point Pleasant to Long Branch were wrenched from their pilings, picked up and blown into beachfront homes and restaurants, or washed down streets.

The wall of water crested and broke smack down on the Asbury Park boardwalk and rolled west to Kingsley Avenue, taking boardwalk, shops and restaurants with it, spewing merchandise and money in its wake. Asbury's famous walk was a total loss, along with all buildings east of the promenade. Officials later described a "50-foot wave" that tore apart the fishing pier, leaving the superstructure scattered like matchsticks along the six miles of beach.

Ocean Grove had celebrated its Diamond Jubilee Year during the summer — Dr. Norman Vincent Peale had preached a celebratory sermon two weeks earlier — and the community had just completed payment on losses from a previous storm. Now every pavilion was wrecked and not one foot of boardwalk remained. Torn-off sections crashed into beachfront hotels and restaurants. Timber and debris showered buildings along Ocean Avenue.

But, remembers Ray Timms, a boy at the time, it wasn't only disaster that rained down. "Teddy bears and toys, prizes from the boardwalk amusement galleys, were lying all over. They were ours for the taking."

"This was the worst storm since the northeaster of August 25, 1893," said Nelson Lillagore, who had been there. "Everything went from the north end to the south end, inclusive. That was a double-header. What escaped the storm of the twenty-fifth was finished by a second storm three days later. The new boardwalk was then laid sixteen feet further west."

If Jersey Central Railroad received any hurricane warnings, it didn't stop commuter service to the shore; in fact, it barely slowed it down. Point Pleasant resident L. Patton Brown left Camden on Train 999 at 5:10 P.M. and arrived home at 7:12. He credits the courage and skill of engineer Bert Longstreet and fireman Joseph Packer, as wringing wet when they arrived as though they had swum the whole way.

At Browns Mills, Brown was jolted when the train stopped suddenly to avoid a large tree blown across the tracks. Aided by the crew, the engine shoved it off and didn't stop again until Toms River. A number of passengers disembarked there and, according to Brown, "one man foolishly tried to use his umbrella which was instantly turned inside out. It blew across the platform and struck a woman, breaking her glasses and cutting her face."

The gale was blowing northwest by the time the train reached Ocean Gate. Between there and the Barnegat Bay railroad bridge, Brown saw hundreds of especially thick and tall pines down on the wires and across the track. "The branches of one fallen giant were so large that they brushed all the north side of the train windows as we eased ahead, giving them a thorough washing."

At that time, the railroad bridge ran for two miles across the bay, and as Train 999 crossed, visibility was about two hundred feet. Brown described the "torrential rain being driven across the bay in such a solid sheet that it simply beat the waves into submission; all we could see was a sea of mud!" After Seaside Park the remaining passengers and crew gathered in the car vestibules to watch "the sights produced by this gale. It was like having a grandstand seat, and much as we regretted the destruction which met our eyes, we realized it was a once-in-a-lifetime experience."

The tracks paralleled a wide avenue from Seaside Park to Point Pleasant where train passengers saw some cars marooned and others navigating through two feet of water. Brown observed "all manner of objects floating — boards, trees, chairs. At Normandy Beach, there was still light enough to see; at this point, the strip of land separating bay from ocean is only about 200 yards wide and the ocean was breaking through the dunes and rushing down the streets into the bay. We saw what appeared to be a small tidal wave break through, and sweeping a fence before it, come charging in our direction. For the next several miles, the water was level with the bottom steps of our train, and it was difficult to know whether we were on land or sea. By the time we reached Mantoloking, all lights were out of commission. We were thankful to reach Point Pleasant only 25 minutes late."

One and a half miles of Bay Head's boardwalk washed two blocks west. Point Pleasant's, from Jenkinson's Pavilion to Manasquan Inlet and south of Arnold Avenue to New Jersey Avenue, and all oceanfront properties south of New Jersey were wrecked. The wind picked up a section of the walk,

*New Jersey State Police (3)*

**The sea claims part of the beach at Ocean Grove and dumps a tug onto Jersey Central tracks in Atlantic Highlands, opposite, top and bottom. Ramparts at Deal crumble, above.**

moving it as neatly as if by hand to a miniature golf course, with seats, benches and light standards untouched by the flight.

Belmar's recently finished Tenth Avenue pavilion and new boardwalk were a memory in minutes. The shrieking gale blew the bathhouse attached to the pavilion clear across Ocean Avenue, and the sea reached as far back as A Street.

Commercial beachfront development — boardwalks, fishing piers, restaurants, bathhouses, shops — broke the force of the storm surge and saved many private homes from devastation by the waves. Kiddie rides, game centers, novelty shops — mostly small wooden buildings on the boardwalks — blew apart and became projectiles, damaging more substantial structures. The herculean Atlantic even twisted the iron railing around the Asbury Park Casino, but only slightly damaged the building itself and the huge brick Convention Hall.

Mantoloking, just two blocks wide, suffered four breakthroughs. Dunes were flattened as the ocean washed through to the bay. On

*New Jersey State Police (top); Keansburg Police Department/Picture Collection, New Jersey State Library (above)*

Downer Avenue, waves lifted a small house owned by the volunteer Air-Watchers Service and dumped it in the center of Route 37. Protected by dunes, most oceanfront homes were damaged but not destroyed.

Towns between Keansburg and Long Branch took the hardest blows. Long Branch's beach still hadn't built up since the previous October's northeaster. Now, sustained 74 mile-an-hour winds demolished every structure on the beachfront. The 50-year-old Chelsea Pavilion crumbled into the waves. The boardwalk buckled and warped, iron guardrails ripping and snapping like so much thread. Where not destroyed completely, the walk heaved up two feet or more. The *Daily Record* said, "It appears as though some titanic jack had lifted the boardwalk, where huge timbers, driven by the powerful force of street-level waves, lodged endwise through the foundation to elevate it, leaving a wavy, scenic railway effect."

About 150 bathhouses splintered. The rear of the town's recreation center collapsed, and the roof and walls blew against the carousel, reducing it to twisted steel. At Seaview Avenue, the fishing pier cracked in two as the land end shifted, turned completely around, and landed intact 50 feet inland on Ocean Avenue.

William Martin, a U.S. cooperative weather observer in Long Branch, reported that winds reached 80 miles per hour and damaged his "wind-reporting machine," so he climbed the 78-foot-high steel tower and repaired it. Martin said the velocity broke a half-century record for the bureau: In 1938, gusts only reached 60 miles per hour.

The noise of the wind is what reverberates most vividly in author June Methot's memory:

*...the ear-splitting, mind-boggling, completely intimidating noise. The wind did not shriek or howl — it roared, for about 12 hours. We then lived on the east side of a point projecting from the north shore of the North Shrewsbury River; the northeast wind had a clean sweep for the length of the river toward our house, which stood about 30 feet above the normal high tide level. It began in late afternoon, suddenly, as a squall wind comes with a thunderstorm, quickly increasing to full force, something well in excess of 100 mph. The pitch of the sound was deep and nearly constant, varying not more than one or two notes of the tonal scale, indicating a minor variation of velocity. Conversation inside the house had to be shouted into someone's ear to be heard. Rain was driven horizontally against the front windows with the force of a large hose.*

*Out a rear window, before dark, I watched an elm tree, 60 to 70 feet tall with a two-and-a-half-foot diameter trunk, fall flat, uprooted, but did not hear it hit the ground although it was no more than 40 feet from the house and I could feel the vibration when it landed. It appeared to fall in silence. Strange, strange sensation.*

*After several hours of darkness during which we anxiously checked windows and doors for leaks by candlelight and our one functioning flashlight, it seemed likely the house would hang together and we decided we might as well go to bed. It was then that we discovered that the force of the wind was apparently compressing the house. The upstairs floor was rising and descending two or three inches with the small variations in the velocity of the wind!*

*The next morning we saw that a sturdy 100-foot dock, 50 to 60 feet of solid concrete bulkhead, and one-third of our riverbank had vanished. The water was still high and the color of mud. The air was heavy, oppressive but absolutely still — not a ripple disturbed the surface of the river; it seemed as though nature, too, was completely exhausted.*

New Jersey State Police

**A bayside location in Keansburg doesn't save the boardwalk from being rendered into kindling, left and above. The excursion paddlewheeler *Smithfield* beached at Keyport, opposite top.**

Along Raritan Bay, the hurricane left the small communities of East Keansburg and Port Monmouth practically unrecognizable with nearly fifty summer homes destroyed. The water lifted the Pew Creek bridge and washed it intact onto a nearby road. In the bay, the surge picked up a 60-foot fire barge and dropped it flush across the spur track of the Jersey Central.

Jack Miller watched his Ideal Beach home move two hundred yards and land upside down in the marshes. Joseph Smith's house shifted only eight feet from its foundation, but his brother-in-law's place next door circumnavigated Smith's with not even a dish broken or furniture disturbed. The plate glass from a patio table in Arthur Barnes' yard sailed about a hundred feet and dropped onto a gravel path. He found the glass later without a scratch or nick in it.

*New Jersey State Police*

**Misplaced dunes line First Avenue in Manasquan.**

Miller heard women screaming for help outside their small cottages: "There were five of them, panicky, and I guess they would have gone down if I hadn't heard them and pulled them over to safety." He never knew who they were. "Lord knows. Some women who lived up the line. One of them told me she lost a roll of bills with $600 in it. I hunted and hunted and found it after a while, but she didn't even thank me."

North Jersey newspapers had a descriptive field day; the poesy pouring from journalists' pens attempted to compensate for the lack of photographers on the spot. Charlotte Johnson wrote in the *Asbury Park Press*:

*It was a night for the ages — a strange contrast of Stygian blackness and eerie searching light, of tempestuous fury and a heaven of stars like tinseled baubles on a velvet drop, of stars you could almost reach out and touch, of roaring, terror-filled sound and interludes of frightening hush. Shapeless, indistinguishable figures, little arcs of flashlight beams preceding them in the darkness, moved spookily through the night. A terror-gripped resort fresh from a summer scene of laughter and crowds was suddenly enveloped in a close-up nightmare. Disaster swept down on us like the crack of doom, and the terrible and primitive passion for self-preservation took hold. But there was an order to it as life moved upon the face of the waters.*

And a disaster it was. For the first time since 1938 New Jersey had an inkling of what a Burmese monsoon, a Japanese typhoon and an Caribbean hurricane are like. "The people got a real tempest to provide new food for contemplation of men's frailty and divine omnipotence," preached the *Jersey Journal*.

When it was east of Florida, the 1944 hurricane packed the same intensity as 1938's, but with a gradual filling of the depression after passing Cape Hatteras, the wind velocity dropped. Also, this storm struck New Jersey obliquely, with the shore on its left, or weaker, side, and the storm tide created by the stronger winds in the righthand quadrants expended most of its force at sea. No tide heights approached the 20- to 25-foot level reached in 1938. The 1938 and 1944 hurricanes traveled the same tracks as the powerful ones in 1815 and 1821 — coincidentally, both pairs occurred six years apart — but few rigid man-made structures stood in the path of the earlier storms' furious wind and waves.

The hurricane swallowed 390 victims. Watery graves claimed 344 sailors: The destroyer *Warrington*; two Coast Guard cutters, the *Bedloe* and the *Jackson*; the lightship *Vineyard Sound*; and minesweeper *YMS-409* all went down. Had it not been for radio silence at sea imposed by wartime regulations, the crews might have been warned.

Death came circuitously too. A man on Long Beach Island tried to close his garage door but the wind smashed it back against him, breaking his hip. Karl Held Jr. went with the Coast Guard doctor to help. "He was a Christian Scientist and wouldn't take the sedative left for him," said Held, "and when they got him to the hospital in Toms River the next day he wouldn't have his bone set. When I was back on duty in the Pacific, I read in the paper that he died."

And the *Jersey Journal* commented, "Timid women died of heart attacks during what seemed like a reign of hell."

## Aftermath

The floodwaters receded and troops of gawking tourists followed in the hurricane's retreating wake. In most communities, the Navy's Shore Patrol greeted the merely curious, turning back everyone except homeowners, who had to produce a deed for identification and admittance.

Asbury Park roped off its oceanfront, but visitors could see the twisted debris, swarming with rats and mice. Ocean City became headquarters for

Coast Guard reservists from Camden, Philadelphia and Trenton, who turned back all casual visitors for four days. Cape May and Long Beach Island officials called in Army units from Fort Dix to help prevent looting. State police set up roadblocks in Manahawkin and Ship Bottom. Twenty troopers were stationed on either side of the bay and closed the causeway to nonessential traffic until September 27.

Snow-white sand covered Long Beach Island. Behind the police barricade, front-end loaders heaped up a mountain of the misplaced beach; the traffic circle was totally covered. An anonymous *New Jersey Courier* writer captured the surreal scene:

> *Sand piled in windrows, smashed homes and stores, uprooted trees and poles, glades cut in from the sea nearly to the boulevard, cruisers, houseboats and smaller craft lying drunkenly about the streets and on lots blocks from the water's edge; houses perched at crazy angles in the streets, surrounded by debris from the storm-tossed sea; personal effects, furnishings and other objects strewn about; streets blocked by sand, acres of macadam ripped from the surface of streets scattered about the landscape; small lakes of sea water twinkling in the light of day, now several blocks from the ocean, in vacant lots, at street intersections, in the middle of the road; scenes of utter desolation which serve as a reminder of the strength of the sea and the inability of mere man to cope with the fury of the elements.*

cream dealers, realizing that their stock would quickly melt, unloaded it at ten cents a pint. An order from the federal Office of Price Administration allowed perishable meat, cheese and butter to be sold immediately without ration coupons. Long Beach Island's War Price and Ration Board eased restrictions on rationed items such as boots, gasoline, fuel oil and stoves.

Firemen pumped out cellars and stores and transformed bulldozed piles of house sections into blazing pyres. Power company crews dynamited trees to clear utility wires. Power was out for days in most places, for weeks in others. Damage to electric lines was erratic enough to provide service to one house and not the next. An extension cord stretching between neighboring homes was not unusual. Shortages of materials hindered utility companies despite the highest priority given to them by the War Production Board. A dispute arose in Beach Haven when borough officials sold salvaged lumber from the boardwalk to Atlantic City. Beach Haven Councilman Charley Yocum said, "I'm not shaving off my beard until we get our boardwalk back," but the valuable boards were sold.

The New Jersey Bell Telephone Company brought in linemen from as far away as Vermont, Maryland and Ohio, and they worked from dawn until dusk. With phone service restored, additional operators handled the heavy load of long-distance calls to shore residents from worried friends and relatives.

Residents hauled water from homes and institutions with unbroken water mains and then boiled it. Six weeks after the hurricane, the Harvey Cedars' mains were still not repaired and the local board of health complained that some families were drinking unsafe water. Officials urged residents to have typhoid shots.

The Salvation Army set up mobile kitchens in fire halls and community centers to feed homeless families as well as those whose homes lacked power. A Red Cross official who assumed the crowds would taper off once electricity was restored found that they were increasing instead. One man, when told the station was only for the homeless, replied, "Look, lady, you give me that piece of pie and I'll give you what's left of my home."

Housewives despaired as butter, at sixteen ration points a pound, melted in useless refrigerators. There was a run on blocks of ice, where it could be found, and homeowners who still had old-fashioned iceboxes shared cold storage with their more modern neighbors. Matawan ice

*New Jersey State Police*

**"Mrs. John Whitten, age 65 ... who lost her recently purchased home when storm swept it off of the foundation and into bay, at Holgate. Mrs. Whitten lost everything but sweater and bag she took with her when she went to the mainland before the storm. She is shown standing at what was once a bus stop along Ocean Blvd." — from state police files.**

Where schools had lost power or were full of homeless families, gleeful children enjoyed an extended vacation. They explored the transformed beach towns, scavenging and salvaging where they could. In some communities the entire bayfront was bordered in floating wreckage, most of which had washed all the way to the mainland when the wind blew from the east and back again when it shifted. Yards were a mess of smashed timbers, porches, stairways, refrigerators, cupboards, deck chairs, benches, chicken coops, rowboats, sailboats, wicker furniture, cushions and dead sea gulls.

Thousands of claims flooded into insurance companies from property owners who didn't realize that their policies covered only wind damage, not that caused by high tides or floodwaters. Ocean County Freeholder A. Paul King remarked, "This is not a case of which came first, the chicken or the egg. The clue is found in an old sailing expression: As weak as the water without a breeze to blow its spine."

MACBRAYER LOT WHERE HOUSE STOOD

*Betty Bright*

**A circle marks the spot where the McBrayer house stood, above.**

Hundreds of workers — municipal, military and volunteer — began an immediate clean-up operation. Even German prisoners of war interred near Vineland were used briefly. Practically before the tide receded, municipalities began the battle for federal aid. New Jersey Congressman James Auchincloss introduced House Bill 5384, calling for a $20 million appropriation for repair and reconstruction.

Governor Walter Edge declined to call a special session of the Legislature and looked to the federal government. He said New Jersey's $1.25 million erosion budget was "a drop in the bucket" and asked for funding from the Reconstruction Finance Corporation, but the federal government only offered loans at four percent interest.

Editorial writers up and down the coast brandished angry pens. The *Cape May Gazette* wrote:

> *When an emergency arises, Uncle Sam suddenly takes on a hunger for profit and says, in effect, we'll collect our four percent or you can all wash into the sea. It's not good business for the government to reduce its interest rate. We are sympathetic ... but not enough to cut our interest! We know you need seawalls and we have plenty of money to lend ... at four percent. We're in business. We must make a profit ... so we can throw that and more away somewhere else. Four percent ... four percent ... four percent ... that doesn't sound like a government of the people, by the people and for the people.*

Angry letters and articles pointed out that Washington was there with money for victims of the 1906 San Francisco earthquake and fire, the 1933 Midwest Dust Bowl drought and the 1938 New England hurricane. In a

radio address, T. Millet Hand, a candidate for New Jersey's Second Congressional District, spoke about the state's contributions to federal projects.

*The money we seek from the federal government is not a mysterious fund in which we have no rights. Uncle Sam's money comes in a large measure from the great producing states of the East. It comes in substantial quantities from our State of New Jersey, which contributes far more to the federal treasury than it ever gets out. All we ask is that in this great emergency, some of New Jersey's money be spent at home. We have helped build giant dams in Tennessee and Colorado. We have helped in controlling the floodwaters of the Mississippi. This time, let's get some of our own money back to protect and benefit us here at home.*

Governor Edge assured people he was doing all he could to "make the Federal Government realize its responsibilities," and state Senator Albert F. Hawkes said, "People and municipalities can no more protect themselves

The Great September Hurricane was the most destructive to hit New Jersey in about seventy-five years. State climatologist A.E. White said "neither weather records nor old newspaper accounts reveal a storm as damaging since the Civil War."

The Auchincloss bill would not be considered until after Congress reconvened in November, and Democrats called foul, accusing Republicans of bad faith. Democratic Assembly candidate Jack Levin from Long Branch charged that Republican politicians were "shedding crocodile tears over New Jersey's plight of the storm-battered communities." After President Roosevelt opened two Disaster Relief offices in New Jersey, Levin said, "Where Auchincloss gives us nothing more than empty words, President Roosevelt gives us results" and claimed that Auchincloss was only grabbing headlines.

In response to the DRC's four percent loans, the mayor of Beach Haven said that Ocean County banks could easily beat that figure. Atlantic City's commissioners considered the loans, but they really wanted outright aid provided under the National Catastrophe Act, "the same kind of aid some states got after the Mississippi flood."

Cables with damage estimates flooded Auchincloss' Senate office; only Point Pleasant Mayor Harry Roe wired, "Pleased to inform you loss very small...no help is needed...thank you." Municipal budgets for 1945 were held up as mayors held their breath. Nothing but silence emanated from Washington.

The Beach Haven mayor ate his words as some Long Beach Island communities extended their debt limit and borrowed from local banks at six percent interest. Towns floated bond issues, divided large municipal tracts not needed for public use and sold off lots, and scratched for funds where they could.

In April 1945 Harvey Cedars Mayor Yearly took his empty coffers to Washington to talk about beach

*New Jersey State Police (2)*

**The signs are still standing at the Ship Bottom circle, but not much of the towns they locate. At left, a state trooper checks a vehicle at the Ship Bottom circle. "Man approaching trooper just learned that his house had been washed into ocean," says the caption in state police files.**

against the ravages of the Atlantic Ocean than other areas are able to protect themselves from floods. Some coastal sections have been so wiped out that even with the power to tax there is little left to tax."

Long Beach Township, Long Beach Island's largest community, lost $420,000 in ratables, mainly from the destruction of homes in the Beach Haven Inlet section. Harvey Cedars, the island's smallest town, had 20 percent of its homes swept away. Almost all damaged towns from Long Branch south to Cape May passed resolutions petitioning the Disaster Relief Corporation for funds. The governor estimated $33 million in damage statewide, the great majority in the four coastal counties. Included in this figure were $5 million each for Atlantic City and Asbury Park, $3.5 million on Long Beach Island, $2.5 million in Long Branch and $2 million for Ocean City.

erosion with the Bureau of Rivers and Navigation — and more talk was all that resulted. The little town made do with some state and county aid for roads, bulldozed a hay-and-sand dike along the beach, and crossed its crippled fingers.

The War Department's Corps of Engineers turned down a plea to erect a sea wall between Sea Bright and Atlantic Highlands and complaints about federal disinterest in reclamation of the seaboard reverberated up and down the coast.

Four days before Christmas 1945, the state Department of Conservation presented Ocean County with $25,000 and Long Beach Township with $66,000, and township commissioners authorized bond issues for the remaining $50,000 needed to pay for two rock jetties.

Ultimately, municipalities received no federal funds for storm damage.

**Looking south on Bay Avenue from Amber Street in Beach Haven in 1953.**

# 1945-1961

*Poor naked wretches, wheresoe'er you are,*
*That bide the pelting of this pitiless storm,*
*How shall your houseless heads and unfed sides*
*Defend you from seasons such as this?*
— Shakespeare, "King Lear"

T HE GREAT HURRICANE OF 1944 was indeed great by any standards, but generally the constant coupling of "great" with "hurricane" had become so common that its descriptive power had been ground down to a convenient cliché. Any hurricane experienced personally certainly seems great.

The 1938 hurricane was labeled the "Long Island Express" by the New York press. A 1950 hurricane in Miami was called "King"; nobody knows why. There was a gale in November 1950 that sent anemometers spinning at 108 miles per hour, dropped nine inches of rain, drove a heavy dredge like a battering ram into a bridge on Raritan Bay, blew the steamer *City of New York* ashore at Keyport, and caused $30 million in damage. Some called it "half a hurricane" but it was officially dubbed the Great Appalachian Storm, despite the fact that the winds came from the southwest.

One that did match its name was the "Disappearing Hurricane," also called the "Lost Hurricane."

The year was 1947. Radar and hurricane hunter planes were in common use; no longer did the U.S. Weather Bureau have to rely on occasional reports from ships at sea or static-filled radio messages from distant islands. The hurricane was spotted, measured and tracked. Warnings went out. Winds were estimated at 200 miles per hour. Schools closed and evacuation centers began filling up. In some places, thirteen inches of rain fell. Everybody braced for the blow, due at midnight.

But at midnight there was a sudden calm. The calm before the storm? No, the calm instead of the storm. The sky cleared, the winds died, the rain ceased. And that was that.

The Weather Bureau's R.H. Simpson said he didn't know where it went. "It lifted off the face of the earth." Grady Norton, also of the Weather Bureau, said, "It was an act of God," a phrase usually reserved for the appearance of such phenomena but, apparently, equally fitting their disappearance.

The use of the military alphabet — Able, Baker, Charlie, etc. — began in 1951, but people objected to any hurricane being named Easy or Love, and non-English speaking people favored a more international set: Alpha, Bravo, Coco. In many islands of the Caribbean it had long been the custom to use the name of the saint's day on which the storm had occurred, a practice not not favored by the Roman Catholic Church.

In 1950, a weatherman named George Stewart had written a novel called *Storm*. In it he identified a Pacific storm as Maria, "for convenience," he said later. The Weather Bureau claimed there was no connection, but in 1953 it began using women's names to identify cyclonic storms in both the Atlantic and Pacific.

For the first few years, however, the same names were used each year, so until 1955 there were several Alices, Barbaras and Carols. The Carol of 1954 toppled the steeple of the Old North Church, in Boston, where "one if by land, two if by sea" had signaled Paul Revere out of the starting gate. Carol came by land and sea. The steeple was a replacement for the original one which had been taken out by another hurricane 150 years earlier, the Great New England Hurricane of 1804.

Carol cruised by the Jersey shore just close enough to give it what the *Beachcomber* newspaper called "a bitchy slap." At 6:30 A.M., Bond's Coast Guard station on Long Beach Island reported, "It won't hit us direct, but things don't look too good." The storm broke down the steel doors of Asbury Park's Convention Hall and pushed Raritan Bay down the streets of Keansburg. It caused postponement, too, of the Bradley Beach baby parade, as well as the annual New Jersey Tuna Tournament. In a first-person account of the storm, a *Beachcomber* reporter wrote:

> *The wind was tearing the tops off big, swift waves racing across the bay*
> *from the mainland. At hundreds of moorings small boats pitched fore and aft,*
> *filling with rainwater, then with the seas breaking over their bows. Boat after*
> *boat took on its load, brimmed over and sank at its mooring, to rest comfort-*
> *ably and more or less safely on the bottom. In Beach Haven Gardens, a*
> *cricket stridulated cheerfully in the teeth of the rain and wind. An hour later*
> *he and his meadow were drowned in the premature high tide. By late*
> *morning, while the wind still raged and rain spattered, sunlight broke*
> *gloriously over the bay and a remarkable low-slung rainbow appeared in the*
> *west. A collective sigh of relief was breathed. Carol had passed on.*

On to New England which, as the paper noted, was not so lucky, with over fifty people reported dead and another twenty missing. Sol Schildhause drove through rising water to the highest spot in what he called "the bottom-of-the-saucer downtown area" of Providence, Rhode Island, from which he observed "the scene of utter desolation below me — an ambulance impaled on a parking meter, the attendants busily engaged in extracting the unfortunate from the back ... windows being blown out of shops and office buildings ... boxes and file cabinets floating by."

One he remembered with "a small glow of inner satisfaction" was an oaken cabinet. "Opening the top drawer, I saw there were files of a loan company with payment records of borrowers. Hastily I reconsigned the cabinet to a watery fate and wonder to this day who got away with what. Is there a morality conflict for me somewhere in the event? No sleep lost for me."

Carol was followed by Dolly, Edna, Florence, Gilda and Hazel. Edna came close enough to swish its stormy skirts at the Jersey shore, but Hazel came right up the coast "like a screaming freight train," as one writer put it, crashing through dunes twenty feet high, crushing houses and creasing roads. It had killed a thousand people in Haiti, burying some two hundred of them under a mud slide. It dropped eleven inches of rain on the Carolinas, set records for wind speed in Washington, D.C., and in New York City, and lived for two raging weeks, even though half of that was over land, which usually cripples hurricanes. On its way it deposited palm fronds and wooden bowls marked "Made in Haiti." Even after two weeks it could dump enough

*courtesy Dave Wood*

**Northeast winds peel off the roof of the Colony Theatre, Brant Beach, on November 25, 1950.**

rain on Toronto, Canada, to wash away buildings and bridges to the tune of $100 million.

Carol, Edna and Hazel together caused $1 billion worth of damage, a new record for a single year. All had been announced well enough in advance to allow ample time for both protective measures and evacuation, else the total would have been much higher. Hurricane hunter planes were now a routine part of the forecasting procedure, plucking data out of the maw of the beast. Instruments gave the statistics, but radar never saw the hurricane's eye the way meteorologist R.H. Simpson did:

*The plane flew through bursts of torrential rain and several turbulent bumps. Then, suddenly, we were in dazzling sunlight and bright blue sky. Around us was an awesome display. The eye was a clear space 40 miles in diameter surrounded by a coliseum of clouds whose walls on one side rose vertically and on the other were banked like galleries in a great opera house. The upper rim, about 35,000 feet high, was rounded off smoothly against a background of blue sky. Below us was a floor of low clouds rising to a dome 8,000 feet above sea level in the center. There were breaks in it which gave us glimpses of the surface of ocean. In the vortex around the eye the sea was a scene of unimaginably violent, churning water.*

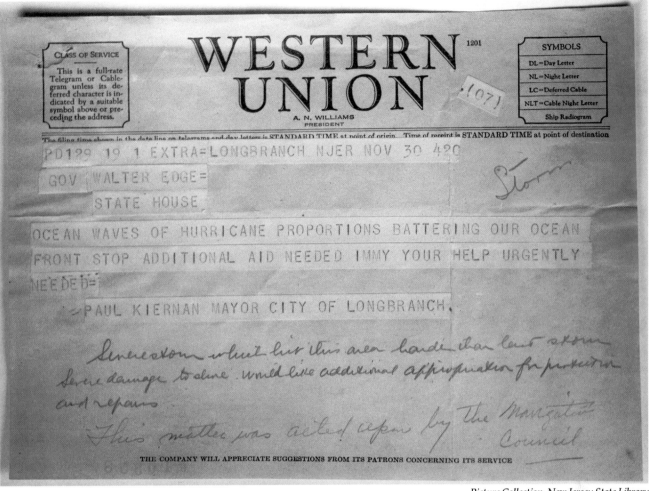

*Picture Collection, New Jersey State Library*
**The mayor of Long Branch appeals for help during a 1947 storm.**

The first hurricane of 1955 was probably a leftover from 1954. It showed up on New Year's Day and, as if realizing its mistake, disappeared almost at once. Nonetheless, the Weather Bureau named it Alice. By the time the regular season got under way, though, the bureau had decided to go to new names each year, so the August 1 hurricane was not Barbara but Brenda. It launched the worst storm year of the century; August had only four clear days that year.

Connie was the first to rattle its way up the coast, spawning a few tornadoes on its edges, sloshing the waters of Chesapeake and Delaware bays, then heading overland to Lake Huron. But Connie wouldn't be more than an entry in the logbook had it not been for Diane, which followed along the same route a few days later. The Northeast was saturated with the waters of Connie. The ground couldn't hold any more, and the rivers were already fat. Diane set records in flood damage, hitting the billion dollar mark all by itself, a first in hurricane history.

Peggy Hostler Davis from Altoona, Pennsylvania, visiting a college roommate and her husband, rode out the storm on Long Beach Island.

*We were in the last house on the last street in Barnegat Light, right up near the inlet, which seemed awfully close to the water to me. There had just been one a few days earlier (Connie), but this was much worse. My friend was pregnant with her first child and we were all nervous for her because there was so much water coming over the dunes and down the street that we couldn't leave. It was a tiny, old, fishing-shack sort of house and it cracked and shook. We were drinking to calm our nerves, but the house shook so much that the scotch rippled in the glass. All survived, including baby.*

The storms did some damage to the Jersey shore but not as much as the reports of their coming did, according to John Mecleary. Head of the Long Beach Island Board of Trade, he complained that "overdramatization" had cost shore resorts millions of dollars. A newspaper account of the group's mid-August meeting said Mecleary urged local business people and residents "not to be a part of this deliberate panic stirring by repeating stories of past hurricanes, the majority of which are exaggerated," adding, "the season is short enough without making it shorter."

Coming up behind Diane were Edith and Flora, with the whole Eastern seaboard watching, the way a mouse watches a snake. Both, however, curved back out to sea. Gladys stayed down around the Gulf of Mexico where it unloaded twenty-five inches of rain. It seemed there could not be any water left in the sky, but twelve days later Hilda brought more. In late

September, as meteorologists watched in wonder, Ione came in with thirty inches.

Janet was termed one of the most vicious hurricanes ever spawned, with winds over 200 miles per hour. It wiped out Swan Island, a weather station in the Caribbean and caused the only loss ever of a hurricane hunter plane. Lt. Cmdr. G.B. Windham radioed that he was about to penetrate the eye wall at seven hundred feet. For two hours there was nothing but static. Then nothing. They never found the wreckage.

The storm beat heavily into the coasts of Texas and Mexico. Bodies floated far out into the Gulf of Mexico. Seemingly not content with its own killing, it drove hordes of rattlesnakes out of the marshes and sent water moccasins to seek rooftops on which human survivors clustered.

Then there was Katie. It cruised around, feinted east-northeast, then drifted harmlessly out to sea.

And then there were no more. The great storm year of 1955 was over. Final tally: $2 billion in property damage and fifteen hundred people killed.

For the rest of the 1950s, hurricanes stayed south and relatively mild. Only Audrey, in June of 1957, attracted any attention. Coming up out of the Gulf, where early-season hurricanes often form, it loomed off Louisiana. Warnings were sent into the bayous. One woman reportedly said, "I wasn't much afraid because the Lord told us He would never destroy this earth with water again." Audrey flooded the coastal area, wiping out one town, killing six hundred people and driving the rest to hummocks where they had to battle alligators for standing room.

In 1960, Hurricane Donna passed about one hundred miles off the Jersey shore. Although it had rocked Florida, knocking out about half the citrus crop, and pounded that favorite hurricane target, North Carolina's Outer Banks, it almost overlooked New Jersey.

A northeaster on November 7, 1953 destroys the 25-year-old Portnoff house on 85th Street in Harvey Cedars, top. The newer home on Third Street in Beach Haven was saved by its pilings.

*this water came gushing past. My mother grabbed me and my two sisters — the youngest was less than a year old — and we ran to the car. All this debris was floating all over and she got stuck on something, and then water was coming into the car at this point and we had to abandon the car. My mother had the baby in her arms and my other sister on top of her shoulders.*

They headed for a neighbor's house on higher ground, along with others who had been similarly surprised. Norman remembers the water being up to his neck by this time. His sister fell off his mother's shoulders and was pulled out of the flood by one of the neighbors. They made it to safety but, Norman added, "My mother called my father and was cursing him out for going to work and leaving her with three kids in a hurricane."

The Norman house was built four feet above the ground; when the family returned after the storm, they found the watermark inside was three feet up the wall. There was no serious damage from the storm, however, and only one life lost, when Charles Stanley dropped dead of a heart attack while helping to push the rowboat that had rescued him.

Donna did hand the shore a couple of surprises as it passed. Its eye stretched out in a northeast-

*collection of the* Beachcomber

**Milton Britz in front of his Centre Street bar when the November 7 northeaster flooded downtown Beach Haven.**

The shore was ready for it, however. Evacuation plans were broadcast from Sea Bright south to Sea Isle City. Raritan Bay extended its domain into bordering towns, turning Keansburg from a waterfront community to an underwater one as rising tides poured forty inches of water into eight hundred homes. The bay, though large, is a kind of cul-de-sac for sudden tidal flows that push past Sandy Hook, and the water quickly flooded the lowlands. Harry Norman was a boy, living about a half mile inland:

*My mother was on the phone with my aunt who was calling to see if we were all right because she knew how this area was. She said there was supposed to be a tidal wave coming. My mother was saying, "So far everything's all right." I was looking out the window and all of a sudden all*

southwest line, one end skirting the shore and dropping the barometer to a startling 28.55 inches, the lowest reading here since the record 28.38 during the blizzard of March 1, 1914.

The following year Esther showed up, far enough offshore to stir little more than sailing winds and surfing waves. The Secret Service took the advance storm warnings seriously, however, evacuating President Kennedy's children, Caroline and John Jr., from the family compound in Hyannisport, Massachusetts. But for the most part there were just the usual Jersey blasters, the northeasters and southeasters that nip in and out of the coast, scooping some sand out of one beach to spread it along another, always rearranging the shoreline but never really changing it.

Until 1962.

The view from the tower of the Harvey Cedars Bible Conference looking east across Harvest Cove and Long Beach Boulevard — from Barnegat Bay to the oceanfront — during the worst of the six high tides of the Great Atlantic Storm of 1962.

# CHAPTER FOUR

# 1962

*This appalling ocean!*
— Herman Melville, "Moby Dick"

THERE IS NO STORY TO THIS STORM. It didn't have what's needed for a story — a beginning, middle and end. It was all middle. It came all at once, without warning. It stayed for three days. Then it went away. It was nothing like a hurricane, with notices and watches and advisories to herald its approach, flags flying, satellite pictures of its beady little eye and flailing arms — Is it heading here? Is it heading out to sea? — and then it comes and blows and bellows and spits and rages, and then the calm eye passes over — God's eye, some have called it — and then you get hit with the backside, furious, mighty, unassailable, unanswerable, and then it goes off to unload on somebody else.

A hurricane is a progression: the sound of distant cannon, the attack, a lull, redoubled violence, and then peace. This storm was nothing like that. This storm was five high tides, the highest 8.6 feet, just 4.8 inches below 1944's 9.0-foot record, water that just kept coming. It was a northeaster more ruinous than any hurricane that ever happened here, a demonstration that nature is a hard mother, a reminder that those who dwell beside the sea are always only a wave's length away from sleeping with the fishes. "A savage gale, with pounding tides, towering seas and heavy snows," said the *New York Times*.

It was unexpected and unannounced, sudden and surly, inundating, devastating, mutilating, obliterating. It battered and bludgeoned the shore until there was no more shore, until it was all running water and milling debris, until almost every trace of a human presence had been washed away. Then it was gone.

But not, to this day, forgotten. One newspaper called it "a scene of human misery unparalleled within the memory of longtime resort residents, exceeding that wreaked by the hurricane of 1944."

While there was no one story to the storm, there are a thousand stories of the storm.

Capt. Paul McGill, a professional pilot, flew over the shore midway through it.

*It was the worst sight I ever saw. I flew over Louisiana after Hurricane Audrey, but this was worse than that. I thought Hurricane Donna was bad but this looked like an atomic explosion compared to it.*

It was actually two storms that joined up or, as some meteorologists insisted, really two "developments" of the same "system." One storm had formed over Iowa on Monday, March 6, gathered strength and purpose somewhere in West Virginia, then moved east, spreading as much as twenty-six inches of snow in some spots. It snowed as far south as Alabama, and the temperature in Miami dropped to thirty-one degrees. The other storm formed off the coast of Georgia. The landward low reached out and joined it, and the new low-low then started a slow saunter north.

And then it stalled, held in place by a cold front that had moved down from Canada. Its winds rose to almost hurricane force. Over a stretch of about six hundred miles — its fetch — the wind pushed the water ahead of it in long swells that rose thirty feet high in open ocean. By the time these neared the shore they were traveling at freight train speed. As they reached the beaches, they mounted to the height of a three- or four-story building; records are incomplete because the storm destroyed the recording devices on the Steel Pier in Atlantic City.

It happened close to the spring equinox when high tides are higher than normal. It also coincided with a new moon, one of the two times a month when the sun and moon are in alignment, which also causes higher-than-normal tides, known as spring tides no matter what time of year they occur.

The Jersey shore had never seen anything like it. The weather report out of Atlantic City for Monday was "Cloudy today and tonight with a chance of some rain developing this evening. Mostly cloudy and cooler on Tuesday."

Instead, as recorded in one newspaper account:

*Never in the memory of anyone living along its 140-mile length of sandy geography had the Jersey shore been dealt a heavier blow. Weathermen were to explain later that the deep low-pressure system alone would have produced a dilly of a northeaster. "We kept waiting for the wind to shift," said the mayor of one tide-battered community. "It always does, you know.*

*Charles T. Higgens/*Philadelphia Evening Bulletin/*Temple University Urban Archives*
**Homes are destroyed by an uncontrolled fire as the ocean meets the bay in Ocean City.**

**The Inlet section of the Atlantic City boardwalk is damaged by three days of pummeling surf.**

*As soon as it backs around to the northwest everyone starts to breathe easier." It didn't get around to shifting until Thursday. When it was over, it took another day before the full import of what had happened began to dawn on the rest of the state. Newspaper editors sitting at their desks listening to their reporters' descriptions just didn't believe it all until the photographic evidence came in. Their hard old eyes hadn't seen anything like this in decades.*

Karl Held Jr., then a nine-year-old on Long Beach Island, says his mother "was mad for years at this guy, Wally Kinnan, the Weatherman. He was talking about early spring and picnics and stuff, and instead we got battered."

Mae Allen had moved from Atlantic City after the 1944 hurricane to Ventnor and a house at the corner of Vermont and Gramercy. "We had no idea whatsoever this was happening," she recalls.

*I woke up in the morning and I saw the cars and the water was over the hubcaps. I could have wakened everyone and told them, I guess, but I didn't. I went back to bed, I was so upset. Water didn't start coming in the house until the second tide. The tide would go out but only a little. Then when the new tide came in, the water went up higher. We never got rid of the water. It was much more devastating than the hurricane. The hurricane was one day and we cleaned up and then it was clean. We were in there 'til Thursday without any food. I had a large loaf of bread and a jar of peanut butter. Everything was damp, the bedding was damp, oh, it was miserable, it was horrible. We were in there and no one could get to us, we didn't have any electricity, the sidewalks were all torn up, the boardwalk...a friend had a house; it disappeared; it just floated away.*

Maurice Nathanson had also weathered the 1944 hurricane and now owned a "luncheonette/grocery/cigar store" at the corner of Sovereign and Atlantic avenues in Atlantic City.

*I came into the store that morning, drove my car over. I opened up for business. The water came up during the day. However, there were three*

*establishments that stayed open: my store, Nickelson's Bar on the opposite corner, and the Caldwell Liquor Store across the street. These were the mainstays of the neighborhood. The water came up approximately eighteen inches above street level at Pacific Avenue, about two hundred feet from the boardwalk. The lot where the Bally Grand stands now was completely covered with water. The water met from the bay to the boardwalk in many locations. Hundreds of automobiles were damaged. The Chevrolet agency at Boston and Arctic had to move all the vehicles. After that none of those cars could be sold as new cars. Every car had on the title "Flood Damaged," no matter how little or how much. It was quite prominent on many vehicles in this area for many years.*

Mike Allan was eight. He and his younger brother and sister were staying at their grandparents' house in Ocean City:

*We slept in a real cozy attic under the Victorian dormers. The house was on Central Avenue, right in the middle of town on high ground. My grandparents were well aware of the ocean's vicissitudes.*

"Pop-Pop Mike" and "Mom-Mom Helen," as their grandchildren called them, had lost a colony of rental bungalows on Long Island in the 1938 hurricane and a summer house on Fire Island in the 1944 hurricane. Mike's parents had been looking for a place to settle in Ocean City, to move from Montclair. They found a well-bulkheaded, 30-year-old cottage on the beach the day after Christmas.

*The older couple that owned the place wanted a delayed settlement because they couldn't move out 'til March. All was agreed upon. Sale price was $14,500. Settlement was set for Friday, March 9.*

Their parents went back to Montclair, but the children stayed on in Ocean City to continue school.

*The storm really wasn't bad 'til March 6.... It was a cold, blowy, rainy/ snowy day. I well remember that night, the wind shaking the eaves of our house right over our heads. Pop-Pop Mike always got up at 5 A.M. and walked to the boardwalk and back before breakfast. I remember him saying, "Go back to bed if you want because there's no school today. The town's under water."*

*I walked in the street with big tin cans tied to my feet to stay above the water. I looked down Fifth Street toward the ocean and saw it as I never saw it before, all white and big, and I didn't want to go near it.*

*My parents were frantic over the phone. Pop-Pop Mike knew the police chief and arranged a ride in a Civil Defense truck to go look at our new house. When he came back he said it was gone, not even a plank left. So were the houses on either side. The bulkhead was ripped apart except for the pilings. Mom and Dad spent the whole next week house-hunting again.*

Adolph Wilsey considered himself "one of the lucky ones" in Sea Isle City:

*Those tides! Tuesday morning was a bad one. Waves came banging into the bulkhead like the wrath of God. The bulkheads held but the sea, whipped by the wind, came right over the top of them. That was only the beginning. Tuesday night's tide was worse. The granddaddy of them all came Wednesday morning. It smashed the bulkheads like kindling wood and the ocean came roaring at us,*

W. Earle Hawkins (both)

**An Atlantic City apartment building collapses as the surf undermines its foundation, above. Remains of homes and hotels litter Cape May's oceanfront, right.**

*rushing into the streets. It ripped away an eight-foot section of my living room wall and pounded out two windows. Water and sand poured over my floor. Furniture was knocked over. Between my house and the ocean there used to be three houses. They were swept away. Not a trace of them was left. The night before the last tide I tossed on my bed, fully clothed. Since my wife died in January I've lived alone. Sometimes the house is pretty quiet but it wasn't quiet that night. The ocean was rolling right underneath me. When I got up in the morning, that big tide had done its work. I figured it was time to get out.*

He grabbed a photograph of himself with his wife, eight children and sixteen grandchildren, shut off the gas — the electricity and phone had been out since Tuesday — and waded to the house of a friend, Tom Jefferson.

*It was a little scary. The water was deep and the current was swift. I finally found a board to hang onto in case I got swept off my feet. We went up to the third floor and looked out over the city. It was a sight to see. It was like a vast, half-drowned junkyard. For a while we watched the dismal sight of our neighbors' homes being washed into the ocean.*

They were evacuated by helicopter that afternoon. The last sight Wilsey had of his house it was flat on the sand.

Wilsey, indeed, was one of the lucky ones. He survived. So did his house, though no longer atop a dune behind a bulkhead. The three-story Windsor Hotel "simply disappeared" during the Wednesday night tide. So did the Fean Hotel and the Madeline Theater. So did the Excursion House and the convent house of the Sisters of Mercy and a Catholic vacation home for boys. The fishing pier was washed away. The Amusement Center went, along with the bowling alleys. Almost all the city's 1,200 permanent residents evacuated, the Bartholomew Filano family leaving moments before their beachfront house collapsed into the sea. Almost every house in Sea Isle City was flooded with four to five feet of water.

Whole other communities were evacuated as well. Most barrier beaches on the New Jersey coast are connected to the mainland by bridge. Debris was piling up against some, the approaches to others were under water. Efforts to use boats were hampered in many North Jersey communities by large chunks of floating ice. Two thousand people were evacuated from the Cape May area after losing lights, heat, water and sewage facilities. Army trucks rescued whom they could during the low tides, which were higher than normal high tides. Most, however, were taken out by helicopters whose normal duty was submarine patrol. One 600-pound woman had to be evacuated from Atlantic City by bus.

In Brigantine, all the dunes were washed away and almost every house was damaged. According to one reporter who must have been a statistician at heart, "about 80 percent had water up to the first floor. The Sea Horse Pier was 90 percent destroyed. Fedullo's Pier was 70 percent destroyed." Longport lost 2,500 feet of boardwalk as well as half its fishing pier and the bulkheads along eleven city blocks. The entire town had been under water. In Cape May, waves chewed off thirteen blocks of the fifteen-block boardwalk. In Margate, the intrusive waters shorted out fire alarm boxes, setting off over fifty false alarms.

Other shorts caused fires that firemen were unable to reach, 40-foot torches blazing incongruously above the tumbling waters. One official declared that the eastern section of Monmouth County had been "blitzed." Crews aboard amphibious DUKW vehicles — known as ducks — were sent out to find and rescue anyone they could. County Engineer Leroy Martin got high-powered rifles from Fort Monmouth to blow out the pontoons placed under Gooseneck Bridge to support it during construction; the heavy pipes on the pontoons slamming against the new concrete base were threatening to destroy the bridge before it could be used for evacuation.

Floodwaters cut off Wildwood, Absecon Island and Ocean City. Atlantic City had tides six feet above normal, with waves twenty-five feet high under winds that gusted to 84 miles per hour. Wreckage from a 100-foot barge plowed through the center of the Steel Pier. The end of the pier had already been swept away by the storm, and the tank used for its famous high-diving horses was "carried through the ocean like a green, deep-hulled ship," according to a newspaper report, washing up on a beach in Ventnor City four miles south.

The tides invaded the big hotels, drowning furnaces and boilers and generators. Lobbies disappeared under water, and guests watched from upper floors as the waves ran across the beach and beat against the doors.

In Avalon, Police Superintendent Lloyd Riggall watched his own house at the north end of the island wash away along with everybody else's. "It seemed to split in two, like a doll's house." The whole town was in darkness. "All our firefighting equipment is under five feet of water," Riggall reported over the only working phone. "There have been five or six fires but we couldn't do anything, not even get close." In Wildwood, firemen tried to battle one blaze from rowboats.

In Cape May, fourteen out of the county's sixteen municipalities flooded. Civil Defense coordinator Leland Stanford finally located some fire companies inland and they sent their trucks down, but by then the approaches to the town were underwater and they couldn't get through. "They had to sit at the other end of the causeway and watch the fires burning."

But other help, he recalled, did manage to get through.

*Mercy Hospital called. They were surrounded by water. They had some critical patients and they were getting short of oxygen. We called the National Guard, and they put some tanks on one of those big two-and-a-half-ton trucks and headed for Sea Isle City. But all the access roads were flooded. They got to the point where the water was up to the radiator and they said, "Hey, wait a minute; we don't know whether there's a road down there anymore," because the tide was flowing so hard. So one of the brave guardsmen — believe me, he had to be brave — he got out with a pole and walked ahead of the truck, feeling to make sure the road was still there. He finally got to the point where there was no road, so at that point we called the Coast Guard. They said, "We'll get it up there in a boat, up the Inland Waterway." They got as far as the old swing bridge and they couldn't hold the boat, with full throttle, against the thrust of the tide long enough to hoist the things up. So we called for a helicopter. Flight conditions were hell, but they figured there were lives involved and their job was rescue.*

The delivery was made. But then another dimension of the storm appeared.

*The minute that helicopter showed up, people started coming out of nowhere, saying, "Get me out of here; I want to leave," because, you know, houses were beginning to go, a lot of things were happening. This initiated a helicopter evacuation of practically every one of our coastal towns.*

The choppers came from the Army, the Navy and the Coast Guard, flown by pilots from all over the country, few of whom were that familiar with the area. Stanford recalls one briefing session:

*We had a big wall map and we'd tell them to look for a big, red-topped building and so on. But there was one Navy pilot I'll never forget who wasn't worried about that. He was from Alabama or Georgia, an accent you could cut with a knife. He's listening to all this briefing and he finally says, "Sir, I have a question I'd like to ask. Yesterday, in my operation, I was evacuating people, parakeets, dogs, cats, turtles, white mice, any number of strange animals. Now, I understand this is a Republican part of the world, is that right?" I allowed as it was pretty Republican, and he said, "Thank God they don't make pets out of elephants."*

Bill Wilkin, deputy Civil Defense director for Sea Isle City, quickly converted the Veterans of Foreign Wars hall to an evacuation center because it was the only building big enough whose floor was still above water. Wilkin found that some people were reluctant to leave their homes, however, and often had to be convinced:

*There was one fellow, had a big three-story house on the beach that started to shake every time the surf came in, and his wife got pretty concerned and she said, "We better get out of here." Well, he kind of hesitated a little bit, "Oh, I don't know..." when a big wave hit. So they got their kids together and they started out. They come down the steps, and when he got to the bottom he felt a jerk on his feet, like the steps were gonna fall in, so he jumped off, and he turned around to look just in time to see his house go into the water.*

All four radio stations in Atlantic City went off the air as water rose around their transmitters in the marshlands. New Jersey Bell reported four thousand phones out in coastal areas. The Atlantic City Electric Company couldn't get to all its downed lines. Gas mains ruptured when the ground they were laid in shifted. Streets caved in or washed away or were buried in sand. "We're at the mercy of the sea," Lloyd Riggall said over the phone. "The only thing we can do is pray and trust in God."

Ocean City Mayor Thomas Waldman also put his faith in some city employees.

*The fire hydrants were under water and the firemen would have to go down to couple the hoses. It was bitter cold, the wind was blowing, the firemen would be brought in exhausted, and our public works drivers would give them massages through their clothes to get their circulation going, and then they'd go back out again.*

Fire Chief Ferdinand Taccarino was fighting a blaze at a woodworking plant.

*The men were immobilized by the thirty-five-degree water and we started to lose them. They were dropping and constantly saving each*

*W. Earle Hawkins (all)*

**Only the substructure of Sea Isle City's boardwalk remains, opposite. Debris fills an Atlantic City street as the ocean recedes between tides, top. Wrecked homes in Ocean City, above, jam together, blocking attempts to grade the road.**

W. Earle Hawkins (all)

**An oceanfront motel and a 50-year-old stucco and tile-roofed home in Brigantine, opposite, are left in shambles. Below, the center of the island community.**

other from drowning. *The tide was knocking men down. Fifteen minutes was the limit a man could work.*

With all that, Taccarino's company saved the adjacent gas, electric and water plants.

*Carloads of lumber floated by and fuel oil tanks, normally buried in the ground, were popping up every where. If a man would have been hit by these things he'd have been killed instantly.*

Like fire chiefs in other stricken communities, Taccarino called for help.

*Fire companies from Somers Point, Linwood, Pleasantville and Northfield all tried to get in to help us. At first they were stopped because roads were washed out, but some men left their equipment and walked and swam, when necessary, to reach us.*

At one point the city's Civil Defense director, Scott Burman, put in a call to Stanford for "all the foam you can get me." The flooding tides had burst gasoline tanks at one gas station, and the light fuel floated up and caught fire. The firemen stood in cold water with ice floes banging their knees, sweeping back the fire with brooms. Foam extinguishers were delivered by boat.

During the storm several babies were born at the Civil Defense center. Doctors were kept busy, often with the kinds of problems they might otherwise never have had to face. Mayor Waldman remembers:

*We had one fellow who got sort of panicky. He gave them a lot of trouble. He was complaining that with the congestion in there disease was going to spread. Everybody started to cry, so the police chief walked in, shook a fist under his nose and said, "One more word out of you and you're going in the cells, and there's three feet of water in there."*

The weather grew worse. In some areas the snow turned to hail. Winds up to 73 miles per hour were recorded, just short of official hurricane strength. The tides rolled in like some relentless force of vengeance, or retribution for some unnamed, unknown and ancient wrong. Weather experts said it was the worst storm recorded since Colonial times. "Monmouth and Ocean counties haven't been in such peril since the Battle of Monmouth," said one state official.

Irene Panunto's family tried to leave Strathmere.

*The water had already started coming up. There were five of us in the car. It was new, only two days old, a Chevy Impala. The water was so deep on Asbury Avenue; it had already broken in from the ocean and was meeting with the bay. The car started to actually be lifted by the water. Fortunately there was a large Civil Defense truck behind us and the soldiers carried us out of the car. After the water subsided we found the car stranded on a pile of sand five or six feet high on someone's front lawn. But it was so exhilarating to be at one with the elements. We lived near the water all our life and it didn't frighten us.*

Loretta Thorton, Irene's sister:

*I was very excited. I was not afraid. Perhaps if it all happened now I'd be afraid, but I was only a sophomore in high school at the time. The destruction, though, was unbelievable. I hope I never see it again. Down at the northern end the sand dunes were just totally gone. It was amazing that so much sand could wash out in one or two nights. That really threw me.*

In Long Branch, a thousand feet of boardwalk was carried away "as if it were made of pick-up sticks." In Ventnor, the entire boardwalk was destroyed. In Point Pleasant, the Lovelandtown Bridge collapsed into the canal. The Passaic River rose, halting train service on the Hudson and

Manhattan Line. The Pennsylvania Reading Seashore Line had to shut down when water flooded signal boxes. The Jersey Central Railroad Ferry couldn't tie up. Train service to all inland cities was suspended.

In Sea Bright, George Moss Jr. watched from the third floor of the Peninsula House. "The mountainous waves literally pulverized one section of bathing pavilion. The unforgettable sound of splintering timber was heard above the roar of the wind and pounding surf. Twisted and tortured, bathhouses and boardwalks slowly disintegrated under the savage onslaught of the sea."

An officer at Fort Hancock logged conditions at Sandy Hook:

*The storm first struck this peninsula with high winds at about 2300 hours, 5 March. The winds drove the snow against lampposts, trees, buildings and telephone poles with such force that snow adhered to the north side of these facilities while opposite sides remained clear. Water stood on parts of the road for some three days after the last high tide… deep enough to make movement by rowboat mandatory. The force of the tide action successfully moved huge seawall boulders near the Main Gate, which were strewn in a random pattern across our main highway link.*

It also moved a Sandy Hook harbor pilot all the way to France. Having guided the ocean liner *United States* through the Verrazzano Narrows and into Raritan Bay, Capt. Harold Kaiser prepared to climb down the ladder to the pilot boat waiting on the lee side. But the seas were rocking both vessels so steeply he was alternately banged against the steel side of the ship or dangled precipitously above the waves. He finally gave up and took an unscheduled thirteen-day cruise to Le Havre.

**The destroyer *U.S.S. Monssen* beached at Holgate.**

Other ships at sea radioed distress. A 500-foot Liberian molasses tanker, the *Gem*, broke in two, leaving twenty-seven men, including one stowaway, in the stern section, seven in the bow. The Navy destroyer *Stribling*, with assists from two other destroyers, the *Huntington* and the *Noa*, managed to get the men off the stern, including the chief engineer, who at first refused to leave in order to prevent the ship from becoming salvage. (The *Noa* was the ship that, just a month earlier, had picked astronaut John Glenn out of the Atlantic after his pioneering space flight.)

About an hour later, the cruise ship *Victoria* of the Incres Line, returning from a Caribbean jaunt, spotted the *Gem's* bow bobbing in the bumpy sea and pumped two tons of oil on the water to smooth it out, then launched a lifeboat to pick up the men as they jumped into the sea. The next night, two salvage vessels located the still-floating sections and attached lines.

"My ship just snapped in two," said Capt. Karl Heinmaa. She had fought heavy seas and pounding waves for two days.

The U.S. destroyer *Monssen* was under tow from Bayonne to Newport, Rhode Island, when the cable snapped. The *Monssen*, with no one aboard, was driven hard onto the sands at the south end of Long Beach Island. The destroyer had survived World War II, when she saw intense action in the Pacific, including a fierce battle off the southern Japanese island of Kyushu while protecting aircraft carriers whose planes were making raids on the mainland. Now beached by an even more implacable foe, she would sit in the sand for six weeks before being floated off again.

Three other ships were disabled. A Chinese tanker, the *Chun Lee*, lost her rudder. A U.S. ship, the *A.H. Dumont*, also had damaged steering gear, and the Coast Guard lightship *Chesapeake* slipped anchor and went adrift. All eventually made it to port but not until the mountainous seas had subsided into foothills again.

Three fishing trawlers out of Point Pleasant did not make it back, however. Two days before the storm, the captains at Carlson's Fisheries had commented that there was "weather" coming, but they had fished stormy seas before; the North Atlantic was their livelihood. Fifteen fishermen were lost.

Storm havoc was not confined to the seashore. Delaware Bay was churned into froth and fury, sending an oil tanker aground on Brown Shoals and driving water up the Delaware River with such force that it pushed water, in turn, back up the

*W. Earle Hawkins*

**Splintered wood drifts like snow against a house in Sea Isle City.**

Schuylkill and Cooper rivers, all of them spilling over their banks to flood waterfront areas in Philadelphia and Camden.

John Waters lived close to the edge of Delaware Bay with his wife, Virginia, their eight children, and his mother, who was blind. As the waters reached out toward their five-room house, he loaded everybody into the family car, but the water had flooded the engine. They sat for a while, waiting for the tide to recede. Then Waters decided they should wade to an oyster-shucking shack that stood on stilts nearby. He and his wife went first so she would be there to help settle the kids, ages fifteen months to twelve years. On the way a wave knocked them down, momentarily stunning him.

> *She dragged me to a spot where I could get my head above water. I got her in the shack, got John Jr. out of the car and my mother and started back for the rest, but my wife kept hollering that I wouldn't make it. I did have my doubts.*

Pushed by winds, the tide had risen fast. Waves knocked down Waters again and then pushed him back upright. His wife saw the car get carried away. One of the windows rolled down and seven-year-old Eugene started to crawl out. "A wave or something must have broken his hold. I knew he was gone." National Guardsmen found the car with five bodies inside. Those who had gotten to the shucking shack survived. Alisa, nine, was somehow spared as well. At the hospital she kept repeating, "Mother, they're all dead," recalled her mother. "She didn't know us. She just kept saying, 'They're all dead.' "

Some newspapers dubbed it the Ash Wednesday Storm, despite the fact that it started Monday night and wasn't over, finally, until Thursday morn-

ing. It lay off the coast for the better part of three days, sending hurricane-force winds, freezing rains interspersed with snow and hail, and sweeps and rushes and piles and gouts of water against shorelines from Florida to New England. But by some quirk of mismatched meteorology and geography, it bore down hardest on perhaps the least imposing of the "barrier" beaches.

Long Beach Island was described in a 1962 *Asbury Park Press* editorial as "an 18-mile strip of sand precariously adrift in the Atlantic." The island has long boasted that it is "six miles at sea," which is almost true. Like its cousin sand bars, the Outer Banks in North Carolina and Fire Island in New York, it is more exposed to the elements than other sea-edge resorts. It rides the ocean like a ship, weathering its gales and squalls, open to its breezes, far enough from the mainland so that, once there, a trip over the causeway does seem like going ashore.

Just the year before, Hurricane Esther had whipped up 72 mile-per-hour winds that sent waves over the dunes in a half dozen places, narrowed beaches and even nibbled at beachfront homes, as if sampling them. Some people elected to move their homes back a few blocks from the beach. Harvey Cedars began replenishing its beaches with sand dredged from the bay. Owners of beachfront homes guarded their dunes with the vigilance of Minutemen. One, chasing away a casual, and startled, stroller, growled, "Every grain counts."

The '62 storm caught that island as unawares as it did the rest of the coast, maybe more so for here preparations had begun for the season, and

*collection of Reynold Thomas*

everyone was busy. Even the weather, which does command attention on a ship at sea, was noted only in passing. People went to bed — fishermen and barmen, motel keepers, bait and tackle dealers, shop owners — some grumbling about the late snow coning in the streetlights, all anxious for the sun and the coming summer. It was the time of the new moon, pitch black. The wind played its familiar song, more lullaby than alarm. And during the night, no radar pinging, no satellite watching, without heralds or proclamations, the worst storm of the century came upon them, a true nightmare calling up pasts to be remembered and futures to be respected.

What happened then can be simply put. The high tide early Tuesday morning took out dunes and undercut sea walls and bulkheads. The high tide that night wiped out the beaches. The high tide Wednesday morning floated houses off their foundations, broke roads and dug new inlets across the island. The high tide Wednesday night pushed the debris into whatever structures were still standing. The high tide Thursday morning was remarked on because it wasn't quite as high as the high tide the night before. By Thursday night the storm had begun moving out, but the last high tide laid in yet more water which washed through the new channels.

W. Earle Hawkins

**Waves break over Long Beach Boulevard in Harvey Cedars during a high tide, opposite, leaving the roadway bent and broken when the water retreats, above.**

Friday morning was clear and sunny. The sea was back in place, curling and cooing like a new baby. Gulls scalloped through the sky and plucked crabs out of the surf. Everything was calm and peaceful. Except there were no dunes, little beach, few houses, and what had been one island was now divided into five.

From the diaries of Robert and Alice Heck, in Surf City:

*Tuesday, March 6 — Robert: At 6 a.m. high tide the beach and sand dunes are eaten away by high seas and all storm fences are gone. Some waves are splashing over and running down the street. Alice: Over to the firehouse we went. The water came halfway up my thighs and was rushing so hard you could hardly walk. If I would have fallen down I wonder if I could have gotten up again.*

*Wednesday, March 7 — Robert: Water and waves are starting to break over the end of the street and running down the boulevard. Water is coming to the curbside outside the firehouse and running down the streets toward the bay. Alice: It wasn't a very nice sight to see, waves as high as a house breaking and coming down the street. At noon I helped in the kitchen getting TV dinners ready and hot soup. At night we had meat loaf and spaghetti (not bad). Robert: High tide about 6:30 p.m. We have about 50 people sleeping on cots and two guys snore from 10 p.m. to about 6 a.m., steady, good and loud. Alice: The best part of sleeping at the firehouse was you could not hear too much of the storm.*

*Thursday, March 8 — Robert: Up at 6 a.m. again to watch waves breaking over the end of the streets and flooding the boulevard. When it would stop, two and a half hours later, the bay would have high tide. Boy, some fun! Each morning when it got light enough I would look to see if my garage was still standing. Alice: Came home around 8 a.m. to look around.*

*The streets were a mess with furniture, clothes, logs and wood, plus wet sand. Went back to firehouse for it was high tide again around 11 a.m. Waters came over again but not too bad. In the afternoon trucks came through picking up logs, etc. along the Boulevard. For dinner had hot cheese sandwiches and soup.*

*Friday, March 9 — Robert: Watched the high water under the house. About noon a tow truck came up the street and put a long tow cable to the end of my car and pulled it slowly out of the garage. No damage to the motor. Started the car and parked it over by the firehouse. Alice: Stayed around the firehouse as it was cold and windy. Talked to lots of people, so time passed. Dad was all over the place talking to State Troopers and Police. It sure was interesting. Friday evening had spinach, potatoes and goulash. The ladies were very good workers. Another night to sleep at the firehouse. It was a noisy night. State Troopers and Police coming in for coffee, and they had just installed a phone which kept ringing. We slept in our clothes for four nights, changing a blouse by day. Everyone started to look a little on the untidy side, but could not be helped.*

*Saturday, March 10 — Robert: Tide did not spill over into the street, so we came home. Everything OK. Took some pictures of the houses washed onto the beach. Alice: The house warmed up in no time as the sun came out, but by night the electricity was gone again so we sat with an oil lamp, but glad to be in our own home. Had no meat as I had to throw it all away. Robert: Slept at home. About 12:30 a.m. the fire siren went off and Mom got excited and screamed, "Fire!" I woke up and looked all around; no fire here. Mom was getting dressed — she took about five minutes to dress — and she bawled the hell out of me to get dressed. Finally I calmed her down and we went back to bed. First good night's sleep in four days.*

*Sunday, March 11 — Robert: Wind still from the northeast, tides not high. Mom and I wheeled about 40 loads of sand by wheelbarrow to fill up the hole in front of the garage, and it still needs about 40 more. Alice: You could never believe the sand which is in every street, and how wonderful those bulldozers work. We have such high dunes of sand now, high as a house. They had to work fast, for if we had another storm it would just be flooded again. I hope I never have to see another storm like this.*

Doreen Spreat's parents lived on the oceanfront in Brant Beach.

*They started calling us Wednesday, saying, "Well, the cabana has gone." "Well, the retaining wall has gone." That kept up till about five or six o'clock. They decided to stay there but by then the ocean was actually washing under the house. Early the next morning they called and said, "We're not staying here another night. We didn't sleep at all!" As we got to Ship Bottom, we couldn't even figure out where the streets were. There were houses scattered all over. The tide was down at that point, and it was just sand roads weaving around houses. At that point we realized, hey, this is really a bad storm.*

In Harvey Cedars, Frank and Madeline Milano went to bed feeling snug. Although it blew all night, Frank had faith in the protective sand dunes.

*Bill Kane*

**A house is launched by the tide, above, and sheared-off walls leave interiors intact, opposite.**

*The galvanized garbage cans were rattling against the house and Madeline said as long as she heard the noise she knew we weren't floating away. I never really worried about the tide coming up that high because we had a dune that we had been working on since 1932. We put everything in that dune — bedsprings, debris off the beach — and it was right smack in front of our house. We just felt that nothing would come through that dune. In the morning I began to see water coming over that dune.*

The house was a split level, and as water began filling up the lower part, the Milanos started bailing with the garbage cans.

*When I was dumping water on the bayside of the house I suddenly saw water squirting out of the foundation wall, straight out thirteen to fifteen feet, just a straight stream of water. That's when we decided we'd better get out before the whole thing just burst.*

They stuffed some blankets into a wicker basket and set out with their two children.

*At that point the ocean was coming through there like a river. We got out the door and the water was just above our knees, but the minute we stepped off our property we were hip-deep. We were trying to decide, "Where are we gonna go?" We picked a house we thought would stay, one of the Troast mansions on the bayside. I think we had to break the door to get in. Freezing cold. We made a little fire in the fireplace, broke up a couple of chairs to do that. At that time it was a matter of survival. We really didn't know whether that house was going to stay. Everything else seemed to be floating.*

The house stayed put, and eventually friends found them and took them to their house in North Beach, from which they all had to be evacuated just before that one was washed away. The Troast house cracked in two the same day.

Since the storm sat in place from Monday night to Thursday night, low tides never really happened. The weather front acted like a dam or a one-way valve. Each succeeding high added to the pile of water that never had the chance to slip away. As one eyewitness put it, "The tide just couldn't seem to get back out to sea." Another observed, "It looked as if it wasn't going to stop until it hit Route 9," about six miles inland.

It caught Karl Held Sr. napping, literally, in his bayside home.

*My wife was sending the kid off to school, and he comes back in and says, "There's water in the street," so she comes and tells me, "There's water in the street," and I says, "Well, keep him home." A little while later I hear this banging against the house, and I says, "What's that?" and she says, "That's the damn waves hitting the house." So I got up.*

Held, a builder, had some houses on the oceanside, one at the south end of the island.

*My brother went out there during the first night and watched the houses go down. He said a wave would come and hit 'em and shake 'em and knock 'em off the foundations, the second wave would bring 'em down into the dirt, and the third wave would knock 'em apart.*

Some of his houses survived; some did not. "Funny thing, too, because they were all made basically the same way." One of them floated across the island and settled on a bayside lot. "Fellow bought it from me eventually." Karl Held Jr., who was "five or six," thought it was fun.

*All I knew is I wasn't in school so I was happy. We were drinking bottled water, which was neat, for me. I was having a good time. We had a block of weeds and bushes south of the house and I remember mice swimming around, getting washed out of the weeds, swimming right down the street.*

Ken Smith was a junior in high school.

*The day the wind and the rain set in it didn't seem like any big deal to me. I'd lived through the hurricanes of the 1950s, the houses falling into the ocean, the beach torn up. We were used to it. Even when we were let out of school around 10 A.M., I passed the weather off as another rainstorm ... until we reached the top of the causeway bridge. We noticed then that our driver, Earl Ford, had all he could do to keep the bus from blowing off the bridge, and I will never forget the pasted smile on his face as he joked with us, I guess to keep us calm. I vividly remember the sweat on his forehead and the whiteness of his knuckles as he fought to get us down off that bridge.*

"Worst storm I ever saw," said Joe Sprague, who has lived through every storm on Long Beach Island since the turn of the century.

*Salvatore Pinto, courtesy Dorothea Pinto*

*I've seen hurricanes, I've seen northeasters. This was nary. It was out of this world. It was a three-door northeaster. The wind got right up here in back of you. First place, you got to realize that all the houses built in the olden days were built on footings — three-block-high cement blocks — beachfront, bayfront, backfront or any other front. That's all they knew. And they built them right up on the oceanfront, all the way up. And that storm, for three days and three nights, just kept digging, digging, cutting the beach away just like that. And just taking the houses...thirteen houses went from Sixth Street where I was.*

*Now a hurricane is entirely different. A hurricane will come up, it will come up the beach and rain, blow and just keep right on going; an hour later it's all over. When we were kids on Second Street, the ocean washed right through the sand hills and the next day the tide would recede and I'd be out there on my knees playing with boats. I didn't know anything. Things were all dirtied up, but you kept right on living. But the '62 storm just kept cutting, cutting. I would take a hurricane in preference anytime.*

Sprague stayed. He always did.

*I've never left in a storm, and I wouldn't leave. Most people, though, they don't leave soon enough. If they know they're gonna get hurt, if they don't want to be here, don't wait till the last minute when the storm is right there in Atlantic City and expect to beat it. They get in their car and what happens? They get halfway up where the water's like that and they get stuck, the guy gets a damaged car, somebody's in a fight, and they're hooked. What they should do when they're caught like that is stay in a house, tie everything down, close the windows, close everything, take a drink and go to bed.*

Tom Pancoast remembers his parents wouldn't leave. "Because of the dogs. We had the boat tied to the back door. That was our escape."

Some got off in time, then turned around and came right back. Margaret Crossley was twelve.

*Our house was okay. You could stand on our back porch and watch houses up toward the beach falling into the ocean. You could see the ocean coming down the street and the bay coming up the street. We weren't too worried because you get used to that when you're a kid and you grow up here. But my brother had muscular dystrophy and his circulation was bad*

*and we'd lost all our power and heat. We got kind of worried and ended up going on Army trucks to Manahawkin to my cousin's house. What happened was my aunt was a real pain and we ended up coming back on the island. We thought we'd rather take our chances on the island with the storm than with our aunt.*

Joel Montgomery grew up in Barnegat Light. "I remember seeing houses washed away when I was a kid." In 1962 he lived there with his wife, Wanda. They'd been married eight months. She worked at the Beach Haven Bank, fourteen miles down the island. On Monday morning they climbed into his pickup. They got a few blocks down the boulevard. Wanda:

*From there on down all you could see was water. Joel said he'd never seen that, so we went back. I called the bank and there was one guy there and he said, "Wanda, whatever you do, don't come in. It's really awful." The water had reached the electrical outlets and he was running around with a ruler knocking the plugs out of the wall. Apparently he reached down and grabbed one with his hand. They took him out in an ambulance.*

That night their own electricity went out and with it the heat. As it got colder, they debated whether to leave. The storm decided for them. Joel:

*It didn't seem unusually windy at first, but then the big picture window started to bow in and out. We got in the truck to go to the firehouse. At the boulevard I saw a big wall of water coming at us. It was just like standing in the surf. The water broke over the truck and filled up the inside. We were sitting waist deep in the water with our dog, Duchess.*

The motor died. They were sitting in cold water. It was snowing. The truck started rocking as the gravel washed out from under it. Joel thought they should get out and get back to the house. Wanda:

*I said, "Are you crazy? As cold as I am now, if I get knocked down by a wave I'll never get up again." I didn't want to leave the truck and he's telling me we should, so I opened the truck door and I said, "Come on, Duchess, we're going home." Now this was a Chesapeake; she'd swim through anything. And she put her head down between her paws and started to whine. I shut the truck door and I said, "If that dog won't go, I ain't going, either."*

They sat there for a while. Waves broke against the truck, which shifted uneasily. Things bumped them. The

W. Earle Hawkins

*Frank Carletto*

**Utility lines were among the first links to civilization to go as the sea cut new channels across barrier islands all along the shore, opposite. The tides flipped trucks as if they were toys but left most stilted buildings standing.**

snow had turned to rain. Joel decided he'd go for help. "I got out to try to make it back to the house, but it was like a river. I was afraid to make a break for it."

Hunched in the racing current, the wind blasting his ears, the rain batting his eyelids, Montgomery thought he heard a motor.

*I finally saw something like two little flashlights, not headlights. It was a guy in a truck and the dashboard lights were reflecting off his glasses. I jumped on the sideboard and pounded on the window. The guy thought the devil had him.*

It turned out to be a Coast Guard truck. The couple, and Duchess, were safe.

Ed and Pat Hathaway also started out for the Barnegat Light firehouse with their two-year-old son, but they never got as far as the boulevard. Pat remembers:

*When Ed saw how deep the water was he said we wouldn't make it. So we turned around just as the ocean washed over the end of the street. We had the lights flashing on the jeep, and Jimmy Givens saw us from the boulevard. He and Teddy Weeks and Eddie Eliasen came and got us. By then the water was higher, just that fast. Two of them had to stay out front clearing debris out of the way. The truck had all flat tires.*

*The firehouse was totally surrounded by water. We had to wade. The water came over my hip boots. I don't know where it all came from. I got a wet butt out of that. We were the first people in the firehouse. One woman came in and she was so damn mad because somebody's house had washed into her new fence. She was just ranting and raving. It got crowded then, and they started evacuating people. The electric linemen were saying, "Heroes first, women and children second."*

Hathaway was a nurse and was kept busy. She managed to find morphine for a teenager who was in bad shape. She also ordered supplies.

*Dr. Gove wanted a bottle of camphorated oil. I type real bad, and we ended up with a whole case of camphorated oil. It hung around the first aid building for years. We finally threw it out, a whole case of little bottles. What we used for contact was the ambulance radio until the battery gave out; the ambulance was leaking oil so badly we couldn't run the engine. Daddy broke into Fleming's garage and got the police car out. Daddy was in charge of public works, which really didn't include the police, but he was the only official left in town, so we used that for communication. Then I dragged George Svelling out of a poker game the next night to use the ship-to-shore on his boat. I didn't give a damn if he was winning or losing. I needed the phone.*

❛ ❛ ❛

Hurricanes were given names in those days, but northeasters were just storms. Some called this storm Miss Surprise. A radio announcer dubbed it Jezebel, because "she was certainly wicked." Betty Hornby, who lived on the bayside in Beach Haven, called it "The Roar of March 6."

*There have been other storms with high tides and winds but none that roared so loud. The evening of March 5 was disquieting but my husband, Reeves, and myself were accustomed to these storms. As the black clouds rolled in from the sea, we automatically made sure that everything outside was secured, just in case the tides would come ashore. Without giving the storm any further thought we turned in.*

*At 6:30 A.M. our sleep was shattered by the shouting of my stepbrother: "The tides are rushing in on us!" While he was waiting on the corner for his school bus, the water rose with such speed he barely had time to make it back home. We hurried downstairs to find out what was happening. Confronting us was a foot of water. Worse than that, our parked automobiles outside were completely submerged with just the rooftops peering up, like a string of submarines. This was unbelievable!*

*The ocean and bay met, making the houses look like houseboats. People were standing on their upper decks unable to do anything but watch and hope the tide would ebb and that would be the end of it. This was not to happen. The first day the tide level never went down; the second day the tide rose higher and kept building up the three days.*

*Dressed in our warmest clothing and high boots, we waded through the deepening water inside the house, trying to lift water-soaked furniture up higher. We got so numb from the cold water we had to go back upstairs frequently where we had a kerosene heater to get the feeling back in our hands and feet. A moving figure outside caught my eye; it was a neighbor, fighting against the strong winds in the cold water. She stumbled and fell; Reeves waded out and brought her upstairs. Luckily we had camping equipment and set up our propane stove to prepare coffee. We waited, to ride out the storm, talking about what we should do if help never arrived. I cooked pancakes and sausage on the stove. Our sons, Paul, 6, Bruce, 8, and Ray, 10, thought this was a great sea adventure. We heard a voice over a loudspeaker outside. A Coast Guard amphibious boat filled to capacity was tied to a telephone pole. The boys were excited.*

They were told to get ready, to take only what they were wearing, no luggage. Betty Hornby worried whether the boat would make it, wondered when they might get back again and whether the house would still be there.

> *One of the men must have recognized my anxieties and he reassured me we would make it. He said he had experienced other terrible storms at sea. Slowly the boat made some headway towards the mainland six miles away. It was only then that we saw the total horror of the storm. Houses had been extracted like huge teeth and swept into the sea never to be seen again. Others were flip-flopped on their sides, ripped apart, and debris was drifting aimlessly without a purpose or destination. Even though we had abandoned our home, I realized how lucky we were to be getting out of this hell alive. With much difficulty we continued to pick up others. Twenty-five of us were in that boat. With the whistle and howl of the wind, there was a hushed silence. We were too fatigued to speak.*

Schools and firehouses on higher ground were the principal evacuation centers, higher being often only a foot or two but, just as often, high enough keep them dry. The largest shelter was Southern Regional High School in Manahawkin. By Wednesday night there were twelve hundred people there sleeping in the gym, the halls, the classrooms. The "Social Notes" columnist for the *Beach Haven Times* noted:

> *We slept on cots with army blankets. For breakfast we had coffee, bread and butter, and a choice of oatmeal or scrambled eggs. For dinner there was macaroni and cheese, stewed tomatoes, salad, and ham croquettes.*

Before it was over, the school served eight thousand meals and made two thousand sandwiches to go. Supplies were brought in by the Army. One helicopter came loaded with nothing but desserts. The Archbishop of Camden issued a dispensation for Catholics to break the Lenten fast until the state of emergency was declared over. Milk companies delivered water in milk cartons. The Philadelphia Society for the Prevention of Cruelty to Animals sent food for evacuated pets. "They have to eat, too," reminded a spokesperson.

The Red Cross tended the high school, the Salvation Army was at the firehouses, and the Coast Guard tried to get everybody to one or the other. Margaret Crossley ended up staying at a police station:

> *We had the Salvation Army right outside the door. I would take them any day over the Red Cross. They fed us, they clothed us, they kept us warm. The Red Cross wanted some sort of compensation. The Salvation Army just came in and did it.*

A Red Cross spokesperson issued this statement:

> *Red Cross disaster relief is not charity. It is neighbors helping neighbors through the Red Cross, which acts as the agent of the American people. Red Cross help is designed to enable each storm victim to continue to hold his head high.*

Dick Clements, who ran a boat business on the boulevard in Haven Beach, recalls that one of his summer neighbors, hearing on the radio that some people had been flooded out, phoned to offer his house to anybody who needed it.

> *So I thought I'd go out and see if I could find anybody. I got up as far as Ship Bottom and that's as far as I got. Right in the middle of the street, about where the circle is now, was this monstrous sand dune, eight or nine feet high, and sitting right on top of it was a house. I was flabbergasted. I knew it was bad but I didn't know it was that bad.*
> *I never saw an ocean like that in my life. In several of the hurricanes over the years I'd go see what the ocean looked like, but I never saw anything like the ocean that time. Holy mackerel! It was unbelievable...very, very dirty, cruddy, foamy; the water itself looked muddy. Standing on the beach, it looked as though it were higher than I am.*
> *There was a couple of feet of water in the store, and I went down there with boots on — God knows why; might as well stayed upstairs for all the good I could do. And I looked up the boulevard and here's a telephone pole floating right down the boulevard, right towards one of our big plate glass windows. I thought, Oh, my God! We got flooded, everything got wet and ruined, but we hadn't had any real damage, and now this damn telephone pole is going to go right through the window while I'm standing here watching it. And just before it gets to the window it makes a nice turn and goes off down the street.*

The MacIntire family tried to stay in their Harvey Cedars house, "to protect our belongings." Dave MacIntire was the football coach at Southern Regional and wanted to "hold the line."

> *Tuesday morning I went out to get supplies and look around. At first the water was just a trickle, about six inches. At Harvey Cedars, the water broke through the dunes and the waves hit my car and shoved it over. I managed to crawl out and make it to Bob Van Meter's house.*

*Bill Kane, courtesy Jane Smith*

*Karl Von Schuler*

**A hearth without a home, opposite, and a home without a hope, above.**

He got back to his house by the end of the afternoon. His wife, Katherine, was keeping their five children occupied playing games. As roof shingles went floating by the window, each made up a story. "Debbie thought one shingle was a shark with fins gliding through the water," said Katherine. "Joey couldn't be outdone so his became an alligator. But the kids got scared when walls and roofs went floating by."

Dave went out to gather driftwood to make a fire in the fireplace where they cooked dinner, "a special storm stew mixed with embers from the fire."

*The house got cold. The fireplace couldn't keep the place warm. We used blankets and everything we could get our hands on for warmth. I slept with four of the kids in one bed and Katherine slept with the baby on the sofa. That night was the worst time. The kids were exhausted and asleep quickly, but we didn't get much rest with the wind and debris pounding the house.*

He decided to abandon the house Wednesday.

*I went outside and saw other houses swept away by the sea and empty spaces where dunes once stood. I went back in and said, "There's only one house left between us and the ocean. Let's go." I guess I got all my troubles in one year; a 1-7 record and this storm.*

The house survived. The car he had abandoned had been towed to a gas station with some others, but they had all been carried away, along with the gas station.

*One thing is certain. We won't live on the island again. Perhaps we won't ever have another storm like this, but next time we might not be so lucky.*

Others had to be pried from their homes, literally. Jack Lamping remembers the story of "the old chap who wouldn't move out of his house and they found him sitting on the commode, and the sink was right in front of the commode and he had his fingers wrapped around the spigots. We tried to pry them loose; we couldn't do it. He was determined. He said, `I've been here for forty years; if I have to die here, I'll die here.' We didn't want to break his fingers, so Reynold Thomas got a wrench and loosened the spigots. They took the old man out in a helicopter over to Manahawkin, and when they brought him in the old S.O.B. still had the spigots in his hands. It was a great tension reliever."

Lamping also saw the storm perform as a good genie.

*Bill Kane*

**A house awash in Beach Haven Terrace. Below, right: utility trucks sent to repair the damage end up as part of the damage on Long Beach Island.**

*There was that family that has the Sink 'R Swim — father, mother, and the son, John Coyle — they were separated, one, two, three, and each one thought the other was lost. They were brought over at different times, the mother first, to the hotel in Manahawkin. It was great rejoicing when the son was brought in, then there was greater rejoicing when the father was brought in. Oh, that called for a round of drinks.*

*There was a house in Surf City. The poor guy had jacked it up and moved it out into the street. He didn't like being close to the ocean and he'd bought a lot on the bayside. So the ocean came through and moved his house down to within a short distance of his lot. Saved him maybe a couple of thousand dollars.*

But mostly the storm was scary, as Jane Smith remembers:

*I was in the apartment over the Beach Haven Laundry. They all started to work Tuesday morning and then they shut down. Everybody came upstairs, and then they took all the women home and asked me if I wanted to leave but I said no, I'd be fine here, I'd be high and dry. So I stayed. Then the storm hit and we lost everything, heat and electricity, and I was up there by myself and I was scared.*

*I didn't even have a flashlight and I knew there was one down in the boiler room, so I lit a little candle and went down. But I didn't get very far because the water was all through the laundry. So I went back up. I spent the whole night...it was terrible...so long.*

*When daylight finally did come everything was flooded, all around. I watched the steps on Adrian King's house next door. I would see the water come up to the top of those steps. And then it started going down again. I timed myself, to keep away from that window, because I just watched and watched and thought, Oh, it's never going to go out. I timed myself and I went back every hour to look, and then it was going down. Then I went back and looked again and I couldn't see the steps again, and I thought, Oh, my God, the tide's up again. And the next time I looked out the window the steps were floating away. It was just water, water, water everywhere.*

Tom Pancoast went walking in water six miles farther north, in Ship Bottom.

*We were leery because the streets were very mushy. You could feel them coming up underneath. You could walk the Boulevard. It was all sand, no roadway to speak of. There was absolutely no dunes, nothing, strictly sand as far as you could see. There was nothing left from North Beach down; sporadic rooftops here and there, frames of houses scattered all over the place. And you could see the waves break and trickle right on through to the bay. The ocean washed out a house from between two others and took it down and set it in the middle of the boulevard and a couple of weeks later it was still sitting there and there was a rose vase sitting on the dining room table with an artificial rose still in it. Nothing inside was damaged.*

Dick Warren, who had not been evacuated, was one of the first persons to walk back into Harvey Cedars, where he found sculptor Boris Blai's bronze head of architect Frank Lloyd Wright in front of the remains of Blai's house.

*It was lying in the sand. I picked it up. They were telling everybody not to touch anything on account of looting, so I set it on top of a box or something. Then when pictures came out in the paper they said the storm had set it there. They asked me why I didn't take it, but I was afraid somebody might shoot me.*

Carl Joorman watched houses in Surf City open up like dollhouses to spill their contents.

*As each tide came in it got higher and higher till finally it got to the point where low tide was higher than high tide. We could see the bay — it looked just like the ocean. It got to the point where at high tide we'd go out of the house to keep pushing stuff out of the yard, all kinds of parts of houses, bowls, anything that would float when the houses got broken up. I never knew iceboxes could float like corks.*

Todd Nicholson watched houses go by his front porch in Ship Bottom,

*...not in fear, not in awe, just kind of very stupidly. We saw many houses go away, houses that all our lives we had seen sitting there, houses we used to play on, climb the roof in the wintertime because nobody was around, and suddenly they were gone. My family didn't ever consider leaving. That was kind of ingrained in me. We always thought the people who left were less hardy or something.*

John and Betty Brill stayed, but worried. The Brill house was sixth from the ocean. One by one they watched the others go. Water was running through the attached garage. The house trembled. Their dog, Tab Bay, hid under the bed. And Brill carefully dressed up in his best Italian suit, a white-on-white shirt, his favorite tie and a new pair of shoes. "I came into this world with nothing," he said to his wife, "but if I go now, I'm going out in style."

Rob Curran was nineteen, staying in the firehouse with his father, Sam. They used the school bus to get people and bring them in.

*I remember one house in Surf City, around nine o'clock and just about peaked out on high tide. The bus got part way up the block and couldn't get any farther so we got out and walked. There was an elderly woman in the house and you could actually feel the waves starting to hit the front. We got her outside. We'd look up toward the ocean, waiting for each wave to break before going on. I remember turning around at one point and yelling, "Grab onto something," and there was a picket fence and we grabbed it, holding onto this woman, and a wave hit and knocked us all down into the street. Then she says, "Will you please go back and get my cats?" I think she had three or four. I said, "Ma'am, we'll come get 'em in the morning," and, of course, the next morning the house was gone.*

Policeman William Beisel was collecting people in North Beach.

*I had twenty-one lives on the truck and two more getting on. Then we saw a whole house coming at us. I said, "Grab the women and get out," and that house didn't miss us by six inches.*

Margaret Crossley again:

*My dad, Sam, was a cop. He was on duty in the Terrace when an older couple called. They were afraid — their house was moving. He'd picked them up and they'd all gotten in the car when a live wire fell on the car and they couldn't move. The water was almost up to the rocker panels. They were afraid to touch anything. Finally a bolt of lightning hit the main transformer and shorted it out. He never even told us. He didn't want to worry my mom. We read about it in the paper.*

Deputy Civil Defense Director Fred Grosinger was checking houses and watched the incident.

*I saw Sam Crossley trapped in his car with two elderly people he had just picked up. A power line had fallen on the car and was sparking. I radioed Sam to stay put and called the light company, but they didn't have a unit available just then. About that time a wave washed the road right out from under the front of Sam's car. They'd all be gone with the next one. Then, like a miracle, the next wave pulled down the old folks' house and washed it right out to sea — and pulled the wire off with it.*

Linemen worked all through the storm, shutting off dangerous transformers but trying to keep power flowing where it was needed. Getting to the breaks proved to be more difficult than dealing with them.

W. Earle Hawkins

*courtesy Intera Corporation, collection of Barbara Hartman McGehee*

Young Bob Van Meter was in the firehouse at Harvey Cedars and decided to go over to the gas station and bring back the cigarette machine. Some people, it seems, were having withdrawal fits. Dave Ash and Bill Forbes went along for the wade.

*We were down the road when we saw these lights flashing, so we crossed over and it was the electric truck. But the electric men were on top of a house. We'd been asked to look for them all day. They'd gotten out of the truck when it flipped over and climbed onto the house, and then the house moved, from the oceanside over to the bayside of the boulevard. They had water going on both sides of the house so they were afraid to get off.*

*We were on the other side of the channel that was going across now. We tried to cross but the water was up to our necks. They threw us a rope and we tied it to one of their poles and they tied it to the house and then they actually walked across that channel, hanging onto the rope.*

courtesy Dave Wood

Looking south on Long Beach Boulevard, across 79th Street in Harvey Cedars, which became the largest of the many new inlets the sea cut through Long Beach Island. At left, an aerial view of the same location, March 8, 1962.

In gratitude, the linemen emptied their pockets and gave the boys $29.27 for their efforts. A four-wheel drive picked them up, but it took them to Ship Bottom. By then the channel had become completely impassable and Van Meter had no way to get back to Harvey Cedars.

*There were three trucks, but out of all of them we didn't have enough tires to make one run; they were all flat, wrecked by the debris they'd been driving through. So I was in Ship Bottom, but my folks heard a rumor I'd been killed. When we finally got over to the high school the kids said, "Hey, you're supposed to be dead." Emma Pierce kept yelling at me, "Call your mother." But there was no telephone, not even any telephone poles on the island — nothing. There was no way to call. Finally I told her off very nastily. I was days with only an hour's sleep here and there. I wasn't too nice.*

He finally got himself smuggled back on the island in a bread truck that was allowed as far as Ship Bottom. His mother, father and sister had survived, too.

"It was survival time," said Mike Hill.

*For the first time in my life — and I never thought this would happen to me — I seriously considered abandoning people, out of fear of losing my own life. I don't think many people acknowledge that to themselves. We all like to think we're heroes. I'd thought of myself as someone who could survive a storm, that I was a local guy and I could save people. All my friends were lifeguards. We were into that game of macho man; it makes you a better person if you save somebody in life-threatening situations. I never thought I would consider leaving anybody. You know what my bailout was? I figured, they're not going to live through this. Who the hell's going to know, except me?*

His crisis of confidence came two days into the storm. On Monday night his house began shaking in the wind. The next morning the tide was "slopping over the street ends." But all this had happened before. He took his wife, Marion, and the kids to visit her mother on the mainland, but when he tried to get back on the island the state police told him only pickups and four-wheel drives were being allowed on. He traded his car for a friend's pickup and went back to his real estate office in Harvey Cedars.

*I really thought it was a one-tide thing, it was nothing. We worked through the day. It was March, it was getting dark, it was raining — snowing on the mainland. I called Marion and told her I was staying in the apartment over the office. Then the tide started coming in again. Bob Keck, who worked with me, and I went upstairs. He was very nervous. He was from Haddonfield. He didn't understand anything about ocean storms. Then about midway through dinner, about seven o'clock, the power went out. The wind was blowing, we lost our heat, and I said, "Look, why don't we go over to the firehouse? We'll hang out, come back in the morning when this thing blows over."*

*I put on a pair of hip boots, got a pair for Bob, took a flashlight. It was very, very dark, no street lights or anything, overcast, raining, no moonlight, nothing from the stars. It was very, very black. When we walked out onto the little patio behind the office I noticed the water was up to the level of the patio. I told Bob, "You take the flashlight. I'm going to let you go first and I'm going to tell you where to walk." I wanted to be able to hold onto him. He was very, very scared. In the middle of the boulevard it was probably knee-deep. The problem was that it wasn't just idle water, it was moving with force; the ocean was seeking the level of the bay.*

*Keck stepped in a hole and went in over his head, literally. The water had gotten underneath the pavement and it had fallen in. But the flashlight stayed on. I could see it. I reached in and pulled him back to the edge. He was cold. I mean, it was brutal cold. He wanted to go right back to the office. I said, "I don't think we should do that. I think we should go somewhere where there is heat." I walked him up the stoop of Nooney's store. He was really shook. I said, "Hold onto my belt." I worked our way around Nooney's, across behind my brother's pizza parlor and where the liquor store is, and then across the water coming down Eightieth Street, big time, to the firehouse.*

There were already thirty to forty people there. There was a radio set up. There was heat and light. In the middle of the night, when low tide was due, Hill went outside again to look.

*There was sand all over Eightieth Street. You know how the beach looks at low tide with all those ripples in the sand? It looked just like that. And I looked up toward the ocean and there was no sign of a dune. It was flat. I mean flat. I could see the waves breaking, at that distance, even though it was black night.*

Hill thought the storm was over, though. The tide was at ebb, and the streets were passable. They decided to go back to the apartment. It was dry. They fell onto beds and slept.

*I woke up at daylight and looked out. And saw a phenomenal amount of water coming down the street. It was piling up against the east side of Worme's house, and then rushing around and down toward the bay. It looked to be halfway up the first floor, piled up by the current. I'm watching and all of a sudden I see the house tip over. It went over and leaned on the house next door. And I thought, this storm is something different; this sucker is serious. I went back and I woke up Bob. Now he is really scared. He hadn't gotten over last night's exposure yet.*

Hill wanted to get to his own house a few blocks away. He could see it from the window of the apartment, still standing. "The ocean had touched it, just touched it, but it hadn't undermined it yet. The tide was coming in again, though. The waves would crash and just slop up to the edge of my house." He convinced Keck to go along.

*We started hauling stuff we could carry out to the porch. There was a window in the bedroom that faced the ocean and a big picture window in the living room. We were just between those two when a wave crashed and took them both out. At that point I said, "We're getting out of here." We left everything.*

At about that time he became aware of a memory that had lodged in his mind like a piece of flotsam. The night before, just before the electricity went out, he had noticed a light in one of the new Cape Cod cottages in the next block. "You know, you live here all winter and you get to know who to expect to see, where there should be a light and where there should not." Now he wondered whether anyone was there.

*Norman Anderson, courtesy Nick Anderson*

**In Harvey Cedars, above, and elsewhere, tides are no respecters of property as they turn barrier islands into sandbars.**

*Dorothy Oldham*

**The view over Harvest Cove and Long Beach Island from the tower of the Harvey Cedars Bible Conference, looking southeast toward the ocean.**

*The waves were coming down the street, and I said to Bob, "We've got to go check on that house. I was afraid that if they were lightweights, if they were women, they were going to have a tough time. Keck looked and said, "You know, I really don't want to go over there." But it wasn't as if the first aid squad was around the corner or the fire company was around to make a rescue. There was nobody around. Everybody was hiding out. So I said, "I'm going over there and if there's anybody there I want you to come and help me get them out." And he said okay.*

*At this point you had to move very judiciously. When I got to Eighty-second Street, there was a slew of water coming down and I waited until it calmed down and got over to Eighty-third Street and banged on the door, hoping like hell nobody would answer. I knocked and knocked and knocked and all of a sudden somebody answered the door, a woman, in her sixties, I'd say, and behind her, sitting halfway up the stairs, was her mother. And they were scared to death.*

*While I was standing there, a wave hit the house and jarred it off its foundation. The fireplace, in the east wall, was undermined and toppled, leaving an opening, so now the seas came in and inundated the living room. They got up on the steps, and every time we'd catch a serious wave the house would bump, maybe six inches or so. I thought, "This is not good," and started waving for Keck. Conditions were getting progressively worse. I mean, the night before the water was up to my knees; now it was around my*

*hips, and I'm six-one. In addition, telephone poles had been uprooted and they were coming down the street. If you ever got pinned underneath one, it could drown you.*

That's when he thought of saving himself, abandoning the women.

*I never thought this would happen to me. I thought of myself as a heroic person. I was twenty-six. I thought of myself as someone who could survive in such conditions. I was still wrestling with that decision when Keck appeared. He came up the steps and he said, "Well, is there anybody here?"*

They made a seat of hands between them, "the way we learned in the Boy Scouts," took the mother first, gauging the waves, going from the shelter of one house to another, using porches to rest, until they got her to one porch where it was relatively safe. Then they went back for the other woman. By now the torrent coming down the street was up to their waists.

*We got to the middle of this trough and I looked around and there was a wave coming. I said to Bob, "Lean into me real hard," so I was at about forty-five degrees when it hit and went over my head, but we stayed on our feet. We were soaked and she was soaked, but she was a gutsy lady and she wasn't complaining about it. She was fighting for her goddamn life and she had a lot of spunk in her. The ocean at this point had gotten underneath the pavement on the roads. When a wave came, the pavement went up and down, like a sheet flapping on a clothesline. I could feel it going up and down under me.*

They got the two women into the office. Hill figures the whole thing took about an hour. Eventually, other rescuers came by in a boat and took them to the firehouse. "And that's the last I ever saw of them, forever." He still doesn't know who they were.

❝ ❝ ❝

There were other pockets of refuge — some police stations which were built on raised slabs, some houses, some stores, and the odd building that had survived other rages of nature and stood as some sort of testament to human tenacity. Or stubbornness. Or, perhaps, something else.

In the middle of Harvey Cedars, a point sticks out into the bay like a crooked finger to form Harvest Cove. On it stands an old hotel dating from the 1850s. There used to be a dozen others on Long Beach Island, all lost to storms, fires and taxes. In 1941 this one became a Presbyterian resort — now the Harvey Cedars Bible Conference — whose four-story-high tower room provided Reverend Al Oldham and his wife, Dorothy, an unmatched view. The building became a shelter for the suddenly homeless, a checkpoint for Coast Guard launches and helicopters and a refuge for adventurers.

*No one told us there was a major storm coming up the coast. Someone said it was like a thousand-mile fetch of wind that all of a sudden let loose, like an ancient sling. We didn't know what to expect. We got some candles out and just stayed there and watched the tide coming up higher and higher. There were rowboats floating by, and oil tanks bumping into the house. It was cold. It had snowed the day before. We put plenty of wood on the fire, put on overcoats, put blankets on top of the kids, just tried to keep warm through the night.*

He remembered two widows who lived nearby and, thinking they would be frightened, he put on a pair of old sneakers, rolled up his pants and waded out.

*I got over to Mrs. Stratton's place and found she was high and dry and snug as a bug in a rug. She had one of those little kerosene heaters, seemed chipper, wasn't at all upset. I went over to Mrs. Nolan's house and found she was the same, all toasty warm. I told them both that if I perceived any danger for them I'd come get them. I started back to my house.*

*It was exceedingly dark. I got a little ways and I saw this thirty-foot launch, nice white boat, floating in front of me. And I stepped into a hole. It was a shock to my system. The water was intensely cold. The boat was going by and I wondered, "What have I done? Have I stepped over a bulkhead?" I didn't know where I was. I stayed perfectly still. I didn't recognize any landmarks because the road was under water, the bulkheads were under water, the gardens were under water. But I saw the flicker of a candle that Dorothy had put on the table in our living room and that was my guiding light and I followed it home. I frequently use that as a sermon illustration, that it only takes a little flicker of light when a person is in deep trouble to find a way. I got to my house and stood up all night in front of the fireplace.*

*Bill Kane (both)*

**Navy helicopters, as here over Beach Haven Terrace, fly more than 300 missions lifting people off Long Beach Island.**

With daylight, people began arriving at the hotel. The land it sits on is five feet higher than the street, and the building is raised another five feet or so above that.

*We had close to fifty people there by the time the next high tide came. We set up in the lounge. We had plenty of firewood; it was floating all over. Some of the fellows went out to collect food from the houses, especially canned goods, and we gave them big kettles from the kitchen to get water out of the tanks. We gave everybody a knife and fork and spoon and told them to keep it because we didn't have water to wash things with and we didn't want sickness to start to go around.*

*We were actually having a great time. People brought their cats, their dogs, so we set up some rooms for them and put papers on the floor for them so they wouldn't mess the whole place up. We sat around and sang old camp songs. It was two or three days before the helicopters came to take us out.*

*We went up to the prayer tower in the daylight and as the tide rose we watched strange things happen to the houses. There were some houses that were not as well built as others and as a result, just as a blow to the solar plexus makes a man crumple up, some of those houses crumpled and boards and furniture started washing away and the houses just deteriorated. We watched this little stream of material wash away as the house disappeared. Other houses that were better built rose up off their concrete foundations and just floated away, out into the bay. I understand some floated all the way to the mainland. It was fascinating to watch.*

The third day, helicopters started flying over. Oldham spotted a sheet hanging out of the second-floor window of a house across the cove.

*I said to my wife, "Honey, that sheet wasn't there yesterday." We took a big mattress box we had in the attic and wrote on it, "50 people safe here. Check house across cove," and drew a big arrow. When they got to the house, the window flew open and people started waving at them. They were some people who had rented a cottage nearby and when the storm came they abandoned it for the bigger house. Every house on that road disappeared but that one.*

The community at the hotel grew as rescuers collected people through-out the three days. There was food, warmth, safety and, perhaps most important, companionship.

*We got closer to one another during that experience than any other we ever had. We needed one another. The only people that got really irritable were the people who ran out of cigarettes. They started to get so hyper. It was really interesting to see that.*

Everyone who made it to the Bible Conference made it through the storm. At the southern end of the island, in Holgate, the storm was also carving new profiles in the sand. The Coast Guard was rescuing people from roofs and windows in a DUKW and taking them to the station. But the exposed station was considered un-safe and it was decided to run groups north to Beach Haven where Ralph Parker headed Civil Defense efforts.

"They never should have left the station," said Lester Parker, Ralph's brother.

*It was about 4:30 in the afternoon and he told them, "Don't come out anymore tonight." But they did. They came out and instead of heading straight up the island, staying on the bay side and coming up over the meadowlands, they came out of the station and headed right into the ocean. I guess it was habit, you know. They headed up toward the boulevard, which wasn't there anyway, and when they made their turn to go north, they got broadside to the waves and they capsized. The thing turned over and dumped them. They formed a human chain, hooking their arms together, to get back to the station, but the water broke the chain and that's when they lost four people. Some got back; I'm not sure how many.*

Mr. and Mrs. Gus Lindell and Mr. and Mrs. Robert Kinney, all elderly, were the four victims. The driver said later the vehicle hit a washed-out spot:

*Night was coming, the wind was howling. We got out. The water was up to our waists. We stood in a line, each holding the other's hand. It was a human chain rescue job. I was holding Mrs. Kinney's hand. She was holding her husband's hand. And behind them were Mr. and Mrs. Lindell. Then came the others. Suddenly I stepped into a hole and I went down, over my head.*

At that point, a wave hit. The Kinneys were seen struggling in the surf when another wave went over everyone. When they came up, the two older couples were gone.

John Fullerton owned the Texaco station in Beach Haven and had one of the few four-wheel-drive trucks on the island. He was helping haul people to the first aid station.

*I had the Kinneys and the Lindells and was looking for others. They transferred to the DUKW because it was bigger. Problem was, the guys operating it were from Manasquan. They had no idea where they were going.*

Holgate is where the U.S. Navy destroyer *Monssen* went aground the first night of the storm and where some of the first houses became seaborne.

**Few houses in Holgate survive, although the Coast Guard station in the background, built high, stays firm to shelter the suddenly homeless.**

One of the island's lowest sections, it was often awash in winter storms, said Lester Parker.

*In the morning my brother came to my door. "You got rain gear?" I said, "Yeah." "Get it on," he said. "We're going down to the inlet to evacuate some people." He had a dump truck, a stake-body, had it for years. It was like an army truck with a canvas top on it. We picked up Ernie Senior, who was a Beach Haven policeman, on the way. There was water on the highway.*

*The main damage had already been done, the dune line was pretty well gone. We took the truck as far as we could and then we got out and started to walk when we saw a township truck, bright orange, the lefthand-side wheels still on the macadam but the passenger-side wheels in the sand so it listed toward the bay. The door was open and there was a camera on the seat and nobody around. The wind was blowing to beat the band. We were getting hit with the flying sand and we were getting hit with sleet. We looked around to see if we could find anybody out of that truck. Looking toward the bay, I saw this guy with a yellow slicker on lying in the tall grass. No hat or anything. I could just see his arm moving. That must be what attracted my attention. We went over and it was Leonetti.*

Angelo Leonetti had just been made Long Beach Township police chief. Earlier that morning, he had told Bill Hodgson he was going down to Holgate to see about a friend of his who was crippled and might not be able to get out on his own. Kenneth Chipman, a township commissioner, and Robert Osborne, who owned a news agency, went with him to survey damage. On the way, they stopped to talk to Fullerton:

*They said they were going down to look at the destroyer. I said, "You know, that'll be there tomorrow. It's not going anywhere." Leonetti said, "Yeah, but we want to take pictures."*

They were followed later by another policeman, Wally Allen, who saw a 500-foot section of sand dune "float across the road."

*Water didn't come over the top; it just pushed the whole dune. A sand dune is basically a pyramid. What was happening was that the water would get the dunes so wet that the bottom of it would act like a skid.*

With that, Allen turned back. There were no witnesses to the accident except the victims. Leonetti was still alive, but barely. Parker:

*The only way I can describe it was that he looked like hamburger, his whole face and anything that was exposed, where the sand had beat him....Ralph told us to try to get him inside somewhere while he went to the Coast Guard station for help. He headed across the meadowland and got about twenty-five or thirty feet and I saw him go down and I went over and he had tripped over Osborne's body. We rolled him over. He was dead. His face was black as could be, which is a sign of a heart attack. He was a member of the Beach Haven First Aid Squad and he was dressed to be down there, but he was overdressed, really, because he had so many clothes on that if he got soaked he wasn't going anywhere. Which he didn't.*

*The only thing we could figure, in piecing this thing together, was that they panicked. The camera was still on the front seat. If a wave had washed them out of the truck, it would have taken the camera, too.*

*Bill Kane*

**Looking as if it has been chomped by giant sharks, a house in Holgate leans over its former foundation.**

*Ralph went on toward the station and I went back to Leonetti. I said to Ernie Senior, "Ernie, we gotta get him and us inside a house somewhere. If we don't we're gonna be right down here alongside him." There was a house across the road on the oceanside. It was on pilings, way up there in the air. All the decks were gone, the stairway was gone. It was built on the dune line, but the dune line was gone. You could look right under the house and right on out to the ocean. It was all just as flat as a pancake. The wind was blowing a gale. How the heck were we gonna get up into that building? I grabbed a two-by-four and threw it like a javelin through a window; it knocked out the whole thing, frame and all. I got up on Ernie's shoulders to reach the window sill and pull myself up. But I didn't know how I was going to get them up. The place had been closed for the winter and I found garden hoses coiled up underneath one of the cabinets, so I hooked them together and dropped them out. Ernie wrapped them around Leonetti and he hoisted and I pulled and we got him in the house.*

*Then I went back out with Ernie and we got Osborne and brought him back. We stripped them completely of their clothes and wrapped them in all the bedding and sheets we could find and proceeded to work on them, massaging them, trying to get circulation back in them, giving mouth-to-mouth — just anything to get them going, even though we were pretty sure Osborne was gone. We got Leonetti to the point where he was responding. He never talked to us, but I'd say, "Lee, move your arm, raise your right arm," and he'd raise his right arm and then I told him to raise his left leg and he'd pick up his left leg. So we had him to that stage.*

In the meantime, Ralph Parker had reached the Coast Guard station and returned with several men. He spotted the broken window. They had a stretcher with them but didn't think they'd be able to make it back without a vehicle. Ralph headed out again and found a tow truck with a radio and called for a doctor, who managed to get through in a four-wheel drive, bringing a nurse and oxygen tanks. But it was too late.

Angelo Leonetti had been a navigator on a B-24 bomber which was shot down over Munich in World War II. He was the sole survivor, spent the rest of the conflict as a prisoner of war but emerged unhurt. It had seemed as if nothing could kill him.

They took the bodies back to the first aid station in Beach Haven. "Never did find out whose house that was," Parker said. "We just left everything, oxygen tanks and all, and the next morning only the pilings were there; the house had been pounded off and it was gone."

Kenneth Chipman's body washed up on the beach six weeks later.

Lester Parker headed back to his brother's house on Delaware Avenue in Beach Haven Terrace. At the beach end of that street, the old four-story Clearview Hotel was breaking the waves, effectively sheltering the house. They had electricity all through the storm and water. Even the television worked. "It was unreal," he said, "totally unreal." They went around the Terrace and evacuated all the people on the bayside, all the elderly they could find, anyone else who was flooded.

> We wound up with seventy-five people for three days. It was wall-to-wall people. Among them was Bud Palmieri, who was manager of the A&P store up in Beach Haven Crest. It had no electricity, so there was a whole great big store loaded with food that was going to spoil. So Bud said to Ralph, "Do you think you can get me over to the store?" So we had plenty to eat for the whole three days.

Each day they thought that the storm would be over, that the tide would recede, the waters run back into the ocean and the bay.

> All that happened was, when it came time for high tide the water just got higher. When it came time for low tide it went to a certain point but just stayed. We never got dry the whole three days. I won't ever forget it.

Later, Hank Biernat, who had experienced the 1944 hurricane, would say, "I learned one thing about these storms. If you know a bad one is coming, lock up and leave. If you're staying, stay put. Most people got in trouble because they were going from one point to another."

Word of the deaths at Holgate spread almost as quickly as the flood waters. Now everybody took the storm seriously. Helicopters from the Lakehurst Naval Air Station flew more than three hundred rescue missions. In Sea Isle City and Avalon, Lts. (jg) Kenneth Kingston and Frank Garruto carried 549 people to safety in a cargo chopper that could hold twenty-four people at a time. "The winds were rough," Garruto said. "At one point, they were registering sixty knots, but the headwinds were forty." He told a reporter about seeing "houses moved like checkers and docks ripped up as though a bulldozer had gone drunk." Lt. Cmdr. Joseph Gardner had been on similar rescue missions during floods in Ceylon. The difference? "The people there are smart enough not to build right on the beach," he said.

Norman Henry was in charge of a Marine detachment on the ground:

> We got some people out of a house in Brant Beach and before we'd gone fifty yards with them, the house collapsed. Up near Beach Haven, we found a 92-year-old woman who was sitting in a car. The water went up around the door handles with every wave. I don't know how it kept from getting that high inside the car. We took her out and a couple of minutes later she said, "You have to go back." We asked her why and she said, "I need my bedpan." So we went back and got it.

Some still refused to go. One pilot used a ruse to convince holdouts in Barnegat Light, telling them they'd have to sign statements absolving the government of any responsibility for their safety if they didn't get on board. Others wouldn't go unless they could take their pets, despite being told the weight might be needed for other people. One pilot reported that fifteen women smuggled small dogs under their coats. Sarah Ashcroft gave her cat a tranquilizer before bundling it into a wicker basket.

There are no rules for those times when life runs off the tracks. Just keep calm and act rationally, they say. But reason tends to wrap itself around the situation. Faced with the prospect of yet higher water in Harvey Cedars, Mike Hill reasoned he had to get himself higher still.

> I made up my mind that if the tide was higher Thursday might I was going up the water tower. I figured that sucker would stay. It's still got water in it, it's heavy, it's got a concrete base. This storm can take out all the houses in town but that water tower is gonna be the last thing to go. I'm going up that sucker. We didn't know how bad it would get. Even the guys who were a little indifferent before were serious now. We were talking about how to get out of there. As far as I knew we were the only people left. We were talking about boats. Bummer (Howard Baum) had a boat; we'd made it across the bay in some serious weather and survived. I had some reservations, though. All I knew is that night when the tide came up, if it got any higher than the water mark on Don's car I was going up the water tower, climb all the way up and sit on top of that sucker until things quieted down.

The tide did not get that high that night. And the next low tide actually left some ground uncovered. By Friday night the tides had returned almost to normal. The storm had moved on.

❛ ❛ ❛

Correspondent Robert Holland was one of the first to fly over the area:

> You can see giant puddles and gashes where the ocean laps at the bay in places that used to be part of Long Beach Island. A north section of the island below Harvey Cedars reminds you of what would happen if a little boy swept his hand across a sand pile, crushing his toy roads and trucks.

Back on the ground, he began collecting stories of the storm, citing the heroic and the not-so:

> ...such as an excitable Philadelphian who somehow caught the second helicopter out, ahead of most of the women. This gentleman said he would pay "whatever it costs" to get to the mainland and offered to buy — from

*weary women who had been handing out free food for two days — meals for his rescuers. The Marines at Long Beach School had a name for him. I hitched a ride onto the island on the back of a high-wheeled utility truck. We passed a housing development east of Mud City that proclaimed, "Every Home on Large Waterfront Sites."*

Charles Roberts, seventy-seven, took a last look as he headed the other way. "Everything's gone," he whispered, "everything's gone."

But it was over. Under the headline, "Nature Lifts Angry Hand From Storm-Torn Shore," reporter Victor Keller wrote:

*The mood of the island people was almost festive. The terror ended in a kind of reckless gaiety, like a peace following a war. People who had stayed on the island mostly gathered together to eat and talk, counting the big blessings, discounting the loss. Thousands of others evacuated to the mainland camped out in school buildings and made a game of it. The reckonings had not yet begun.*

Flying over Sea Isle City, Adolph Wilsey said, "This resort looks like a huge lumber yard." Reporting from Wildwood, Steve O'Keefe said, "I never saw such a display of sustained power and fury." Far across the Atlantic, the coasts of Ireland, southern England and France were battered by gales that churned up waves as high as fifty feet for two days. On this side, some four hundred bulldozers went to work to create a new dune line as people began sifting through the sands.

Marion Rapp found a Bixby Ink bottle setting on a stump in front of her house. It bore the inscription, "March 6, 1883." For almost eighty years it had lain under the sand waiting to be uncovered. The rudder from an old sailing vessel, twelve feet long, eight inches thick and clad in its original copper, washed up at Holgate, not far from where the *Monssen* itself lay beached.

Dave Wood found George Otto's Coke machine in the bay the next summer in about six feet of water, "still full of Cokes, plus six bucks in quarters. Those old, thick, green bottles — you can't kill 'em." Wood and his friends spent the summer poking around in boats.

*Cars...I remember just south of Gunner's Point this big black car sunk there. It was very ominous. To this day, when I get near something that's sunken and man-made like that, a sunken boat or some wrecked thing, it gives me the heebie-jeebies. We were kids, having a good time. There were a lot of wrecked houses lying around. You could just go play in them. And in the bay, too. We rowed through one, right through it. It was a lot of fun.*

*I got cut constantly that summer, walking in the bay and stepping on stuff. But everything was a treasure. I still have one weird thing, sort of a black, lacquered affair, some kind of Japanese art thing, I suppose, very exotic.*

*We watched a gang of kids pour gasoline in one half-sunk house. They spent all day chopping holes in the roof to ventilate it so it would really go up on July Fourth. It was great.*

Richard Plunkett had his antique store on the causeway then.

*There was a large mantel that had come through the storm and we found out it was Boris Blai's, come all the way from Harvey Cedars to Ship Bottom. There were whole houses that ended up underneath the bridge, totally intact. They had to be dynamited to let boats get through the channel. We'd go out day after day helping people try to find things. I remember the sadness of one lady. She had just bought her house and moved in a month before the storm. She couldn't even find one shingle. She said that it would have resolved her life if she could have found one shingle.*

Plunkett did find a piece of furniture he had sold to Naomi Coyle some years earlier. A lot of "found" objects, of course, were never returned. Looters came in boats from the mainland by night even before the storm was over. But Margaret Crossley remembers some who were neighbors:

*They were some ladies that lived on the next street. We called them the Gabor Sisters — because there were three of them, not because they were glamorous. Here it is high tide and they're up to their waists in water, looting. Martial law was established after that.*

Atlantic City policeman James Kelly had evacuated his family from their flooded home, then gone on around-the-clock duty. When he finally returned, he found $3,525 worth of goods had been stolen, including his wife's engagement and wedding rings.

Those who had been evacuated to the Southern Regional High School soon found they had something else to worry about, as Doreen Spreat recalls:

*Well, the place was mobbed, just filled with people, and some of the children were running around with either chicken pox or measles, so for the next three months everybody's kids had chicken pox or measles.*

W. Earle Hawkins (both)

**Atlantic City's Steel Pier loses its link to land, along with the tank for the famous high-diving horses which washed ashore on the beach in Ventnor.**

Dick Clements watched the water level subside in his store, and watched the Army trucks making wakes along the boulevard that threatened to flood it all over again. He began to clean up, piling his own truck with debris and taking it to the town dump.

*Coming back, it's a beautiful afternoon, the sun out, gorgeous, and I'm passing the Esso station and I see in one of the repair bays this unholy mess of stuff piled all over. And there, at the back, just sitting there, is Jake Jakobowski, who owned the place. We used to go fishing together once in a while so I pull in and get out to say how'd you make out and everything. And he was barn-stinking, stone drunk. He couldn't move, he was so drunk. I started to laugh. I said, "Jake, you're the only one on this island that's got the right idea."*

**The exposed remains of a Sea Isle City cottage top a pile of broken homes.**

It had been, everybody agreed, some storm. It did more damage to the Jersey coast than any storm before or since. Newspapers wore out adjectives trying to describe it. Finally the U.S. Weather Bureau gave it a name, not a sissy girly-boyish name, either. It became The Great Atlantic Storm.

"The magnitude of the storm, it seemed to us, made it necessary to give it a classification, an official name," said Charles Knudsen, a New Jerseyan who headed the bureau's headquarters in New York. And so it stands, a record to shoot for. "Northeasters have come and gone in this area since time began," Knudsen added, "and they'll come again."

The storm prompted new laws in many communities, setting construction standards that, among other things, dictate that new buildings must be on pilings, well above the highest imaginable tides.

Estimates of the damage in New Jersey were put at $130 million, almost half of the total suffered by all six of the states the storm hit. No point on the shore escaped unharmed. Mat Adams, state conservation commissioner, reported that the sea broke through Island Beach in eight places. In Dover Township, Mayor John Dalton reported, "The beach is just about completely wiped out." In Cape May, it was all wiped out. Most of the boardwalk in Seaside Heights was uprooted. Out of about four hundred homes in West Wildwood, ninety-two floated off their foundations. One newspaper said, "The Jersey coast resembled a beachhead battlefield after a Marine invasion." Another called Long Beach Island "18 Miles of Disaster"; another, "A Ravaged Strip of Death and Destruction."

Loretta Thornton remembers getting back to Strathmere: "It was as if the homes there never even existed. The only homes that stood through it all were the very old homes. All the new ones were just washed away."

Avalon Police Superintendent Lloyd Riggall stood on a patch of sand on Dune Drive: "This was my home. It's gone, scattered all over town. My car is gone. I have no idea what I'm going to do. There goes my life, my entire life."

In Bradley Beach, three feet of sand buried Ocean Boulevard. In Long Branch, it was Ocean Avenue. In fact, the Ocean avenues of Monmouth Beach, Ocean Grove, Sea Bright and Sea Girt all seem to have tried to live up to their names. A report from Sea Isle City:

*Wreckage is piled eight to fifteen feet in an unbroken line along what once were streets. Scores of cars are under water, only their roofs showing, abandoned when high water overtook fleeing families. Scores, possibly hundreds of refrigerators are bobbing on the surface of the water. This correspondent had to go 16 miles to find a phone that worked. To cross the four-mile causeway required 45 minutes as drivers dodged debris. Pleasure Avenue used to be the first block back from the beach. Today it is just a memory.*

Reporter Carl Sheppard filed these impressions:

*Of the curious way the sea tidied up after itself, like a good housekeeper following a rampage. Long sections of oceanfront were left neat as a pin, but many houses that front the spotless sand and creamy surf today stood one row back on March 6. The first row is gone without a trace, along with the lots on which the houses stood. Of the startling yardsticks left by the fierce excavator to measure his work. Manholes that were in streets now sprout like concrete mushrooms, four feet tall, halfway down the beach to the water. Homes stand isolated atop pilings ten feet high. Brick chimneys that once touched earth at their bases cling to house sides far above the new beach level.*

Houses had been pushed around as if they were toys. Even the massive boulders that formed jetties all up and down the coast were pulled apart like so many piles of gravel. Trailers were scattered, trucks rolled over, cars set up on their noses.

The National Rural Electric Cooperative Association was holding a convention in Atlantic City when the power went out. One member from North Dakota commented, "This is the first time I saw the Atlantic Ocean. I didn't know it ran in the streets."

*Lawrence F. Wagner*

**In Loveladies, the Army Corps of Engineers and others work to put Long Beach Island back together as bulldozers find the roads and remake the dunes.**

On Long Beach Island, the storm had sliced that twenty-one-mile strip of sand into five islands. Three of the channels were quickly closed, but the cut through Harvey Cedars at Seventy-ninth Street was sixty to seventy feet wide by Wednesday and some twenty feet deep in places — a new inlet where part of the town had been. Harvey Cedars also won the unenviable distinction of being named the most heavily damaged on the Jersey coast. At the time, Mayor Reynold Thomas estimated it had lost one-third of its ratables; later, it would turn out to be closer to 50 percent.

Jack Brewer, who had seen a lot of weather on the island, explained, "Down in Harvey Cedars I don't think the people realize it, but that used to be a marsh down there." In the south end of town, the rushing waters had uncovered ancient cedar stumps, remnants of the forest of swamp cedar Henry Hudson saw there on his voyage in 1609, the last of which had been blown down in the hurricane of 1821. Remarked Thomas, "The 1962 storm made the hurricane of 1944 look like an April shower."

By the weekend, the tides were still running a bit above normal. To the benumbed disbelief of those who still bothered to listen to their radios, a new storm had formed off the Georgia coast and was headed north. It fell apart before it got to the Mason-Dixon line.

The Army Corps of Engineers' assessment of the damage along the Jersey shore was more than four thousand buildings destroyed or so structurally damaged as to be unusable, with ten times that number suffering severe flood damage. The Red Cross put the death toll for the whole East Coast at forty, a quarter of those in New Jersey.

The affected communities were declared disaster areas by President Kennedy, with federal aid and loans promised. Each community hurried to submit damage estimates. As state Senator Charles Sandman of Cape May said, "The areas that were hit the hardest are those which depend on the resort business for their economy. We have only eleven weeks to get them back on their feet." The Legislature agreed to extend the horse racing season by nineteen days to finance some of the rehabilitation, but nothing seemed adequate. *The Philadelphia Bulletin* reported:

*A dazed woman is walking across a rubble-strewn marsh. She picks up a Chinese lacquer box, a high-heeled slipper, a copy of* Lorna Doone, *a bag of coleslaw still sealed and fresh. "These were in my house before the storm," she says numbly. All that is left of her place now is a few jagged posts on a clean-swept beach. A New Jersey state trooper puts his arms gently around her shoulders and leads her back to his car.*

Barnes also found some happier stories. The summer home of Mr. and Mrs. Carl Schlingmann was one, and the reporter joined the Schlingmanns as they walked up from the causeway.

*"It's there! The house is there! I can see the roof," she exclaimed suddenly. We struggled through the bulldozed sand. The entire lower floor had been carried away. The level of the sand had been dropped about 12 feet. The floor and two walls of Mr. Schlingmann's workshop had been wrenched off. His tools still hung on a remaining wall. Fishing rods were suspended in the gutted garage. The hose of a vacuum cleaner hung in what had been a closet.*

This was a week after the storm. Like visitors to a foreign country, people were admitted to the island only if they had permits. Police manned barricades at the causeway and the National Guard patrolled the streets, guarding against looters. Those who had been evacuated were returned by the same trucks and buses that had taken them away. One account by Fran Burtaine in The *Beachcomber*:

*At the home of each passenger, Civilian Defense workers entered the residence and checked it for heat, light, water...if all was OK the residents were allowed to remain. We were lucky. Everyone was allowed to return home. The oceanfront in Brant Beach was shocking. Every oceanfront property dipped drunkenly into the ocean, if it remained at all. We saw almost no people. They told us we shouldn't drive our cars, we must boil water for fifteen minutes before drinking it, we should stay close to our homes, we must not be out after dark.*

A loosely imposed martial law discouraged roaming about. Army trucks ran errands and made deliveries. The buses returned to take people to the market.

*The mood was changed now — people were back in their homes and almost giddy with relief, exhaustion, and unbelief. We shopped and picked up half-gallon containers of safe water. Our water from the faucet is so spiked with chlorine it is all but undrinkable.*

There was no time to swap stories, commiserate or even, like Jake Jakobowski, tie one on. "We will be ready by Memorial Day" was the cry.

The island had eleven weeks to clean up for summer. The task was formidable. "The bleeding has stopped," another paper proclaimed, "but the wounds inflicted by the pounding waves and swirling flood tides are still raw."

The most obvious wound was the channel that had cut across Harvey Cedars at Seventy-ninth Street where the water had taken out the dunes, the street, and any house unfortunate enough to bear that address. Efforts to close it were begun even while the sea was doing its best to keep it open.

The Barnegat Bay Dredging Company dredge had returned to its home mooring in Harvey Cedars just before the storm hit. The company was owned by Mayor Reynold Thomas, and his son, Michael, was a practiced hand at the dredge. (This is the same Michael who figures in his mother's account of the 1938 hurricane, then just two years old and being comforted by Little Bo Peep.)

Mike Hill had been saved from spending a night atop the water tower and was thinking of getting off the island. He never did.

*Mike [Thomas] said, "We gotta plug up the inlet through here." We got in the cove and Bummer and I, we didn't know much about this thing, what to do. Mike got the dredge in the position he wanted and says, "Okay, throw the anchors over." They had these 250-pound anchors on steel cables. I couldn't move a 250-pound anchor if my life depended on it. That was twice my weight! I tugged at it. Bummer helped but we couldn't move it. Mike was in the lever room pulling levers and he runs outside and says, "Jesus Christ," and he runs over and grabs it and goes, "Boom," and throws it overboard. Then he runs around to the other side and throws the other one*

*Norman Anderson, courtesy Nick Anderson*

**The storm makes its deepest cut across Long Beach Island at 79th Street in Harvey Cedars. It grows to 200 feet wide before the flow can be stanched.**

*in. By himself! I never knew anybody could be that strong — 250 pounds of steel two guys couldn't slide off the boat!*

Thomas' plan was to put a sand dike at the ocean end of the cut where it was, paradoxically, the shallowest. Toward the bay, the channel was "over your head at low tide," according to Hill, but the ocean end was already beginning to shoal up by the natural action of the waves. Rolf Englesen helped lay the pipeline that would ferry the sand from the bay back across the island.

*The Ship's Wheel was totally wrecked, all twisted around, right where we had to lay pipe. We ran the line in a sliding door and out the window and started pumping. The ocean was coming through the break so hard it was almost a waste of time. The bulldozers got there and they were trying to push sand but they couldn't close up the hole because the water was coming through so fast. We kept pumping; I guess we pumped three or four days. We were pumping only two shifts because we didn't have enough people. We worked as long as we could until we were so tired we just dropped. And the bulldozers kept inching the sand out and we finally got it closed off.*

Mike Hill, again:

*I really felt good about that. Here's this private guy who's never going to get a nickel for the work he does, out there closing up this inlet. He filled the damn thing all the way to the boulevard. Covered it up. When Mike pulled the dredge out of here there was no more inlet — it was sand. The Army Corps of Engineers came on Saturday. We could see the bulldozers coming, building the road as they went, moving the sand. It was a wonderful feeling. It was like, "Here come the liberators." We were feeling isolated here, just been through the ravages of hell and these guys are building it back already and the tide is hardly even out. I thought, "What a country we live in."*

Don Wood had been skiing in New England with Harry Marti when they heard of the storm back home:

*Harry got a message, something about, "You better get home 'cause there isn't gonna be any home." Mommy Marti used to get a little bit excitable, like all mothers. I kept saying, "Oh, man, come on, it's a damn old northeaster, that's all."*

*courtesy Barbara Hartman McGehee*

**To close the new inlet, sand is pumped from the bay in a pipe laid through the Ship's Wheel.**

He says, "No, no, we better go," so we left. I was pissing and moaning. We drove all night long, listening to the radio where they're saying there's no island left. Got to 'Hawkin there's a lineup of about three miles there of people trying to get on the island. So we left the car somewhere, walked to the head of the line, bullshitted this lieutenant and got on one of those landing crafts and got over. We met Davy Ash and stayed at his place. We planned to stay awake, in case the house got washed away, but we didn't, and it didn't. Next morning we saw the bottom of a house broken up with an outboard motor hanging on the wall, so we snagged that, found a can of gas, threw it on a boat that was floating around, took it around to find out what happened to Harry's mom.*

They ended up at the firehouse in Harvey Cedars, where they found everybody safe. Mike Thomas promptly enrolled them in the dredging project.

*We were having a royal time, really. They were flying in ice cream and steaks and all that. The liquor store had been busted down. You'd scuff your foot in the sand and out would come a bottle of Chivas Regal.*

They worked eight to twelve hours at a time on the dredge but the in-between time dragged.

*Everybody played cards. I never got much of a thing out of playing cards, probably because I always lost. After four or five days I decided I'd had enough of that. The juices were flowing in me and the Moan (Marti) so we kind of geared that little boat up, went over to Moaner's house to get some good clothes; he had a closetful of bee-bop, doo-wop, you know, he was famous for them. And we took off across the bay, went over to Jimmie's tavern.*

*We walked into that place and it's crowded with a lot of people from the island who were evacuated and dang, man, we found out we're heroes. The press had been making this thing about these guys in Harvey Cedars, saving the town and all that. So we stayed there until they closed. They had to pour us out of there. And we forgot, of course, about the martial law.*

*The Coast Guard had a great big cutter laying out in the bay, because people were starting to come over from the mainland to loot at night. We got about halfway home, cruising along about half slow watching out for debris, when all of a sudden this searchlight went on. It looked like it was on top of the Empire State Building or something. I mean here's this big, dark, looming shape about a hundred yards to starboard with this big beam stabbing at us. So I put the pedal to the metal and we sped out of the light, but they tried to catch us again, swinging back and forth, and we were dodging in and out of little coves through some real treacherous territory. And we ended up burning the motor up, running it aground so many times trying to lose that light. We finally made it back into Kinsey Cove and it seized and we paddled the last hundred yards.*

It turned out the boat and the motor both belonged to a lawyer who did not regard the young men as heroes and brought charges. Mayor Thomas interceded and they went back to work.

*I remember us thinking the town was done. And then all of a sudden we looked up and here comes all this machinery rolling into town, bulldozers and scrapers pushing up dunes so the ocean wouldn't come over. And when*

Lawrence F. Wagner

*they let the people back, it wasn't but a couple of days we started getting orders for pilings; people who had lost their houses wanted to rebuild them again. Amazing.*

The borough hall had split "like a coconut." Temporary quarters were established in the Marti house. The Army Corps of Engineers went to work on the beach. Mike Hill:

*It was impressive. They'd line up six or eight bulldozers, blade to blade. These were blades eight or ten feet wide, so that's sixty to eighty feet across the face of this thing. They'd move a whole wall of sand.*

But the temporary dune they put was well behind the old dune line, behind even some houses that had survived the storm. That presented Mayor Thomas with a dilemma.

*The Army wanted to condemn anything east of the dune. They were really lobbying for that. "We'll rebuild your town from here back, but not from here out because it's only going to happen again." But the mayor didn't want to throw people off their property. That dune line was only two-thirds of the way from the boulevard to the oceanfront. He'd already lost a big chunk of his ratables. He fought them tooth and nail.*

Thomas finally took the engineers to the southern end of town, where the island narrows. There he pointed out a house on the oceanfront and proposed the dune line be established just east of it. The engineers agreed, not realizing that extending the line would save a lot of properties they had written off.

In Ocean City, Mayor Thomas Waldman had his own run-in with federal authorities:

*There were certain things that had to be ordered and I was the one that did it. I was charged with theft for ordering the break-in to supermarkets to*

*get food. They claimed I was violating procedures, that I didn't go through due process. But they dropped it. We fed our people.*

Other decisions were harder.

*We had to close off some areas of town because the streets were just big canyons, but we had people trying to slip through, like the Berlin Wall, to go home and get clothes or whatever. Some would get caught, but what are you going to do with them? We'd plead with them not to do it anymore. One guy went down there to walk an animal. He'd run this gamut of policemen twice a day to walk his dog.*

Help came from unexpected places.

*The Amish people came down, from somewhere in Pennsylvania. We didn't have anything to give them, food or shelter. They brought their own, lived in the buses. They worked around the clock, didn't ask for anything. They brought their own shovels, asked which section to start on. We gave them the worst area and they'd go in the houses and shovel sand. The sand was two or three feet deep. They'd do the whole thing. Fantastic people.*

The town got a chance to reciprocate when Allentown, Pennsylvania, suffered a bad storm some years later. Ocean City hurried to help, and Waldman was made an honorary citizen.

On Long Beach Island, recovery was slow. Residents were not allowed back for weeks, then many had to live in trailers. The water supply was unreliable. The storm had so altered the landscape that bulldozers, unable to find landmarks in the piles of sand and debris, kept rupturing the mains. Mike Hill:

*There were all kinds of problems. There were cats running all over. What were they going to eat? Somebody said they carried rabies. One of the geniuses said, "I think we ought to shoot all the cats." Bummer, who was a cat lover, said, "For every cat you shoot, I'm shooting two dogs."*

A newspaper account a week later reported:

*Nobody lives in Harvey Cedars anymore. There are no roads. There is no drinking water. The permanent residents have been evacuated. Wreckage is everywhere and where there is no wreckage there is just sand, in some places four feet deep. Even the houses don't offer evidence of where the roads were. The houses are everywhere, in no order, sometimes piled two or three together. Around them crushed and mangled cars and trucks lie half buried.*

Correspondent James Brown added:

*Everywhere shattered wreckage. Everywhere the roar of huge bulldozers and earthmovers. Everywhere sand and mud, the stench of diesel smoke, the stench of ruptured cesspools, the burning smell of overheated engines on trucks and tractors bogged in hub-deep sand.*

Mayor Thomas promised, "We'll be back to normal soon." Pointing to an American flag flying from an almost totally destroyed house, he added, "I guess that will show you that they intend to win this battle."

Martin Berger, an airline pilot, picking through the rubble, said, "I'm going to stay." He'd lost his seaplane and two garages and the house was badly damaged. "I'll have it fixed up. It's all I have." Sue Danner was moving things out of her house, which had been pushed from its foundation. "We're putting things in storage until we can get the house back up. We shall return."

Carole Youngman sat on the tilted windowsill of The Ship's Wheel, right where the dredge pipe had rested, and raised a cocktail glass, one of the few items to survive. "We've already made plans to rebuild," she said over the litter of stained clothing, broken pottery and corroded toys. The Ship's Wheel II opened Memorial Day.

Nat Ewer was luckier, or wiser. After the 1944 hurricane had wiped out his store on the boardwalk in Beach Haven, he bought an old coastal schooner, moored it on the bayside, filled in sand around it and opened for business again. The *Lucy Evelyn* became an island landmark and also proved herself a good ship and true. Ewer said, "The old ship just rose with the tide. Everything was dry as a dance floor. She may not settle back as low as before but we'll just put in another step or two at the door."

Henry Gsell looked at all that was left of his summer house — the roof. "I think I'll jack it up and make a carport." Raymond Gantt was found fishing in the debris-filled surf. "I worked all week cooking for the workmen and the police. I'd like to catch a striper before I go home."

The city newspapers called it "The Shattered Shore," "The Battered Shore," "No Man's Land," but Ralph Parker wrote to the *Beach Haven Times*:

> We came back after the 1944 hurricane and we will do the same again. I for one will not see any part of Long Beach Island made into a park, or give one inch to the sea. What does Holland do when they lose a dike? I have not heard of their giving in. Please help us, not in strength — we have that — but in silence.

And Aniela Harris, writing the Surf City news in the same paper:

> We are arising from an act of God, with the will and the courage of a dedicated people for a good and even better life on the island than we had before. We have confidence and faith that He who made the earth tremble will also show us the way to again make this island the joyous and invigorating place it was for the weary and exhausted peoples of surrounding inland states.

Correspondent Leonard McAdams wrote:

> This was the picture that emerged from the sea mists and surf spume of southern New Jersey's battered barriers: the determination of man to repel the invader sea, to reclaim, to rebuild, to recapture his way of life. The disdain of man for the senseless might of the elements was shown as damaged homes took on new faces. Masons and carpenters and painters swarmed all over them. New homes were rising as if to say, "So what?" to the madness of March.

An editorial in the *Beach Haven Times* two weeks after the storm put it as a challenge:

> Long Beach Island is picking itself up out of the heap of dripping, burnt rubble. This is a time when optimism must prevail. Many Islanders lost everything. The fear felt during the storm may still be felt now as they look to the future. If that fear is conquered with positive action, as it was in the storm, the Spirit of Long Beach Island will be strengthened.

Cape May City Manager Jack Sweitzer said, "Our beaches will be better than ever. We'll be in A-1 shape." At Sea Isle City, Mayor Vincent Lamanna said, "By Memorial Day we're going to have the most beautiful beach this town has ever seen." In Avalon, Mayor John McLaren said, "The beach is in pretty good shape. I think we'll be cleared up for Memorial Day." And Mayor Harry I. Conklin promised, "You won't know Beach Haven had a storm when you look at our beaches."

They were talking it up. They had to. It was simple economics. Already hard hit, the shore resorts would be hurt worse by a poor tourist season than by the storm. The tourist business in New Jersey amounted to $1.6 billion and employed more than 40,000 in fifty-five communities.

But one major tourist attraction was gone. Six weeks after it had beached, the USS *Monssen* was floated on a morning tide. It took two seagoing tugs and four salvage vessels, "engines going full blast," as one paper put it, to pull the 2,000-ton destroyer into deep water. The destroyer, it was pointed out, had seen action in the Solomon Islands during World War II, done convoy duty, rescued downed airmen in mine-infested seas, all without incident. Altogether there were some seven hundred salvage technicians in Beach Haven during the six-week operation. A columnist for the *Beachcomber* wrote:

> We met one of the young men in a launderette. He said he was living in the tent city at Holgate. When we commiserated that it must be pretty miserable he said, no, they were comfortable, but that there was a great deal of sand!

One officer, Lt. (jg) Thomas O'Malley, had been killed in a previous attempt to free the ship when a tow cable snapped. Finally, dynamite was used to clear a channel back to sea. Total cost was figured at $106,070.

A suggestion, said to have come from Navy men, was made that the 15-foot deep cove left by the vessel's departure would be a nice spot for surf fishing now and, if the ocean does not fill it in, a good summer swimming area.

But swimming was dangerous, due not only to the debris that kept washing in, but also to that which was hidden under thin layers of sand. Nurse Meribah Walker of Southern Regional High School made up a pamphlet of precautions to observe, "otherwise the March storm will continue to take its toll." They included inspecting all water for debris before swimming or diving or skiing or boating. Capt. J.D. Craik, commander of the Third Coast Guard District, issued a warning to small craft operators to be alert for "destroyed, misplaced or unlighted aids to navigation," but it didn't look as if many small craft operators were going to be operating that year. Carl Sheppard reported the storm had delivered a "haymaker blow" to boating.

> The greatest tidal rise on record surged over docks and storage lots to undermine shoring, while screeching northeast winds bowled over craft like tenpins. Smaller boats floated away, many never to be seen again. Others, their bilge plugs knocked out when they were propped up high and dry for the winter, simply filled and sank during unscheduled launchings. Boats tucked away "safely" inside buildings rose through the roofs.

Karl Von Schuler

**Attempts to free the beached *U.S.S. Monssen* from the sands of Holgate attract tourists.**

rather than water. Eventually, this led to the establishment of national flood insurance but then, as one headline announced, "Few Insured by Storm Policies Can Collect on Wave Damage." As an insurance executive pointed out, such coverage would have been so expensive as to be beyond most people's reach anyhow. Still, companies put 150 claims adjusters on standby.

They were to bear heavily on Dorothy Oldham. She had taken pictures from the four-story prayer tower of the Harvey Cedars Bible Conference of the houses being lifted, floated and smashed by the sea. Several appeared in an article on the storm in *National Geographic*. Insurance companies seized on these as proof that the damage was water-inflicted, not wind.

*I don't know how many subpoenas I was handed to appear in court. It meant being against your neighbors. I was heartsick anyway and to have this on top of it made me feel even worse. Everybody sustained damage, and there was no monetary help anywhere. It dragged on and on. I felt like burning all my prints and negatives.*

Sheppard also reminded his readers of one law of the sea that does not apply on land.

*A boat discovered adrift or sunk does not belong to the finder. Even advertising the craft won't establish the finder's title. The legal owner can come along and take the boat away at any time.*

The fishing industry recovered first. One paper commented, "The storm failed to affect one way or another what has been an extremely poor season to date." But fishermen are nothing if not optimistic.

*True, the contour of the entire coast has been changed — changed in some areas almost beyond recognition. New bars and new sluices have replaced once-familiar sand formations. One-time favorite "fishing-holes" have been filled, but new ones have been opened by the unrelenting surge of the surf.*

Shore facilities were largely a shambles. But the fish, of course, were unaffected, and stories of clam beds being smothered in mud proved to be untrue.

As always in such storms, insurance covered very little of the costs, unless a building's owner could prove the damage had been caused by wind

The good news was that you could deduct any property loss sustained from your federal income tax. The Internal Revenue Service prepared a pamphlet entitled, "Hurricanes, Floods and Other Disasters" to tell how, including tips on what to do "if your loss exceeds your income for the year." But, by law, local property taxes were still due, even though a house and the land it was sitting on might have been washed away by the sea. Harvey Cedars' Mayor Thomas balked. "What kind of a man can enforce this?"

The resorts started their long pull back to normalcy. Although they didn't exactly "Bounce Back," as one headline had it, they did a fast hop, skip and jump. Here's William Lawrence's bird's-eye look as the season opened:

*An airplane flew the length of the South Jersey seaside on Thursday (July 5), and those who rode it saw spread below the serenity of a bright and warm summer's day at the shore. Few of the scars of March remained. But everywhere men and machines were still mending what the sea had wrecked.*

*Four months ago, Long Beach Island was under water — ugly brown water awash with all sorts of debris, from floating houses to drifting seaweed. Four months ago the sea was a free-for-all of fighting giants. Now it broke in the slow, lazy rhythm of summertime, swimmers ducking its creamy surf, fishermen tugging at it from the shore. Atlantic City's boardwalk looked as though no storm had ever touched it. The Steel Pier was whole again. Ocean City sustained heavy damage but little of it is visible now.*

*Here and there a charred piling rises above the sand. Smoke from fires set by cleanup workers burning debris spiraled skyward at Strathmere and Avalon, Sea Isle City and Stone Harbor. At Stone Harbor some 50 nuns were walking on the beach. They wore long, blue, old-fashioned bathing suits and white bathing caps. They waved at the plane. The South Jersey shore has come back.*

Correspondent Joe Carragher filed this report after his tour three weeks later:

*Old Glory flapped in the breeze...a woman cried in despair...a fisherman hurled his lure into a pool of stripers...a bulldozer nudged a pile of sand...and the once destructful giant was serene as she gently rose and fell. That's how it is along the Jersey coast — life goes on or, that is, the comeback to life goes on.*

*Salvatore Pinto, courtesy Dorothea Pinto*

**Bulldozers push aside wrecked homes and move tons of sand in Harvey Cedars, above, and all along the coast.**

The comeback to life included the ancient and honorable art of salvaging, an unquestioned right at sea, less clear on its fringes. Long Branch issued an order against people taking any lumber from the beach or "anything, unless they can prove it belongs to them." Much of the timber had formerly been boardwalk. Mayor Thomas Farrell declared martial law in Sea Bright. Only those who could prove residency were allowed in, and then only on foot. Similar measures were taken in other communities. Sea Isle City mayor Vincent Lamanna warned people to leave boats be. Some owners had spotted their craft, only to find it gone when they returned to pick it up. Looting was widely rumored but seldom reported. Determining whether the vandals had been storm pirates or Mother Nature was impossible, and most people were more concerned with beating the calendar.

"The seashore is governed by the weather," said Asbury Park restaurant owner Louis Karagias. "If the weather is nice the summer people will come to the shore; you can't keep them away."

"A lot of prime properties on the waterfront are gone and that's that," said realtor Alma Blair in Ship Bottom, "but people will come; they always do. Of course," she added, "we can't rent houses that aren't there." But as proof that for a real real estate salesperson there is no such thing as an all ill wind — or tide — another observed: "With a lot of the oceanside properties hard hit, this should be a good year for the bayside."

But nature itself threw in another stopper — rainfall in June was 33 percent above normal.

By the end of July, newspapers headlined, "Tourists Decline at Jersey Shore." As one shopkeeper put it, "Too many people think this resort is still a wreck." Sightseers continued to come down on weekends, "but they don't even get out of their cars." Even one real estate agent complained, finally, "Business isn't good."

The storm had moved a lot of sand around. Now it had to be moved back. Sand removal ads ran in the newspapers right next to sand replacement ads; sometimes it was the same ad. Nelda Iacovo in Brant Beach recalls:

*We had four feet of sand piled around the house and we couldn't get anybody to shovel it so we could get in. One wanted $300, one wanted $400 just to move the sand. So we let it stay until the following year and then all the young people that came down, they shoveled it.*

Associated Press editor Robert MacDonald, who had moved to Brigantine from Philadelphia seven years earlier, did it himself.

*I pushed a snow shovel much of the weekend. I didn't shovel snow, just sand — hard-packed, black wet sand. Wheelbarrow after wheelbarrow I pulled across a road to where the ocean had washed a deep hole in "our" protecting dune. There I dumped the sand. It was a feeble gesture, I knew. One good wave could make it disappear. But the sight of that huge gap in the dune being closed by even a foot-high pile of sand made us feel better. For that dune had saved our home.*

Some people were trying to rebuild their dunes with beach sand. The army complained that the "unauthorized removal of sand" from the beaches was hampering the work of the Corps of Engineers. Col. T.H. Setliffe noted that the best beach protection is provided by a gentle slope that absorbs the wave energy before it reaches the dunes, and warned that taking sand from the beach to create what he called "unconsolidated dunes" removes that runway.

Dredges worked all through the summer pumping sand from the bays, where a lot of it had gone, back onto the beaches. At one time there were six working, some of which had come from New England to help, each moving a minimum of 250 cubic yards of sand per hour. The Corps put up nineteen thousand feet of dune wall from Barnegat Light to North Beach. Reporter Norman Collie was there:

*Night and day, 12-inch dredges suck sand and clay from the bays and spew it in a thin, black gruel onto the beaches, where hundreds of sea gulls and sandpipers grow fat and lazy banqueting on clams and bloodworms, eels and winter flounder disgorged with the fill. Flowing and ebbing tides spread the material, setting up a new first line of defense against future storms.*

The idea was to construct a wide beach, backed by dunes that were at least fourteen feet above mean sea level. For those who doubted whether this would be enough, the newspapers ran ads enticing people to a surer shore: "Attention Flood Victims — Why Run Risks? Build on Safe Land. Lake Manahawkin. High and Dry."

Some joked that Manahawkin would eventually be oceanfront. Jack Brewer was not so sure it was a joke:

*I've noticed in the time I've been here this island gets narrower all the time. Instead of wide and low it's getting narrow and high. They keep making the dunes higher but, boy, the island itself is getting narrower.*

He also had his doubts about sea walls and bulkheads.

*We had a place down here, built by the president of American Express. He built this place and the ocean wasn't going to wash him out. He built this tremendous bulkhead to go around his place. It was 20 feet high and it had a concrete base and creosoted timbers. And he offered to bulkhead all Harvey Cedars oceanfront, too. My grandfather, Ephraim Jones, was mayor then (1927) and he said, "No, it's only going to wash out. Nothing is going to stop the ocean." The '62 storm took out that bulkhead just like it wasn't there.*

The house itself, according to a newspaper account, was "bent into a pretzel by the tides." But farther north, George Moss Jr. credited a sea wall with saving one community.

*Only the protection of the massive sea wall and bulkheads built in 1914 and strengthened through the decades saved the borough of Sea Bright from annihilation. Without these the huge waves would have swept over the entire borough, leveling everything in their path. Only these man-made bulwarks against the sea prevented the rebirth of the Shrewsbury and Sandy Hook inlets.*

The U.S. Coast and Geodetic Survey sent a team to study Little Egg Harbor, Absecon and Barnegat inlets and started recharting the shore immediately. Capt. Lawrence Swanson said it was the first time a major survey had been prompted by a single storm, calling it "one of the biggest natural changes this century."

By the end of July, the *New York Times* reported:

*There is still much evidence of devastation, but the comeback has been spectacular. Row upon row of new, neat, brightly painted cottages, motels, apartment units, stores and concessions have been erected to replace structures washed out to sea.*

There were flood damage sales, but property values did not drop, as some had predicted. People kept finding things all summer long. Bottles of liquor turned up, seals still intact but labels gone. "The only trouble was," remarked an islander, "if you found something you liked, you didn't know what it was."

Stephanie Schnatz found a gold ring in North Beach, "up by the Cox's, what was left of their house. I tried to get in touch with them, could never find them. I've still got it; I keep it in my jewelry box." Everybody kept a memento, some leaving a wall unpainted to show visitors the high-water mark. The most popular souvenir seemed to be a set of 105 storm photos that Bill Kane of the Nor'easter shop in Beach Haven Terrace put together and was selling for $15.

The Great Atlantic Storm left its stories scattered amid the debris. And its memories. Betty Hornby wonders, "How many remember it as I do?"

*Chief (Angelo) Leonetti and his wife were so much fun. He called her "the bride" even though they'd been married for thirty years. Bob Osborne was kind to all the kids who hung around his magazine racks, reading everything they could and never buying; he never seemed to mind. Kenny Chipman, always active, always helping those in need. They have been washed away with the sands of time.*

The *Beach Haven Times* put the sentiments of a lot of people into an editorial:

*Tuesday, February 20, 1962, the culmination of man's mastery of science sent a man out of the earth and ionosphere to circle the world. Tuesday, March 6, 1962, man's puny scientific skill in predicting the vagaries of nature brought incredible terror, destruction and death to a strip of this earth. If scientific calculations can send us into orbit, why can't they warn us as to what's going on down here?*

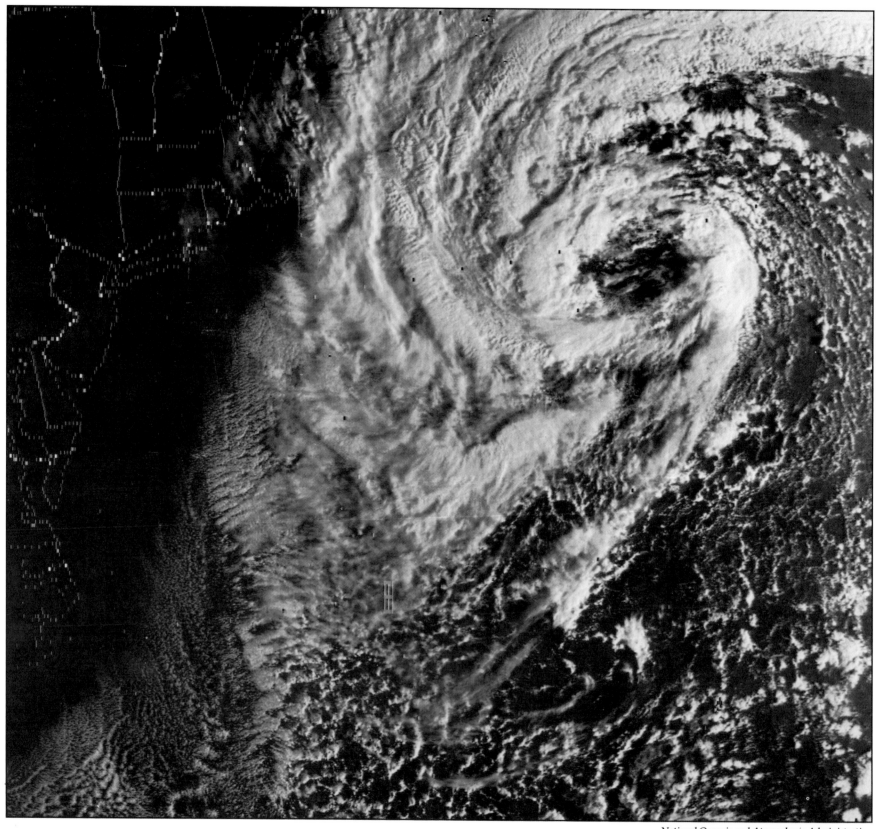

**The Hallowe'en storm, about 750 miles off the New Jersey coast, as seen from the NOAA 12 Polar Orbiter satellite October 30, 1991. Even at this distance from the shore, the storm caused extreme tidal flooding.**

# CHAPTER FIVE

# After 1962

*Think of the storm roaming the sky uneasily like a dog looking for*
*a place to sleep in; listen to it growling.*

— Elizabeth Bishop

IF THERE IS A STORM GOD, it was either satiated with its three-day feast of beaches and bungalows in 1962, or it had used up so much energy it needed time to recharge. Whatever the reason, the weather along the Jersey coast quieted down considerably after 1962.

There was tropical storm Doria in 1971, which spawned a small tornado in Cape May and flooded the Raritan Valley, and ex-hurricane Agnes in 1972, which was little more than damp air by the time it reached these latitudes. There were other northeasters — a winter without northeasters is as unlikely as a sea without salt — but nothing out of the ordinary, nothing to stir the ink. So when Hurricane Belle came along in August of 1976, the news media tried to make as much of it as they could. As a story in the *Beachcomber* told it:

*Some newscasters stumbled over their words in their excitement to get out the "Big News"; the over-enthusiastic reporting of "30-foot tides" and "a worse disaster than 1962" were not geared to calming already nervous residents, and the station that played the Rolling Stones's "We're on the Eve of Destruction" at least six times probably did not help soothe evacuees.*

Dubbed "Bicentennial Belle" because it came along a month after the nation's 200th birthday celebration, it was the first major storm to threaten the Jersey shore during the summer season since 1933. August is the busiest seaside month, and a snarl of traffic in the best weather. Warnings went up early and most people heeded them. According to Long Beach Township Mayor James Mancini, some seventy-five thousand vacationers managed to get out in just under five hours.

Although there were no thirty-foot tides, there was plenty of water.

*Contrary to most hurricanes, damage was heaviest on the bayfront. Learning from his experience in 1944, Al Houghton sank all his rental rowboats before the hurricane hit and they didn't go anywhere. Others were found tied to telephone poles and street signs. Nine boats were counted in a heap at one street crossing.*

Dave Wood remembers the storm as "Hurricane Rat." He had holed up in a gunning shack on Sandy Island in Barnegat Bay:

*I had advice from all the local duck hunters that the place never had any damage, never even had any water on the floor. But it did get rats. I hate rats! I had this big, black dog, Charlie, I got from the S.P.C.A., part Newfoundland and part who knows what. He was never allowed in the house. He had this habit: He'd pick out a spot — a knot in the wood or a grease spot on the floor or anything — and go nuts on it, barking and growling and jumping around.*

*Before it gets dark the water is already up. All you can see is the tops of the bayberries. The dock is under water, so I let Charlie come inside. Well, in the middle of this hurricane it's blowing about seventy, it's pitch black out, you can't see anything. It is really eerie. And there I am, waiting for rats. And here goes Charlie into one corner and he's barking like crazy and I'm sure it's the rats. I mean, where else are they gonna come out from? They're gonna come out from the corners. But he's over there barking at a spot on the carpet! Scared the hell out of me.*

*I'm constantly going outside, checking the boat, checking everything and drinking whiskey. I see the old outhouse has blown over and it's lying there like a big wind scoop and I'm afraid it's going to get picked up and crush the boat, so I figure I'll tie it down. I get my flashlight and shine it on this thing and it's covered with rats! Maybe fifty rats. So I look at it and I figure, well, maybe it'll be just fine the way it is.*

*Back in the house, I'm belting down another shot of liquid courage and thinking, My God, I just restored that sneakbox. This is the first time it's been back in the water. And it's my father's. He'll kill me if it gets crushed. So I get all stoked up and go back out with a rope and hammer and nails and I'm gonna do it. I'm batting rats off the outhouse with the hammer ... it was very strange.*

At one point he got blown into the water. Normally about two feet deep there, the bay was now over his head. And the water was full of swimming rats.

*They were swimming for their lives. They were attracted by the light, and they went for my legs. It was gross, terrible.*

He gave up trying to tie down anything and sank the sneakbox instead. In the midst of his efforts, he looked back toward the cabin.

*I had an oil lamp on a table by the window, and Charlie, he'd never been in the house before, and so he had no house manners, and there he is, up on the table, looking out the window, his tail wagging and banging against that oil lamp. If he had tipped that thing over that place would have burnt to the water in about ten seconds.*

As for the rats, the next morning their bodies, by the thousands, marked the high-water line all along the bay shore, spurring emergency pickup operations before they started to rot. Storms always drive animals to seek higher ground, and apparently there had been a population explosion in the marsh's rat population that year.

*Ray Fisk/United Press International (all)*

**In March, 1984, twenty-two years after the Great Atlantic Storm, another major northeaster undercuts houses and eats away beach and dunes in North Beach and Harvey Cedars, above and lower right; the same storm tears up the boardwalk in Atlantic City, right.**

Hurricane David in September 1979 was one of the rare hurricanes that passed by to the west, over Pennsylvania, putting New Jersey under the eastern quadrants of the storm, always more damaging since it is there that the storm's forward speed is added to its counterclockwise circulation, causing stronger winds. Power lines were torn, twisted and tangled all over the state.

In 1984, a gale with "near hurricane force winds" hit the Jersey shore, causing waves that broke through the dunes on Long Beach Island for the first time since 1962. The National Weather Service said it was as close to a winter hurricane as it could get. Newspapers had it "slamming" and "pounding" and "pummeling" the coast, "whipping its way across the Garden State with a forceful vengeance."

By the time Hurricane Gloria came by in September of 1985, the shore was all but deserted. The summer people were gone and the winter people heeded the sirens. Earlier in the year, Neil Frank, director of the National Hurricane Center, had warned that a major hurricane moving up the coast could kill five thousand people in New Jersey. The Pentagon assured the governor of North Carolina it had sufficient body bags on hand to handle the expected casualties. An elderly resident of Cedar Bonnet Island had this advice on his way out: "If the police tell you to leave, leave. You get a bunch of half-assed guys who will tell you they're going to have a hurricane party, but it'll be their last party."

Another weather veteran, stopping at the Porthole Bar in Ship Bottom, hadn't made up his mind: "It depends on how big a party it is. I've stayed for all of them. But I've got a gut feeling this is the one they've been warning us about. There's been too many false alarms."

Gloria spread her spiraled arms three hundred miles wide and chased about 95,000 people from the Jersey shore. Cape May County underwent a mass evacuation, moving 25,000 people from their homes. In Monmouth County, everybody living within twenty blocks of the ocean was ordered evacuated. The advance word on the storm prompted the eleven casinos in Atlantic City to send everybody home four hours early, resulting in an estimated $7 million loss. "I was on a hot roll," complained Stephen Rokicki, the last person at the craps table. Even the White Castle hamburger chain, which closes only on Christmas, closed for Gloria.

As the hurricane came up the coast, winds were clocked at 130 miles per hour. Meteorologists called it "one of the great storms of the century," "possibly the worst hurricane of the century," "one of the most powerful storms to stalk the Atlantic coast this century." Some of those who had experienced some of the other hurricanes of the century were convinced. Mayor Cecile Norton of Sea Bright had survived Donna. "I don't think I've ever been as frightened in my life." Clark Gilman, of the New Jersey Department of Environmental Protection, said, "I think we have a lot to be worried about."

Tides were expected to be eight to twelve feet above normal. "We're lucky this storm isn't taking place in midsummer," said John Weingart, director of the state's Division of Coastal Resources. Schools closed, people boarded up, taped up, shuttered up; hospitals and utility companies put everybody on call.

And still some people would not get out. "About 50 percent of the people here will remain," said Highlands Police Chief Howard Brey. Jim Walzer actually came back to Long Beach Island from New York. "I canceled an appointment to come down and watch the storm." Supermarkets experienced a run on some items. "I ran out of Poland Springs water, but I had Great Bear," reported Martin Foley, manager at the Keyport Shop Rite. "One woman got quite upset because her brand wasn't available."

"Maybe we're due," said Chick Walnut, battening down his porch furniture in Barnegat Light. "It's been twenty-three years." But he was thinking of staying. "I'd hang on if I could." In Beach Haven, Nancy Davis said, "I'd like to stay. I'm sort of curious. But staying would be dumb." Across the street, Wallace Ruoff dragged his sneakbox out of Little Egg Harbor Bay and into his living room. "I wouldn't think of leaving except for the kids and grandmother." In Ship Bottom, a woman who had evacuated in 1962 said, "I just don't want to jeopardize anybody's life who would be coming over to save me." Fred Cramer seemed to encapsule the majority view. "So my house blows down — there's nothing I can do to stop it. It comes down to fate." Meanwhile, the radio blared, "Rock You Like a Hurricane," and a clerk at Shell Liquors reported, "People are really stocking up on liquor."

Southern Regional High School reverted again to its alter ego as Southern Regional Evacuation Center. Dr. Robert Daria, district superintendent, noted that the school's secondary identity was by now almost as natural as its primary one. Having lived through hurricanes in Florida, he had his own way of getting through them. "It's called prayer. There's no sense worrying about things you have no control over."

But, like an overhyped movie star with a shaky script, Gloria failed to live up to her billing. It wasn't "the big one." Coastal geologist Susan Halsey explained that the storm apparently lost acceleration as it neared the New Jersey coast and veered east. Its eye expanded, slowing its internal winds. It also arrived at low tide, keeping flooding to a minimum, which meant minimum damage to the beaches:

> There were some problems in Harvey Cedars, but then there always are. The major problem seems to be groin-induced erosion. Those areas will be affected until we notch those groins. They are too high to permit water to wash over. But we really weren't affected much this time. God must watch out for fools and vulnerable coastlines. At the same time, I hope people got a taste of what it could have been.

Reporter Deidre Carmody wrote, "Preparing for Gloria was like the storm before the calm." A parks commissioner said, "I would say that as the storm of the century this was a washout." Those who had stayed crowed, those who had left shrugged. As William F. Buckley put it in his *National Review*:

> A careful reading of after-storm sentiment reveals many people were disappointed over the modest level of damage done to other people by Hurricane Gloria. Everyone was geared up to seeing that night's television give gruesome details on the holocaust visited on the eastern seaboard.

**Hurricane Gloria in 1985 sends most shore dwellers scurrying for cover, but this Ship Bottom resident checks out the surf at dawn. The storm stays far enough offshore to cause only tidal flooding and big waves, top left. Long Beach Island evacuees wait it out in the Middle School library in Manahawkin, bottom left.**

Since evacuations cost money — $150,000 to $200,000 per mile of coast — the National Hurricane Center received its expected share of criticism. "I'll take the criticism when there's no loss of life," replied Neil Frank. "What I never want to hear is, 'No one warned us.'" An editorial in the *Asbury Park Press* said, "Our narrow escape provides a new danger. Too many people have compared the forecasters and the media to the boy who cried, 'Wolf!'"

If the advance of technology had provided ample warning of approaching hurricanes, it hadn't made much progress in protecting against other dangers. At a state-sponsored workshop after Gloria, coast watchers warned that heavy development since the Great Atlantic Storm of 1962 had left New Jersey particularly vulnerable. The problem was too many buildings, not enough protection.

"What it boils down to," said Monmouth County planner Robert Huguley, "is that in a major storm there will be considerable loss of life."

There were the usual calls for a halt to beachfront construction, a ban on multifamily units within specified yards of the beach, a refusal to allow anyone whose beach house was taken out by the sea to rebuild, a building line that would accommodate natural forces, not oppose them. Long Beach Township Mayor James Mancini said the proposals did not deal realistically with the development already in place. Weingart pointed out that "the federal government is not going to be in a position to bail out New Jersey when there's a storm."

Lee Koppleman, a regional planning official in New York, used another allegorical allusion. "If the hurricane of the century hits our shore, we will be prophets in our time. If it doesn't, the planners will be a bunch of Chicken Littles." The only thing that would convince people, he felt, was "major damage."

By 1990, however, a whole generation had passed without a major storm down the shore. The last big hurricane had been Donna in 1960 and the last big northeaster The Great Atlantic Storm two years later. According to David Ludlum, author of *The New Jersey Weather Book*, that marked the end of a thirty-year period heavy in storm activity. Tracing back further, he found that the thirty years before 1930 were also relatively quiet, and from the turn of the century back to 1871, activity was again high. He took his research back as far as he could find reliable records and noted what seemed to be a regular thirty-year cycle of destructive storms on the Jersey shore.

In 1991 it seemed that, indeed, the great wheel of mild weather had turned again. It was the year that Hurricane Bob brushed by, hardly more than a good rain here but mean enough elsewhere to leave $1 billion in damages along its track. "We get northeasters that bellow more than that," said one beach dweller.

And on Hallowe'en, they did.

True to the date, it came in as quietly as a ghost just before it says, "Boo!" As the *New York Times* put it:

*A storm with no name and questionable parentage ambushed the Atlantic Coast, smashing homes, washing out roads, stripping beaches. Breakers crashed through windows like vandals, strewing sand and rocks, and left like looters, hauling appliances, furniture, and whole houses out to sea.*

Another account called it "a ferocious, nameless Atlantic storm masquerading as a Hallowe'en hurricane, a monster hundreds of miles wide that lashed like a hurricane but was born in Canadian waters, not the tropics, and fell just short of a hurricane's 74 mph winds." And the *Atlantic City Press* said, "The whole event appeared to be an abnormality, a sort of unnatural natural disaster."

And if the Bobs of the world hadn't endured enough ego punctures, Red Cross worker Donna Nelson said it made Hurricane Bob "look like nothing." Harbormaster Erik Anderson added, "Bob was a shower compared to this." Emergency worker Gil Hanse Jr., said, "Hurricane Bob was a pussycat." Wharfinger Stuart Smith said, "It makes Hurricane Bob look like a breeze."

The Hallowe'en storm was called deceptive, dangerous, and "one of the worst of this type to hit the area in twenty years," by the Weather Service's Gene Salerno. It didn't show up as a one-eyed bogeyman on satellite photos the way hurricanes do and it didn't carry much rain, but the winds were strong enough and long enough to push mountains of water ashore all along the coast.

Officially it was classified as an extratropical storm. Newspapers tried dubbing it "E.T." but the name didn't stick. "To the people affected, it really doesn't matter if it's a hurricane or not," said meteorologist Robert McElhearn.

It began as a classic northeaster, forming somewhere off Nova Scotia. Some weather watchers thought it might have gotten added power from Hurricane Grace, which was petering out over the Atlantic. What surprised them was the path it took. Jack Beven at the National Hurricane Center in Florida explained that a high pressure system over Canada prevented it from following Grace northward, and the system's clockwise winds sent it down the coast instead. Meteorologist Keith Arnesen of Rutgers University said, "When you get a high pressure system near a fairly strong low pressure system, the winds in between are very strong."

Waves broke over the top of the 100-foot high Minot Lighthouse on the Massachusetts coast. An Air National Guard helicopter was knocked out of the sky. Two teenagers in a boat were rescued three miles out at sea after "the wind just sucked them off shore." In Sea Bright, Police Chief Kenneth Johnson reported the whole beach had been wiped away, the whole town evacuated. Emergencies were declared on the Outer Banks of North Carolina and beach erosion reached as far south as Palm Beach, Florida. The storm also invaded and "severely damaged" the summer White House of President George Bush in Kennebunkport, Maine. The President told reporters, "It's our family strength, being close to the ocean. Unfortunately, the sea won this round. We'll see how we go in the next one."

In New Jersey, damages were eventually pegged at $90 million. The *Newark Star Ledger* reported, "The fortunes of many communities changed by the hour as tides that crested Wednesday night barely subsided Thursday morning, only to surge again in the afternoon."

The siege lasted two days. Not nearly as overwhelming as the Great Atlantic Storm of 1962, it was nonetheless notice to a new generation of shore dwellers that they live at the sufferance of the sea.

Jonathan Cohen

**A wave crashes against a Longport sea wall during the 1991 Hallowe'en storm.**

One resident, living on the mainland side of Little Egg Harbor Bay was trapped in his home for two days. "I look out my windows and all I see is water," he told the *Philadelphia Inquirer*. "It's like being on a ship. It's sort of a surreal feeling to look out on two miles of water in every direction."

In Lacey Township, also on the mainland, Larry Whelan said, "The water seems like it's just coming out of the ground. It's as calm as it can be, but it's an eerie calm."

It was not calm on the seaside. Heavy surf roared across beaches and took out dunes nurtured for almost thirty years as if they were so many sandcastles. Dr. Stephen Leatherman, director of the Laboratory for Coastal Research at the University of Maryland, explained:

*In a northeaster, steep waves are coming in very quickly. The beach is submerged, always wet, so it is easier to move the sand. The first high tide takes away the beach, the second starts hitting the dunes.*

There were three high tides. Ten million dollars worth of beach replenishment in Cape May was washed out. Avalon lost 500,000 cubic yards of sand. In Sea Isle City, several years of work, mostly volunteer, plus about $400,000 that had been put into building up the beach was wiped out. The estimate to "get things back in order" was $3.5 million. Despite attempts to fatten the city's beaches with almost two million cubic yards of sand since 1978, the beachfront has gotten progressively thinner. Testifying about the storm's erosion, one coastal geologist said, "There will be some recovery in a week or so, but probably 50 percent or so will stay on the bars and some of that was pushed back beyond the bars and that won't be back."

The *Atlantic City Press* reported:

*Those who stayed in areas threatened by rising water spent the hours before high tide using boards, rags, tape — anything to try to keep the approaching water out. It was a losing battle.*

Gail O'Donnell of Beach Haven Terrace said the water came in her home and lifted the shelves off the walls and floated them away. She saw her "beautifully landscaped garden" turned into mush.

*On my front lawn there are clumps of the worst-looking flotsam and jetsam you've ever seen. I get the prize for the most obnoxious-looking damage. And our trash cans must be somewhere in Tuckerton; I can't find them.*

Jane Kurani in Beach Haven ran an ad for a pink, ceramic pig planter she found that she thought might have sentimental value for someone. Long Beach Township Commissioner Frank Pescatore said, "We learned one thing in this storm. Decorative wooden curbs and posts are very destructive. They float around the streets and become projectiles."

Mud City, in Stafford Township's marshes at the edge of Barnegat Bay, was under water for three days. Walt and Rose Mattis stayed and quickly found themselves surrounded by driftwood and debris. They used a rowboat to get around, trying to save neighbors' belongings. "One of my neighbors called to ask if I'd seen his porch. We looked all over the neighborhood but we didn't find it."

The Atlantic City Red Cross delivered cleaning supplies — mop, broom, scrub brush, disinfectant and sponge — in flooded neighborhoods, as well as packages of Tastykakes and potato chips. The state halted clamming in all bays due to contaminant levels up to ten times normal. Officials wouldn't predict when the waters would be declared safe.

On the beaches of Surf City, Public Works Superintendent Emil TumSuden was surprised that there didn't seem to be much trash mixed in with the estimated one hundred tons of driftwood, which included chunks of boardwalk torn from beaches in northern New Jersey. "The storm seemed

*The* SandPaper

**The Ocean City boardwalk suffers a one-two punch with the Hallowe'en 1991 and January 1992 storms.**

to drop everything it picked up here. For some reason, nature always has the nails pointing up."

Many dune lines held, though most were undercut. Stuart Farrell, director of the Coastal Research Center at Stockton State College in Pomona, gave the dunes credit for saving much of the infrastructure of shore communities. Lavallette Mayor James Boekholt said, "In some places the waterline was higher than the boardwalk. We would have lost the boardwalk if not for the dunes."

Some sea walls toppled, others leaned. In some places, beach elevation dropped as much as five feet. In Loveladies it was estimated that thirty feet of beach was lost. Shore communities hurried to assess damage and apply for aid. Then they discovered there wasn't any. Two years of tight state budgets had provided no funds for shore protection. Coastal engineer Michael Bruno was appalled:

> The Jersey shore is basically the jewel of the state. How many things can this state point to with pride? If we had no funding, most of what we know as the Jersey shore wouldn't exist. So, how do you let it go? I don't understand that.

The Legislature had been debating the issue for seven years, over two administrations, one Republican, one Democratic. Department of Environmental Protection and Energy Commissioner Scott Weiner said, "It's indicative of the scarcity of resources and the very awful choices that have to be made." Governor Jim Florio said he would appeal to Washington for help. To be eligible for federal assistance, a state must declare it does not have the resources to take on the burden of restitution. The governor asked for $72 million.

A spokesman for the Federal Emergency Management Agency delivered the bad news. "The President's disaster fund is out of money," said Marvin Davis, adding that victims of the San Francisco earthquake, Hurricane Hugo and Hurricane Bob were still waiting.

Bruno said that without outside aid, no community could afford to replenish beaches and rebuild dunes. "The real test is to see how much of the beach comes back. Under normal circumstances the sand is removed and deposited offshore and then, during a calm period, the sand comes back and redeposits. But in a large storm like this, a lot of the sand is moved too far out and not given a chance to come back. This sand is gone in a lot of places."

Replacing lost land was called a Band-Aid by some, life support by others. Alan Purcell works in Ocean City. "Every year they dump thousands of dollars into it. When are they going to learn that they can't really fight it? A man-made reef would do it, but that would take away the waves for the surfers."

One of those waveriders is Everett Bauer of Ocean City. "We live for this. The bigger the waves, the more radical, the better. A lot of times at this time of year you find guys traveling to Puerto Rico, Hawaii, Costa Rica. But it's really nice when we get the same quality surf here in town."

Police Sgt. M.F. Cook of Sea Isle City told a reporter most people he knew took it all philosophically. "It's strange, but most of the residents I talked to seemed to be wishing it was worse. One old fellow told me he looks forward to these things. He said it's nature's way of cleaning out a town."

Others were not so sanguine. In resort communities, incomes hang on an easily upset balance. The washup of a handful of medical syringes, the residue of sewage dumping, the rumor of storm-damaged beaches have

wiped out whole seasons. It's estimated that resort business means about $8 billion to the state's economy.

Summer visitor Johann Das came down to look at what one newspaper called an ex-beach in Ocean City. "I just want to see what beach I want to go to next year. I mean, why come here if there's no beach?" Year-round resident Ann Morris said she was planning to leave. "I'm ready to go to a dry island. I'm tired of this." Farrell predicted, "If nothing is done and there's another northeaster, the water will be at people's front doors."

But nature columnist Pete Dunne, writing in the New York Times, pointed out the benefits of periodic flooding to the wetlands that back up the barrier islands and had this observation:

> Coastal storms are a regular occurrence on the coast, part of the dynamic tug of war that goes on between the land and the sea. So instead of looking at coastal habitat as a risky place to live, think of it as a fine, stable habitat with a short-term lease. Then, after a period of quiescence and good living, another storm sweeps the slate clean, and the process begins anew. Sounds a lot like life, doesn't it?
> There's only one problem. People who own oceanfront houses, and the legal systems that enforce the boundaries of oceanfront lots, are not as flexible and dynamic as the beaches are. They cannot just fall back like the dunes. They want the boundary between the ocean and the land to be fixed.

Before they got the chance, the water came charging back up the beaches. On January 4, 1992, little more than two months later and as if to emphasize that the nineties might indeed be the start of a new thirty-year cycle, what one meteorologist called "a tightly wound" storm sporting 60 mile-per-hour winds hit the Jersey shore. Although the tides were not as high as those of the Hallowe'en storm and did not last as long, damage was greater due to the weakened state of the beaches and dunes. Sea Bright police Sgt. Steve Spahr sighed, "Here we go again." He had just finished refurbishing his home with new floor tiles, carpeting and furniture.

This storm, too, took everyone by surprise. According to meteorologist Lee Grenci at Pennsylvania State University, it showed up first as "a reasonable low pressure system, nothing to write home about. Three hours later it was a lollapalooza."

"The low pressure system was the tropical connection — warm, moist air. Think of that as the fuel. At the same time, there was a disturbance in the jet stream, a river of air between 25,000 and 30,000 feet running west to east. Think of that as the match. When the two got together you had an explosion."

In Cape May Point, tides breached dunes that had held on Hallowe'en and flooded half the borough. In Cape May, the ocean carried three feet of sand over the sea wall, and the area known as Frog Hollow was under water. Ocean City lost more of its boardwalk. Concrete benches relocated blocks away from their sites in Sea Isle City. Dunes in Strathmere were "wiped out," according to one witness. In Stone Harbor, the water broke through the bulkhead in five places. In Harvey Cedars, waves scoured away beaches and chewed into dunes that had been carefully nurtured since 1962.

And, as in the October storm, when the high tides on the beaches receded, those in the bay rose to give the narrow islands a one-two wallop. The governor again declared a state of emergency in the four counties of Cape May, Atlantic, Ocean and Monmouth.

**Veterans of a century of storms, Cape May's Victorians get their feet wet again during the winter storms of 1991-92.**

An editorial in the *Atlantic City Press* wondered whether continually trying to rebuild was the answer:

> In the 19th Century, when developers first discovered the value of barrier islands as prime real estate, they had an excuse for ignorance. They didn't know that islands are always growing, shrinking, shifting and changing, locked in a perpetual game of hide and seek with the ocean. The 21st Century will arrive in less than a decade. We approach that new age with a view of nature that was formed around the time of the Civil War. We can't tame nature. Nature ... is unpredictable. The human response, however, is not.

The human response was to rebuild the beaches — some of them, anyway. At Ocean City, where a tug-of-war with the sea had been going on for years, $39 million worth of sand was trucked in to spread like salve on the lacerated shore. At Loveladies, where million-dollar homes had turned the beachfront into the Gold Coast of Long Beach Island, too valuable in ratables to let go, the sand was piped in from the bottom of Barnegat Inlet.

In an attempt to tame that unruly waterway, engineers were constructing a new jetty, giant boulders piled far out to sea, much farther than the old jetty, which had not been able to keep the shifting currents from filling the mouth of the inlet with sand. But as the jetty went up and out, homeowners in Loveladies — and in Harvey Cedars next door — claimed it was causing the currents to pull sand off their beaches. They wanted it back.

Four miles of dredge pipes were laid down the island, and sand from the channel was pumped onto the beaches of Loveladies. None, however, got to Harvey Cedars. Mayor Harry Marti pounded protests into deaf ears in Trenton and Washington, but while homeowners in Loveladies spent the summer sunning on their beaches, homeowners in Harvey Cedars spent the summer hoping the winter northeasters would not come chewing at their already half-eaten dunes.

On Friday, December 11, a winter storm did arrive. Born of an offshore low in the classic manner of northeasters, it kept skirting the definition as its winds shifted around to east by south, then southeast before returning to northeast. Gale warnings went out. Fishing boats stayed in.

There had been notice of minor coastal flooding; the National Weather Service had set a coastal flood watch two days earlier. Old-timers smelled a storm in the air even though the temperature was warm for December. There was a full moon — there had been a full lunar eclipse the night before — signaling the spring tides.

*Jay Mann/The* SandPaper

**High tide, December 11, 1992, Brant Beach: The ocean comes surging in, washing away dunes and pounding the beachfront.**

But no one expected the twelve- to eighteen-foot seas that came in with the morning tide, pushing it to nine feet above mean low water, over ten and a half feet in some of the bays two hours later, coming up through storm drains to flood towns and invade homes.

Kathleen Daniels' house was halfway between the bay and the ocean in Beach Haven. She'd lived there since 1933. "We never had water in the house before. This time there was 14 inches. It didn't roll in; it came up through the floor." Ship Bottom Mayor Robert Nissen had a mark in the garage at his marina on the causeway where the 1962 tide had crested. "This was at least six inches higher."

Later there were arguments whether flood levels broke the record set in 1944. Tide heights were calculated differently then, taking sea level as the mark. When it was discovered that sea level was slowly rising, the mark was changed to mean low water and adjustments had to be made. Eventually it was judged that 1944 still had the edge — but record or not, what the *SandPaper* called "The Storm that Stole Christmas" was wet.

And windy. "If they had said `hurricane' we would have left," said Marion Cleary of Beach Haven Crest, another storm veteran. Hurricane-force winds of 77 miles per hour roared along a front that stretched from Cape Cod to Chesapeake Bay.

Under the press of the winds, the sea rose up on its haunches, shouldering aside sea walls and bulkheads and roaming wild through the streets. Boardwalks flew apart from Sandy Hook to Ocean City. Waves took out the 111-year-old fishing pier in Ocean Grove, too, leaving only the pilings "stuck up from the ocean like the arms of a drowning man," as reporter Steve Chambers put it.

Signs came raining down. Traffic lights spun on their tethers like ballroom mirrors. The Absecon Inlet section of Atlantic City was "beat up pretty good," according to one witness on the now-constant news coverage all channels were giving the storm. The Staten Island Ferry had to suspend service due to high waves in the harbor. Rancocas Creek erupted from its banks 50 feet on either side when the Delaware River backed up. Airports shut down because of the winds that were gusting up to 90 miles per hour. Barometric pressure dropped to 29.2 inches.

Friday afternoon the waters subsided, but not much; the wind was blowing broadside to the shore to keep them pressed against the beaches and bottled up in the bays. Some long-time residents began to have eerie memories of the Great Atlantic Storm of 1962 when a low that seemed to have sent down roots wouldn't let the tides recede, layering new volumes of water over the old for three days.

It was not that bad, but it was bad enough. "It's one of the four or five worst storms of the century," said Jay Kreiger of the National Weather Service. The low rocked back and forth, then centered over the Delmarva Peninsula just south of Delaware Bay, held in place by a high over eastern Canada that also seemed disinclined to move. The clockwise winds circling the high met the counterclockwise winds around the low on a line between New York's Long Island and Wildwood, sending a double wallop against the Jersey shore.

Meteorologist George Prouflis said, "All the energy just came together. It became a supercharged storm." Most of the beaches that had suffered erosion during the Hallowe'en storm in 1991 and the January storm a few months later were unprepared for the new assault.

In some places, four inches of rain fell in 24 hours. Parts of the Garden State Parkway were flooded and shut down. The causeway to Long Beach Island was closed when access roads became impassable. Manasquan Mayor John Winterstella said, "At one point our most passable road had five feet of water." In Monmouth County, where power was out for five days in some communities, 19,000 people were evacuated from the towns of Highland, Sea Bright, Monmouth Beach, Union Beach, Middletown and Dover Township. In Oceanport, a sixteen-foot boat ended up in Donna Anastasia's bedroom. In Point Pleasant Beach, Ray and Vera Bisordi had to be rescued in the bucket of a backhoe. The Red Cross estimated that 3,200 homes were damaged statewide; over two-thirds of those were in Ocean and Monmouth counties.

**Flooding in the streets of Long Branch during the December 1992 northeaster submerges cars and trucks and blocks access for emergency vehicles.**

New Jersey Governor Jim Florio declared a state of emergency, the second storm-driven shore emergency that year. Prompted by the first, Florio had signed a bill just two weeks earlier to provide $15 million for beach preservation. The program was due to go into effect the following July. President Bush also declared the four coastal counties a disaster area.

Late Saturday night the low finally began its slow walk out to sea. Still-stiff winds kept coastal flood warnings in effect, with flood watches set through Sunday, but the waters were seeping away, seeking normal levels. It wasn't until Tuesday that the waters finally drained from the bays and the marshes reappeared. Some residents in the back bays had been stranded for four days.

The storm left a shoreline that looked as if it had been scoured with a fire hose. Ocean City lost most of its $39 million sand pile. In Point Pleasant, the Lake of Lilies had risen up and receded to strand fish on St. Louis Avenue. The wind blew out windows facing seaward in Jackson Township, miles from the sea. The sea wall between Belmar and Spring Lake was breached, and the sea broke through the twelve-foot high sea wall in Sea Bright in two places, strewing two- and three-ton rocks across front yards all over town. On Island Beach State Park, sand covered all the vegetation. In Point Pleasant Beach the sand was gone. "There was 75 yards of beach at this spot until yesterday," said resident Mike Creedon.

Some six thousand people spent at least one night in shelters, according to the Red Cross. One of those was 81-year-old Anna Farina of Sea Bright. "The walls of my house just fell in," she said. In Little Ferry, Frank Balsam said he had sandbagged his doors to keep out the water. "It didn't work."

*Lisa Suhay (top) and Tim Moersh/The* SandPaper

*Tim Moersh/The* SandPaper

**Hurricane force wind gusts lift the roof from this Harvey Cedars home during the December 1992 storm, which also brought extremely high tides, washing away dunes and placing the ocean under homes in Beach Haven, left, and Harvey Cedars, above left, where the tide rushes across Long Beach Island.**

Long Beach Island took the hardest pummeling. Dunes were cut away, in some places leveled, revealing stacks of 1950s automobiles that had been put in to help hold them in place. Mayor Marti stood on what was left of a dune in Harvey Cedars and said, "Right now I'm wishing someone else was mayor."

The wind lifted roofs off beachfront homes and sliced them into the houses behind. Decorative trim and old railway ties became missiles and battering rams. Barnegat Bay flooded over the almost-solid wall of bulkheads that line it as if they weren't there. Brian Cleary cruised about on his surfboard rescuing neighbors' boats. Nick Englebert paddled around in his kayak to check summer houses. Windsurfer Jack Bushko sailed down submerged streets. "I sailed all day and never went out into the bay or ocean." Of the $500 million damage estimate for the state, almost one-quarter was on Long Beach Island.

It was certainly the best-covered storm in history. Hurricanes come and go too quickly to get all the cameras in place in time. Northeasters are much more media-friendly. By Sunday there were as many reporters on the scene as there were insurance adjustors. Pictures not only of wrecked houses but of the waves wrecking them were flashed around the country. Some papers called it the storm of the century. The *Beach Haven Times*, with more experience in these affairs, merely dubbed it the Yule Tide.

Amateur coverage of the storm was even heavier. While emergency supplies were big sellers on Friday and Saturday, they were soon surpassed by film and videotape. Within a week, commemorative cassettes were being hawked for $25. A week later, paint and lumber sold out. Within a month it was hard to see where the storm had been — except, of course, on the beaches, or rather, where the beaches had been.

"Where there were beaches before, there are none now," said Bernard Moore, head of the state's shore protection program. "The storm has radically changed the coastline." A meteorologist on the Weather Channel said, "This storm crossed the line from classic to legendary."

It also changed some people's ideas about living by the side of the sea. Richard Schwartz of Dover Township, whose house was declared "unfit for human habitation," said, "It makes you wonder about shore construction, if it should even be done." Rolf Venzie of Ventnor said, "I'm definitely thinking about selling. I've lived here for 30 years, but there have been too many of these floods lately. You just start thinking that nature is going to reclaim all of this."

But George Pineiro of Ventnor Heights said, "Leave? Why would I leave? This is the best place to live." Edye Marshall of Brant Beach said, "This was my parents' house, and that's that."

The storm started a new round of arguments about saving the beaches. Proponents pointed out that they form the core of the state's second-largest industry, tourism, which accounted for $18 billion annually even during the recession. There was too much invested to just abandon them.

Scientists shook their heads. With enough money, they agreed, the fight could be waged. How much was enough? Stuart Farrell estimated "a cost of $300 million to fix now." Put another way, it would take about $2.36 million per mile of beach to earn $141.73 million per mile. Farrell added it would cost about $30 million a year to maintain.

Mary Jo Hall, professor of Geological and Marine Sciences at Rider College in Lawrenceville, was among those who argued the beaches are migrating westward despite all efforts to retard them. "How many

*Tim Moersh/The SandPaper (top), and Frank C. Dougherty/Sipa Press*

**The December 1992 northeaster brings severe beach erosion to Harvey Cedars, top, and rips up the boardwalk in Bradley Beach, above, scenes repeated up and down the New Jersey coast.**

times do you replenish before you retreat?" In Bradley Beach, Council-woman Janet MacInnes had already conceded. "We know we have to retreat because the ocean is already up to Ocean Avenue."

Nine environmental groups gathered into The Campaign for the Coast and sent a letter to the governor and state legislators:

*It is clear that the cost of trying to hold back the ocean and re-create beaches to pre-storm conditions will run into the hundreds of millions of dollars, and even then the effectiveness of that approach is questionable.*

*It is time to rethink New Jersey's coastal land use laws and an insurance system that encourages construction in high-risk areas.*

After the 1991 Hallowe'en storm, the DEPE made up a list of the nine most-vulnerable areas on the coast. After the January 1992 storm it added three more. After the December storm it threw away the list. "Everywhere from Raritan Bay to Cape May and some places on Delaware Bay are now vulnerable," it stated.

But the winter sea had taken away the beaches before, only to have the summer sea return them. One pilot reported, "All your sand is sitting just offshore. You can see it."

"The damage would normally take five to six years of recovery in the absence of further storms," said Farrell. "Northeasters can occur almost weekly in the winter. There were eighteen in 1982-83, about eight days apart. I think retreat is in the future, one way or another."

*Tim Moersh/The* SandPaper *(both)*

**The northeaster severely floods back bay areas. Along Little Egg Harbor Bay in Tuckerton, day two of the storm also brings snow, top. Above, after the storm, a dirt dike is covered with sand at the Harvey Cedars beachfront.**

**Lightning flashes illuminate the night sky over Barnegat Bay during a severe thunderstorm in southern Ocean County July 21, 1983.**

# CHAPTER SIX

# Other Seasons, Other Storms

*On the whole, the climate of New Jersey is a compound of most of the climates of the world. It has the moisture of Ireland in spring, the heat of Africa in summer, the temperature of Italy in June, the sky of Egypt in Autumn, the snow and cold of Norway in winter, the tempests of the West Indies in every season.*
—*Rev. Jedidiah Morse, "Geography Made Easy, 1800"*

OCEAN COUNTY METEOROLOGIST George Prouflis puts the chances of a direct hit by a hurricane on the Jersey shore at 1 in 200, of a 1962-type northeaster at 1 in 8. But any year the odds are better than even that it will get thunderstorms, snowstorms, hailstorms, even tornadoes.

Thunderstorms are probably the most underestimated of nature's uproars. The weather forecasts often link them with showers, even though the rain may come down like an emptying bathtub. Usually they move too fast to interrupt the afternoon for long, but they often pack more energy per storm cell than the hurricanes that make it this far.

It was once thought that thunderstorms heralded the end of hurricanes. Father Benito Vines, a Jesuit priest in Cuba in the latter half of the nineteenth century who devoted himself to the study of hurricanes, wrote:

*The absence of electrical discharges within the cyclone is a phenomenon so constantly observed that whenever during a tempest the rolling of thunder is heard or flashes of lightning are perceived this is considered as a favorable sign indicating the speedy disappearance of the storm.*

As a bit of folk forecasting, this is true so far as it goes. It is not that the thunderstorms come along only toward the ends of hurricanes, however. It is only then that the thunder which has been there all along can be heard. Lightning, too, darts constantly about, as if stitching the rain bands of the storm together. Indeed, some observers report almost continuous lightning in the interior of tropical storms. Tom Nickerson, caught with his family on a towed barge between Atlantic City and Beach Haven in 1923, remembers the lightning. "It was insistent, it never stopped, just one steady flash, just like daylight."

In 1926 came a bolt of lightning that everyone for miles around remembered. It hit the Naval Ammunition Depot at Lake Denmark in Morris County — 456 acres of military explosives. Two vacationers driving nearby told this story:

*Everything was dead quiet and the storm seemed right on top of us. There was a tremendous clap of thunder and right on top of it, so quick that we were completely stunned, there was a horribly terrific noise that shook the whole earth. A red ball of fire leaped to the sky and our windshield shattered and spilled in broken glass around us.*

Then, in the words of David Ludlum:

*The explosions shook the country for miles around, tore houses from their foundations, hurled vehicles off the highways and darkened the sky with barrages of smoke. For many hours, big shells, depth bombs, cans of high explosives and cases of powder continued to explode as fire or a stray shell reached one building after another. Some debris was found as far as twenty-two miles from the scene.*

The next day, the *New York Tribune* described the scene. "The entire area is charred and smoking. Not a blade of grass or a green shrub remains. Trees are stripped of branches. The ground is pitted with craters. One of them is 100 feet long, 30 feet wide and 50 feet deep."

The loss was put at between $70 million and $90 million. Sixteen people in the depot and surrounding communities were killed. It was a freak hit; the Army's Picatinny Arsenal next door was untouched. But that single bolt of lightning remains the single most destructive yet recorded.

Freaks come out of the sea as well as the sky. Reports of rogue waves that seemingly emerge from nowhere to swamp ocean liners and cover whole islands are disputed by wave experts, but there are seawide seiches, tidal waves and tsunamis. There are also occasional ridges of water piled and pushed by steady winds across miles of open ocean, almost indiscernible until they mount the surprised shore. From a 1931 news account in Atlantic City:

*A terrifying series of mountain waves crashed over the beach here shortly before noon today at a point between the Steel and Central Piers, drowning one man and sweeping 70 other bathers into the swirling waters of the backwash and undertow. Lifeguards fought bravely to assist bathers to return to the safety of the beach and pandemonium reigned as the bathers struggled for their lives. The cause of the terrific waves is unknown but they are believed to have been caused by some gigantic mid-ocean upheaval.*

⁶ ⁶ ⁶

Among the reasons the Jersey shore is so popular during the summer are its winds — balmy breezes and energetic zephyrs, cooling winds and sailing winds. Winds are such a steady feature of this coast it was once proposed that a series of windmills be constructed along the length of the Garden State Parkway to generate electricity.

The most deadly winds of all have occasionally visited the coast as well — tornadoes, those fickle fingers that suddenly lower from the sky to flick away anything in their path. The phrase, "as tentative as a trailer in a tornado," gives only a small indication of their truly scary power. Not only trailers but solidly based homes, fully loaded semis, oceangoing yachts, and long-distance freight trains have been tossed about by tornadoes as if they were made of paper and gauze. Being uncommon here, they are often not recognized until they are banging on the roof. A nineteenth century news item:

*On the morning of August 17, 1876, there appeared in the atmosphere just south of the mouth of Dyers Creek a cloud having the appearance of smoke. When first seen it was to the naked eye about the size of a quart cup.*

*It kept increasing in size and came roaring like several express trains at full speed. From the cloud would run branches waving and slatting fearfully back and forth in the air and, as it crossed the salt marsh, filling the air with the new mown hay. Cows feeding in the pasture were blown to the ground.*

*Mr. Edward Sayre, with a child, sat down close to the butt of an immense tree about 2 feet in diameter and escaped unhurt. They saw the approaching tempest but did not comprehend their danger nor imagine its severity until it was upon them. A young man, Mr. Elisha Scull, living with Mr. Sayre had just gone into the parlor to try on a new pair of pants; he escaped unhurt but the pants had a big hole through the seat as if a brick had just missed his head and punctured the pants.*

*The belt of the tornado was about 200 yards wide and its track over a mile. Corn was stripped of its blades and husks, lima beans were shelled, fences blown flat; trees 12 to 18 inches in diameter were uprooted or broken off, some carried a quarter of a mile in the air without touching the ground, tossed about as if they had been feathers. Where some struck the ground great holes were dug.*

Another descended on Petersburg on July 4, 1881:

*... nearly one-fourth of a mile wide, of sufficient force to blow down three barns, shift buildings from their foundations; one tin roof was rolled up in a bundle.*

And north of Seaside Park on October 4, 1849:

*The occupants heard an immense roar of wind passing over the top of their home but so high up as to do them no damage. It swept down into the hollow near the Lee barn, twisting one corner of it, then crushing one house owned by Samuel Godfrey to the ground and breaking it into fragments without injuring anyone seriously. Then as it rose up the hill it carried away the upper half of Jonas Corson's home, together with his first wife, Rachel, and her sisters who were sleeping in a large room, carrying them eight rods or more.*

The Jersey shore is not a prime breeding ground for tornadoes, and when they do erupt here they generally unravel again within a few minutes, traveling perhaps a tenth of a mile in that time on a track only a few yards wide. There have been occasional stemwinders inland, including one that unzipped the landscape for forty miles between Red Lion and Seaside Park in 1941. The biggest contemporary shore-borne tornado skipped through about thirty miles of lightly populated areas in Cape May County on August 27, 1971. It was thought to be part of the entourage of tropical storm Doria.

The mini-tornado that hopped around southern Ocean County on the evening of July 27, 1983, gave a few people a rare look at this twisted quirk of weather. Louise Hannold was living next to a supermarket in Manahawkin. "I didn't know what to think, I didn't know where to hide. Debris was flying through the air, and it sounded like trains going over the house." She ran from room to room, dodging produce from the market that had turned into deadly missiles. The winds took off her roof and toppled a half-dozen trees in her yard, one of which crushed her car. "Still, I was very lucky. It could have been worse."

John Duane was working at a liquor store nearby when what he thought was a thunderstorm blew open the automatic doors and cracked the front windows. Fearing sheets of glass would "act as a guil-

*Ray Fisk/United Press International (both)*

**Two North Beach homes smashed by a tornado on July 21, 1983. Opposite, the wreckage that greeted Dottie Waite when she escaped from the bedroom in which she had been trapped. Above, another bayfront home, where neighbors found the family huddled in the bathroom.**

lotine," he crouched behind a fortress of liquor cases while sand, leaves and rocks blew through the store. Outside he could see shopping carts sailing by.

On Long Beach Island, Dottie Waite said she heard a whooshing sound. The weather had been "oppressive" and, expecting rain, she ran to the bedroom to close windows when the wind "sucked the door shut behind me." When she tried to get out, the force of the wind held the door, trapping her. She heard unearthly noises on the other side. "Everything got completely black. I felt like I was in *Poltergeist*." She remained captive in her bedroom while the tornado peeled off the roof and wrecked the interior. "It opened closets, it opened the refrigerator door and pulled everything out on the floor, it lifted up furniture and turned it upside down. The front room looked as if it were a doll's house and someone had just taken a spoon and stirred everything around." Three days later the rains did come, soaking everything inside the unroofed house.

Although tornadoes are seldom-seen bogeymen on the Jersey coast, they occur at the height of summer out of clear, sunshiny skies, smashing ice cream stands and beach bungalows, spoilers at the party. Snowstorms, on the other hand, come at the other end of the year, the bottom of winter when the sky is the color of tin cans and old bedsheets and the sea flings stinging spray at anyone who dares to walk upon the beach. When the first soft flakes begin to transform that landscape, even fence posts become magic wands.

But snowstorms are deceptive, both beautiful and terrible, a child's fantasy and a grownup's nightmare. A deep, drifting, down-the-shore blizzard spat out of the mouth of a cold-booted snowstorm disrupts every bit as much as a hurricane, taking control of lives, bringing all activity to a standstill, imposing its own rhythms on the world and making its own rules, the penalty for breaking which can be death. People are warm-blooded creatures who need heat to survive. Blizzards sap the very stuff of existence.

One of the first big blizzards to be recorded on the East Coast was called the Great Snow of February 1717, as described in a letter from New England minister Cotton Mather:

*On the twentieth there came on a snow, which being added unto what had covered the ground a few days before made a thicker mantle for our mother than what was usual. And ye storm with it was for the following days so violent as to make all communication between ye neighbors everywhere to cease. People could not pass from one side of a street unto another. But on ye twenty-fourth day of ye month comes Pelion upon Ossa. Another snow came on which almost buried ye town. For no less than eight and twenty days after the storm, the people pulling out the ruins of an 100 sheep out of a snowbank which lay 16 feet high over them, there was two found alive, which had kept themselves alive by eating the wool of their dead companions.*

During what was called the Hard Winter of 1780, George Washington kept a weather diary that records three severe snowstorms within two weeks of one another that buried the countryside with three to five feet, and then a long cold spell which kept it there. He had no thermometer, but the British, warm and snug in New York City, recorded a temperature of minus sixteen degrees Fahrenheit. It was the only time in recorded history when both New York and Delaware bays froze over with ice heavy enough to support cannons.

In their book, *Shipwrecks*, David Seibold and Charles Adams III wrote, "The darkness and bone-cracking cold of the dead of winter on the seas off Long Beach Island must be experienced to be fully understood." They tell the story of the wreck of the Austrian bark *Kraljevica*, "before modern navigational equipment and creature-comforting conveniences," in February 1886:

> *The bark was sailing close, too close, to the Jersey coast when the shoals of Barnegat punched her and bilged her, adding her cargo of salt to the already briny depths.*

The crew sent up a flare, then took to the long boat. A wave capsized it and the sea claimed eight of the men. Six others made it to the beach and found a duck hunters' shelter where they weathered the night. Meanwhile, the flare had been seen and a rescue boat went out from Barnegat Light.

Ludlum, it "achieved a historical reputation unrivaled by any other," attacking New Jersey with "unprecedented fury." Blocked in its passage by a weather front to the north, much as the Great Atlantic Storm was in March 1962, it marked time east of Cape May for a day, then proceeded slowly to a position east of Long Island where it stalled again. Snow fell on the Jersey shore for the better part of two days. No official reckoning of the amount was possible because the high winds not only made it difficult to measure but blew away most of the instruments.

Snowfall rates rarely exceed an inch per hour, and storms rarely last longer than eight hours. Average annual snowfall at Atlantic City is 15 inches. It has experienced almost double that, but it has also had as little as one centimeter in a season. It was estimated that the blizzard of 1888 deposited over two feet of snow during its passage. Some observers put it up to three feet. Winds were clocked at gale force, rising to 80 miles per hour at times, or over hurricane force. Newspapers were vivid in description:

> *The snow was drifted in huge heaps, and packed so solidly as to bear a man's weight. It was useless for man or beast to brave the fury of the gale. The frozen particles of snow cut the face with acute pain.*
>
> *The air was thick with snow and the frame buildings were groaning and trembling as if they were ready to fly apart. Few people slept.*
>
> *The snow fell continuously and was drifted and whirled nearly to the tops of first story windows, and in some places as high as the street lamps.*

*The life-savers fought against the searing gale winds and rabid surf to reach the distressed bark. Rowing, straining, every ounce of courage and strength being put to the ultimate test, the crew battled its way for two gruelling hours and came to within 50 yards of the stricken vessel only to have their hopes crushed. They had no idea the crew had abandoned ship. The men brought their boat around and made for the shore. But about 400 yards from that sandy haven, a massive swell overturned the boat, drowning three men.*

The Austrian government, in tribute and gratitude, sent money to aid the families of the dead men, and the U.S. Congress authorized marble monuments to them at the Barnegat cemetery.

Heavy snowstorms often follow the same track as many of the hurricanes New Jersey gets, up from the south on a line from Cape Hatteras to Cape Cod. None ever equaled the storm that embraced an area from Virginia to Maine from March 11 to 14, 1888. In the words of David

*Ray Fisk/The* New York Times *(above) and United Press International (right)*
**After a coastal snowstorm on January 11, 1985 cross-country skiers traverse the beach. At right, Lucy the Elephant, Margate's National Historic Landmark, stands unblinking in toe-deep snow, December 1979.**

*The roads are obstructed by fallen trees and telegraph poles, and the rural districts are as unexplored regions.*

*The early train to New York got as far as Red Bank and then got stuck. The engineer loosened the locomotive from the rest of the train and tried to force his way through the drifts, expecting then to return for the rest of he train. He succeeded in getting about a hundred yards and then could go no further, and on starting to return to the train found that the snow had drifted in behind him so much that he could not get back.*

Another train made it from Toms River to Whiting, nine miles up the line, but it took four hours. Snow so filled the streets of Toms River that no stores could open, even if someone could get to them. The second day of the storm was election day but few made it to the polls. Historian Thomas Farner recounts the story of a milkman named Xavier Zwinge who chose to wait out the storm in a local tavern:

*His horse decided to make the trek home to the barn. Zwinge's wife reported him missing. "Alone (a local newsman surmised) he had gone to his reward in that blizzard-swept wasteland." A couple of days later, milkman Zwinge trudged home where neighbors were consoling his grieving widow. "I wasn't dead, just drunk."*

Long Beach Island got not only the snow, but also the direct impact of the northeaster that delivered it, complete with flooding tides. At Beach Haven, water washed over the railroad tracks and froze, covering the rails with three inches of ice. During the night, the schooner *Whim* dragged anchor at Barnegat Inlet and was driven out to sea, stranding on the shoals and necessitating a lifesaving boat to go out in the subfreezing gale to rescue the crew. A sloop full of oysters was waiting out the storm off Little Egg Harbor Inlet when its anchor chains gave way and it went ashore on Tucker's Beach. All the oysters froze.

The *New Jersey Courier* reported that Delaware Bay was "a field of ice." Ocean County received the most snow. Toms River was shut off from the outside world for three days.

*The only team out Monday was Brewer's big sleigh, and after making a trip to the Pennsylvania Railroad station in the morning and getting nearly stalled in a snowbank on Washington Street, Ben put his team up and enjoyed a holiday. On Tuesday morning every storekeeper was shoveling snow — there being little or nothing else for them to do — and by noon they had a good roadway for pedestrians in the business part of town.*

But apparently nobody got that far. The storm had started on Saturday. It wasn't until Wednesday that some trains were able to resume their schedules.

❞ ❞ ❞

It wasn't snow but a blinding winter fog, thick as bad karma and disorienting as a waking dream, that stranded the Army transport *Sumner* on Barnegat Shoals in December 1916 with four hundred troops aboard. She struck right off Twelfth Street in Barnegat Light. The weather was so impenetrable the captain couldn't see the lighthouse beacon. He said he had no

idea what part of the coast he was on. The ship radioed an SOS which was picked up by the Coast Guard station in Sandy Hook; word was passed down the coast. Every station started looking until the Barnegat station finally found her and got everyone off. It was four days before tides and tugs could work the vessel free.

Icy weather returned the next winter, culminating in February 1918, when the ocean off Atlantic City got so cold it froze out to the ends of the piers. But for almost two decades thereafter, bad weather seemed to have found other places to spend the winter. Predicting another mild winter for 1934-35, one commentator noted the unusual wetness of autumn, however, which he said was often a sign of a change in the climate "that is expected sooner or later."

And in 1935, the cold came early, sending Labor Day crowds shivering home. From the *Philadelphia Inquirer*:

*Ray Fisk/The* New York Times *(both)*

**During a frigid spell in late January 1985, the commercial fishing boat *Theodora* has to break through four inches of ice before it can tie up at its Barnegat Light dock, opposite. Above, arctic sea smoke, a condition caused by extremely cold air temperature, rises over the ocean off Long Beach Island.**

*By the thousands they poured wearily back into Philadelphia last night — the same throng that trekked so merrily to the shore for the Labor Day weekend. The movement of more than one million from Atlantic City started around noon, about an hour after a discouraged sun was chased away by heavy clouds.*

This was the same year that fishermen reported seeing icebergs off the coast of Long Beach Island in June. In January came "raging sleet storms that swept into Ocean County from the arctic wastes," later to turn into "raging blizzards," according to the *Beach Haven Times*:

*Wires started to sag and break, roads became skating rinks, streets were filled with men and boys trying to break a path through the drifts. With the fall of night the temperature tobogganed. The car of Mr. and Mrs. C. Burke was stopped behind one of the county road scrapers which was stalled on the Plains road, necessitating a long walk into Tuckerton by the couple.*

*Nearing town, Mrs. Burke collapsed and was carried by her husband until he gave out and was compelled to leave her on the ground and go for help. On reaching the DeLuxe Diner on Main Street, Mr. Burke collapsed and was brought around by Arthur Marshall and the lunch car man. On hearing the man's story, Marshall went in search of the woman and managed to carry her as far as the Methodist Church on North Green Street. It took nearly a half hour to revive her.*

The next year the bays froze, lifting docks five to ten feet out of the water. To free the 300-foot dock at the Beach Haven Yacht Club, workmen cut out blocks of ice thirty-seven inches thick. Even Niagara Falls froze solid that year.

But it wasn't until 1947 that the next blitz hit, when it snowed for twenty-three hours and forty-five minutes and gave the shore its whitest day-after-Christmas ever. The storm "put civilization on hold," wrote reporter Robert McMenimen.

*Buses were helpless. A Public Service dispatcher reported, "I keep sending them out and then I never hear from them again." By nightfall, the company said that 122 of its commuter lines had foundered. Deliveries ceased. Utility wires went down as if scythed. Trains were running, so to speak, but reaching a station to board one became a life and death struggle. Commuters stood in doleful herds at the major intersections, stirred to frantic waving and shouting when a rare bus, already jammed to its baggage racks, hove into sight and almost invariably drove on without stopping.*

Despite the date, the Christmas spirit apparently did not touch everyone.

*Looting of stalled cars became the crime of the night. With variations. Two men tinkering with the engine of an ostensibly stalled car asked a passerby for help. As the pedestrian leaned over to peer under the open*

*hood he was slugged with a wrench and relieved of two rings, a watch and his wallet.*

Another decade passed, another blizzard piled up to twenty inches of snow on the shore. It was February 1958, and the snow fell so thickly that roads had to be plowed every two hours. Many cars had been abandoned where they stalled, presenting an obstacle course for plowing crews who were having enough trouble trying to find the roads. A man in Toms River died of a heart attack when a first aid squad bearing oxygen tanks was delayed by drifts; the doctor forged through the last mile of snow on foot, then collapsed himself. Another heart attack victim died in a hunting cabin near Tuckerton while his son was hiking through snowdrifts to fetch his medicine. Ten men in two trucks, four cars and a snow plow rescued a Boy Scout troop that was camping out in the Pine Barrens. "The boys had enough wood for the night but were short of food. They reused some coffee grounds four times and Sunday dinner was white bread and jam," reported one rescuer. That storm was the sixth of the season.

Twenty years later, in 1978, a single storm spread more snow over the Jersey shore than the total of all snowfalls in between. It was the product of what might be termed a frustrated Alberta Clipper, a cold weather system

that comes out of the northwest. Meteorologist George Prouflis saw it coming five days in advance.

*We get a lot of them in an average year. Usually they are innocent, starved for moisture, and pass out to sea. But there was a storm out there already that blocked it. It slowed down and exploded over the Jersey shore. The last time that happened was 1888.*

The storm started just past midnight on February 6 and continued to just before the following midnight.

*The closer you got to the beach the heavier the snowfall. Usually the heavier snowfall is inland because the ocean warms it to rain here, but this one picked up moisture from the ocean and dumped it right back as snow. By morning the winds were gale force (35 miles per hour) and the snow was falling at the rate of two to four inches an hour. Throughout the day it got heavier and heavier and the winds got stronger and stronger. At one point, I clocked them at 91 miles per hour. I went outside. It was a total whiteout; you couldn't see across the road for hours. There were drifts eighteen feet high. I estimated a total fall of thirty-four inches, which would be a record if it were official. If you classified it on a scale of one to five, it would be a five. It was the worst to hit the Jersey shore in the twentieth century.*

A year later, in January 1979, a snowstorm isolated Atlantic City for three days and the city almost ran out of food. In 1987, Atlantic, Cape May and Ocean counties were put under a state of emergency with only essential traffic permitted. Casinos offered guests cut-rate rooms. Most businesses on the coast closed. "It's not a tough question," said one. "There's no one here so it's kind of pointless to remain open." Sears department store at Seaview Square Mall in Ocean Township stayed open. "Believe it or not, we had customers come in and shop," said manager Robert Butler. "Our snowblowers were sold out."

And in 1989, blowing in before a forecasted white Thanksgiving, near-hurricane force winds caused an "unusual event" at the Oyster Creek nuclear power plant in Forked River. "The strength of the wind changed the direction of water flow from the bay and we were forced to reduce our power output because there was not enough water coming in to cool the reactor at full power," said spokesperson Sanford Polon. An "unusual event" is the lowest of four emergency situations at nuclear plants, a "nonroutine event of no risk to the public or the environment."

Severe eastern blizzards generally involve a vast spread of the country, often covering everything from Chicago east and reaching as far south as Texas and Florida, but they are fickle in local intensity. The otherworldly look they give to the landscape can be exciting and inspiring, but it means, in fact, that the everyday world has changed and cannot be treated the same. Their beauty is as evanescent as a snowflake, but their consequences can be forever.

❝❝❝

It has snowed in New Jersey as early as October and as late as May. That means there are only four months where the chances of seeing snow are those of the proverbial snowball in hell. But a hail ball, that's something else again. Hailstorms occur in warm weather, often accompanying thunder-

storms. The stones have been sized from rice-grains to grapefruit, with peas, mothballs, walnuts and golf balls the usual comparisons. A news account of a June hailstorm in 1742 describes them simply as of "amazing bigness."

*We are informed that in one house they struck twenty-eight holes through the roof. The damage to grain is so great that some who had already brought their last crop to the market countermand the same, lest they should want bread.*

From a magazine article in the spring of 1758:

*I was a spectator at one of the most extraordinary storms of hail as perhaps has been seen in America. At first there came a little rain but was soon followed by some large stones of hail for the space of eight or ten minutes, when appeared to me a most amazing prospect — it seemed as if the whole body of the clouds were falling. The street appeared as another Delaware full of floating ice, and the air seemed a cataract. I tho't in the midst of it of Noah's flood. The thickest of it continued about fifteen or twenty minutes more. After it was over the ground looked as if there had been a snow, some of which remained till night notwithstanding it continued warm after the storm.*

Though usually local, some storms can blast strips up to two miles wide for five or ten miles. From a July 1853 news story:

*The hailstones ranged in bulk from the size of peas and hickory nuts to the dimensions of hens' eggs. Wheat &c were cut to pieces and swept away like chaff. Hundreds of acres of corn and oats utterly destroyed. The window glass of every house within the area was, for the most part, demolished. Poultry, birds, rabbits &c were killed by the pitiless pelting and, strange as it may seem, we learn that two cows fell victim to the icy volleys. A large scope of land was stripped as completely as if a hostile army had passed over it.*

In June 1906, the fall of hail lasted for an hour in some places. In May 1925, egg-sized hail that fell in Ocean County remained on the ground in some spots for three days. In November 1970, Point Pleasant got wind, rain, lightning and hail in one walloping thunderstorm.

❝❝❝

Thunderstorms visit the Jersey shore in summer as regularly as tourists. The state depends on them for much of the precipitation that keeps its farms green and its reservoirs full. But their formative processes are the same as those for hurricanes, and they can be as destructive as a cannon with hiccups. Major Joseph Duckworth, the first person to fly into a hurricane, said he had encountered more turbulence in a fully formed thunderstorm.

Mature storms can rise to sixty thousand feet, dominating wide swaths of landscape. Their tops are flattened into the familiar anvil shape by shearing winds at the base of the stratosphere. Inside, lightning and thunder make it seem as if the gods are indeed at play, or at war. There can be snow and hail as well as rain at different levels, with violent rushes of air rising and falling and, frequently, funnels of incipient tornadoes.

The shore experiences from twenty to thirty of these a season, usually in late afternoon or early evening. Since they don't last long and generally indicate the end of a heat wave or the start of a cool one, they are usually welcome — unless you're in an airship.

*Ray Fisk*

**A summer storm moves out to sea, Harvey Cedars, July 1983.**

The USS *Akron* took off from Lakehurst Naval Air Station on the evening of April 3, 1933, on a training flight bound for Rhode Island. Fog was rolling in from the ocean, so the airship first headed west. Over Wilmington, Delaware, Commander Frank McCord spotted lightning and turned the ship east again and then northeast across New Jersey. By 9 P.M., turbulence and lightning were reported moving up behind her and the *Akron* headed out to sea.

At 11 P.M., the ship was surrounded by intense lightning streaking air to ground, ground to air, cloud to cloud. McCord headed for the coastline and arrived at the vicinity of Barnegat Light about midnight with a hard decision to make. There was too much turbulence to attempt a landing back at Lakehurst. He decided to try to outrun the storm over the sea rather than the land. There was a strong wind, with light rain and fog reducing visibility, and he was wary of obstructions on shore.

He pointed the *Akron* southeast, but the ship encountered a downdraft and began to lose altitude. Ballast was dropped and she leveled off but within moments was caught in another. Her rate of descent was an alarming fourteen feet per second. A desperate attempt to break out by gunning the engines only raised her nose and dipped her tail into the sea. Unable to fight free, the *Akron* was remorselessly pulled under. The ship didn't have enough lifesaving gear. Most of the crew were still green. Of the seventy-six aboard, only three survived, rescued by a German freighter which happened to be close enough to see the airship's lights disappearing into the water. During a congressional inquiry, officials commented that another one hundred feet of altitude might have saved the vessel.

The world's most famous airship disaster was, of course, the *Hindenberg*, at the Lakehurst Naval Air Station on May 6, 1937. There has never been a satisfactory conclusion as to the cause of the explosion that brought it down. Captain Max Pruss recorded:

> *We had bad weather. About two o'clock we were over New York, made a few circles and then went on to Lakehurst. Then we saw a big thunderstorm over New Jersey and we knew we couldn't land and thought it better to go back to the sea. We went along the coast to Atlantic City and back, and we waited for the storm to blow over.*

A little after 6 P.M., Lakehurst radioed, "Conditions now considered suitable for landing." It was another hour before the ship was in position over the field. There was some light rain and occasional flashes of lightning off to the south, but the skies were clearing. Lines were dropped at 7:21, and almost immediately the ship erupted in flames. It could have been a spark or a burst of St. Elmo's fire — static electricity. It could have been sabotage. The gas bags were full of flammable hydrogen, since the United States was the only source of inert helium and would not sell to a Germany it considered increasingly hostile. Almost anything could have set it off, and almost nothing could have prevented it.

Despite the impression given by the unforgettable newsreel that every unfortunate soul on board must have perished, however, almost two-thirds of the ninety-six passengers and crewmen survived.

**Harvey Cedars, after the Great Atlantic Storm of 1962. Major coastal storms may seem infrequent, but their power and destruction can not be ignored.**

# CHAPTER SEVEN

# Irresistible Forces, Immovable Objects

*And everyone that heareth these pronouncements of mine and doeth them not shall be likened unto a foolish man which buildeth his house upon the sand. And the rain descended and the floods came and the winds blew and beat upon that house, and it fell; and great was the fall of it.*

*— Matthew, Chapter 7*

AFTER THE GREAT ATLANTIC STORM of 1962 left the coastline bent and broken, an editorial in the *Trenton Times* pointed out, "The New Jersey shore, as a long history of disaster demonstrates, lives precariously."

Governor Richard Hughes said, "We can't let this happen again," and stressed that "even without the disaster, New Jersey's shoreline is a chronic victim of erosion...We have learned that our shoreline will remain vulnerable until we take the necessary permanent protective measures. Now is the time for clear thinking about the future."

An editorial in *New Jersey County Government* said, "Storms are often like wars. They give man a fresh opportunity to build better and plan wiser. This is the `second chance' now given to the resort counties of Monmouth, Ocean, Atlantic and Cape May. Hard and expensive decisions must be made."

Recommendations ranged from abandoning the barrier islands to the sea to so armoring them with rock jetties and concrete sea walls as to make them impervious to any further attacks. The abandonment forces argued that the islands are supposed to be washed over by storms every now and then. In the process, however, they tend to migrate westward, the storms removing sand from the oceanside and carrying it over to the bayside. Unfortunately they take along anything built on the sand as well. Abandonment as a solution did not find wide support along the Jersey beaches. As James Mancini, mayor of Long Beach Township, said:

> *We know that the people on this island and Atlantic City are not going to donate their property for the benefit of 200 years from now because the ocean is rising. Regardless of whether it's right, wrong, middle, backwards — it's not going to happen.*

The armorers argued that the only way to stop the sea was to create massive structures that would turn it back, a Great-Wall-of-China approach. But, lacking slave labor, there was the question of how to pay for them. There was also the question of what they might do to the beach. To Orrin H. Pilkey, professor of geology at Duke University, there was no question. He described a post-wall beach:

> *Rubble from pre-existing sea walls, groins, revetments and the like clutter the beach in front of the sea wall. No sand is visible except, perhaps, at extreme low tide. The shoreface has steepened considerably and, as a result, wave energy is high. No longer do large waves trip over offshore sandbars. Instead all waves — large and small — impinge directly on the sea wall and are reflected onto a narrowed and usually submerged beach at its foot.*

In his opinion, such structures not only do not save beaches but accelerate their erosion. Supporters of this view cite the examples at Deal, Sea Bright and Ocean City. As the sea sweeps away the sand, the wall is undermined and eventually topples, requiring installation of a larger wall. It's a sort of arms race that can end only in the erection of vast dikes like those in Holland or in the sea having its way.

Two strategies finally emerged: raise the dunes and raise the houses.

"Our sand dunes — quite simply — are all that stand between us and the Atlantic Ocean," said Jerome Walnut, president of the Long Beach Island Conservation Society.

> *Long Beach Island is a sand bar, and sand bars are very fragile, shifting geological formations. Our maps, some of which go back for 200 or 300 years, tell us Barnegat Inlet has moved south by over a mile in the past 100 years, and the island as a whole a considerable distance to the west.*

The Hallowe'en storm of 1991 uncovered the remains of a village on the beaches of Cape Cod said to have been inhabited for thousands of years up to about a thousand years ago. Archaeologists said it was originally five miles from the shore. Noted Walnut:

> *There is very little likelihood that anything that we can put up in the way of jetties, groins or bulkheads will appreciably affect this pattern. Our best recourse is to adopt the tactics used by Nature herself in the constant interplay between the elements. A flexible defense of open, sloping beach backed up by wide, well-grassed sand dunes has held our island in the past, and if we have any sense at all we should use this to protect ourselves in the future.*

Mancini said it depended on the dune. "You have the aesthetic, picturesque kind, and you have the protective kind. There's a distinctive difference. People say, `We had huge sand dunes.' They were worthless as far as protection. You need a sand dune wall." Some of the dunes that had been built up before the Great Atlantic Storm had steel bones to them. "We had a lot of erosion from 1957 to 1962, so we stockpiled old cars to start new dunes." They were among the ones that proved to be worthless, but after the 1962 storm, many of the houses wrecked on the beach were buried in place for the same purpose. Architect Beryl Price advised building the dunes of hay and seeds as well as sand. He said that his grassy dune had held up well, while on either side of it, the storm had taken out those made of sand alone. People took to piling old Christmas trees at the back of the beach — anything to make the sand stand tall.

The Harvey Cedars borough council passed a resolution which among its various "whereases" stated, "Whereas it is in the best interests of the municipality to restore the sand dunes, vegetation and other protections which heretofore existed along the shore line," the borough would now therefore, among other things, "...acquire all lands, easements and rights of way deemed necessary for placement of beach fill and sand fences as required...and maintain the restored and constructed protective dunes."

But there were those who doubted that dunes could do the job. Certainly they had been inadequate under the determined assault of the 1962 storm's five tides. Other methods were proposed, but sea wall advocates countered them all in the introduction to an ordinance in Long Beach Township:

*1. The use of old ships sunk along our beaches as protection: There has been no real experience with these, plus the fact that we have never been able to obtain any, even for trial purposes. 2. Erection of a sand dike, as proposed by army engineers: There is insufficient room to erect a proper dike. 3. Erection of sand dunes and planting of the natural grass: Again, insufficient space, and it would take too long for the grass to grow.*

Bob Bahner

**Old cars that had been used to help nature build the dunes prove useless against a relentless tidal assault in 1962. Some were exposed again in December 1992.**

Concluded the argument: "The erection of a bulkhead ... would give us the best permanent protection we could obtain quickly.

There was, however, a snag. The Army Corps of Engineers had established the defense line considerably landward of that proposed by the township, "leaving exposed to the Atlantic Ocean our most valuable assets comprised of homes, other structures, parking areas, utilities, roads and other facilities." The Army Engineers were, it was claimed, insensitive to the local economy.

According to the minutes of another township meeting, "The people of Holgate inquired whether it was true the U.S. Army Engineers were taking over the old road for the new dune." The engineers had ruled the beachfront irreclaimable at the southern tip of the island and wanted to move the main road to the bayside. Residents objected and proceeded on their own to construct a sand dike ten feet above mean high water. They dredged the bay to restore the beach and planted rows of snow fences to build dunes.

It was argued by some that in another 1962-type storm neither a high dune nor a sea wall would last. What was needed was that "open, sloping beach." The problem was, as U.S. Secretary of the Interior Stewart Udall put it, "Private property. Ninety percent of this limited, highly desirable resource is under private control. The seashore is big business."

He pointed out that areas such as Island Beach State Park in New Jersey and Cape Hatteras National Seashore in North Carolina — "where nature's balance is relatively untouched" — escaped serious damage.

"The question has been asked, `What will the East Coast be like in ten years?' The signposts of the future should be clear." He called for "bold vision and determined action.... To save this priceless heritage we must muster the spirit of sacrifice needed to get the job done. We stand at the threshold of a new — and final — opportunity."

He proposed that a 400-foot strip along the entire coast be cleared, relocating some buildings, buying some, condemning some. Park Service Director Conrad Wirth said, "There is no doubt that it will be less expensive over a period of years than repeating emergency repairs and replacements." The reaction was predictable, if deplorable. As June Methot reported:

*Before the papers were even printed there was another sort of storm created by owners of beachfront property. Each demanded restoration of "his piece of the beach" right where it had been! The Corps of Engineers is answerable to elected officials and elected officials are answerable to voters, so they gave in, despite good advice from all manner of well-informed sources that it was unsafe and impractical and would lead to enormous public cost for future maintenance and protection.*

The Ocean County Board of Chosen Freeholders voted to ask the federal government to consider New Jersey's ocean beaches as a "virtual national park area contributing to the health and happiness of the nation" and to contribute to its protection. The resolution did not deal with public access to sections of this national park that were in private hands, despite Udall's further recommendation that "it may well be the time to encourage dedication of those restored beaches to public use." What most seaside governments have in mind with such proposals is federal guarantees of their tax base, not seeing their ratables disappear under piles of new sand and day-trippers.

*Ray Fisk/*The New York Times

**After a March 1984 northeaster washed away beaches and undermined homes in Harvey Cedars, bulldozers push sand to create dunes over a dirt dike.**

If a wider beach wasn't practical, a higher house was. Harvey Cedars was one of the first to rule that "hereafter, all buildings to be constructed or placed on any site" shall be placed on pilings. None, it added, "may be placed upon the top of or on the ocean side of a sand dune, dike or berm." The seven houses that Beryl Price had designed withstood the 1962 storm. He recommended pilings sunk to a depth at least below that of the sea floor, but noted, "The island is a hazardous place, despite the claims of the Chamber of Commerce and the local Realtors. If we get into a good nor'easter we gotta be lucky, pilings or no pilings."

The pilings requirement was soon adopted by shore communities everywhere. Not only oceanfront buildings had to be set up out of reach of the waves but also any building on lands that had been flooded by storm waters, or were likely to be. Said Mayor Mancini:

*The ambiguity of the '62 storm was that all that was left was a row of sentinels on the oceanfront. Why? Because that was the only place we used*

*pilings. Now we use pilings all over. I would estimate a repetition of that storm would produce only 15 percent of the damage we had. The island is a lot better off because of the storm.... We have flood insurance, we have building restrictions, we have a building line, we have elevation ordinances, we have new jetties ... we have everything that is good for the protection and preservation of our beaches.*

Pilkey disagrees.

*Beaches and buildings are safe only until the next big storm. The methods fail in the long run because human effort, no matter how costly, cannot indefinitely offset the impact of rising sea levels on the open coast and sandy beaches. It is this rise, which began to accelerate over fifty years ago, that causes coastlines to retreat landward. A more sensible approach must start with the recognition that erosion and shifts in beaches are part of a larger natural system. Planning must be based on long-term projections, not short-term objectives.*

*U.S. Coast Guard*

**Cape May Point, 1922. Shore towns and residents build wooden jetties in an attempt to stake the beach in place, but with little success.**

Mancini does not have much patience with that view and challenged Pilkey on the problem at a conference held in Atlantic City:

> *Orrin Pilkey knows nothing about our beach. His whole thing is not to spend any money on beach protection because you could lose it and it's a waste of money. He pointed out where they put in $5 million worth of fill in Atlantic City and it's all gone, so they wasted their money. Then I got up and said, "Hey Professor Pilkey, I certainly respect your knowledge and your theory. You're probably right. I have a better way of saving money. Everybody sitting in this room, in the casino, walking on the boardwalk, is going to die. There's nothing we can do about that. So I propose we do away with medical care because it wastes money."*

Pilkey may not have to win any battles to win the war. Two beachfront homeowners in Ocean City recently sued to prevent the construction of dunes in front of their homes and won. The court's decision was that private ownership precludes the city's right to build dunes. In another case, a property owner actually got the city to remove a dune in front of his house that was blocking his view.

When South Carolina tried to institute measures to prevent the building of new construction close to the beach or rebuilding storm-wrecked houses on the same precarious spots, the resistance from property owners and developers, as well as the towns that depend on constant growth for growing ratables, was so intense that the state cut back its requirements. Attempts in New Jersey to impose limits on construction and reconstruction by the beach have raised similar rants about the heavy hand of government poking into private property and squashing individual rights. But when the sea washes the beach away, the cries for that same hand to reach in and put it back again are even louder. In 1963, New Jersey Commissioner of Conservation Mat Adams pointed out that "the Atlantic Coast states have spent over $200 million since 1946 to repair and rebuild" the shoreline.

It is, perhaps, easy to watch impudent beach houses reduced to used lumber and scrap metal and shrug and say tsk-tsk and refuse to donate public funds for the continuation of such folly. But what about Sam Kartman, who, before the Great Atlantic Storm, owned and operated a colony of fifty-six cabins in Brigantine? He lost fifty-three of them.

> *They went to Pensacola, maybe Siberia. The rest went down to the city dump. Everything in life isn't owning cabins. Still, everything we had in the world was right here. My wife and I wanted to start again but we didn't know how. After the storm there wasn't anyone who didn't think we were finished. But a human being is not finished until he's dead.*

There are twenty different government agencies that have something to do with the coast and its development, some not so obvious as others. It was the federal Small Business Administration that gave Kartman a twenty-year, $200,000 loan to rebuild.

> *I don't know of any country where the government would reach down and pick up a little nobody like me. Without government like that where would people like us be?*

The federal Environmental Protection Agency gave grants for some rebuilding. The Department of Housing and Urban Development subsidized some, and so did several state agencies. Nor was it only official sources that were available to the storm-dispossessed. The Red Cross gave "outright grants with no strings attached" to those otherwise unable to finance rebuilding or repairing "permanent homes" or small businesses. "Of course, we will not replace TV sets or refrigerators and things like that," the spokesperson added.

There are always old-timers on hand, too, to assure that the sea will give back again next season whatever it takes away this. Not only is this piece of folklore measurably untrue, but it seems that when the sea does give back pieces of beach, it doesn't always do it in the same place. In 1971, the beaches of Ocean City were a block wide, while those of Longport were barely able to provide for a decent volleyball patch. Then the situation reversed until the sea was coming all the way up underneath sections of the boardwalk in Ocean City while it added acres to the beach at Longport. No one knows which way it might go in the future.

Some scientists have discerned patterns, however. Robert Dolan and Bruce Hayden, both professors of environmental sciences at the University of Virginia, pointed out that "the Ash Wednesday storm of 1962 caused severe erosion in the same locations as previous storms." The same seems true of the slower processes that change the profiles of the coastline, except that they are accelerating.

> *To date, shoreline rates-of-change measurements have been completed for the 1,000 kilometers (about 621 miles) of Atlantic Shoreline between New Jersey and North Carolina. The shoreline erosion rate for this area is 1.5 meters (about five feet) per year.*

Previous estimates had been two to three feet a year. Some hold it is only about one inch. Pilkey claims that in some places it's closer to fifty feet, more than enough to overwhelm some barrier islands entirely. As Rich Youmans wrote in the *SandPaper*:

> *The sea is godlike in its powers of creation and destruction — an apathetic god whose mystery can suck an island into its currents, pile or retract sand along the coast, and alter a shoreline into a memory.*

Stuart Farrell cites the example of Tucker's Island, once located just south of Long Beach Island and one of the first resorts on the coast, dating back to 1745. By 1807, a beach joined it to Long Beach Island. Some thirty years later it was separated again, only to be linked again in another thirty years. At the beginning of this century, a community flourished there, but by 1930 the sea had cut it off once more and by 1950, Tucker's Island had all but disappeared beneath the waves. In the early 1990s, however, it started to rise again, and Farrell predicted that by the end of the century it would look as it did at the beginning, "provided no one screws around with it."

❝ ❝ ❝

As Josephine Reider was being evacuated from Barnegat Light in 1962, she observed, "The ocean gives us the island and then takes it away. It's just caprice."

Immediately after the 1944 hurricane, editorials in the *Asbury Park Press* argued:

> *The prospect of replacing expensive beachfront structures every decade or less, depending on the whims of nature, can no longer be followed. It is vital that hereafter the possibility and even probability of devastating storms be taken into account before capital is invested along the beachfront. But the only protection against this hazard is to plan now to erect all new structures far enough from the surf reasonably to insure them against destruction.*

*Ocean County Historical Society*

*Ray Fisk/The* SandPaper

**A house that once stood two blocks from Barnegat Inlet provides a view of the water that may be too close for comfort by 1930, left. It was remodeled and threatened again in 1982, and now is fortunate to stand on a site protected by a new $35 million inlet jetty.**

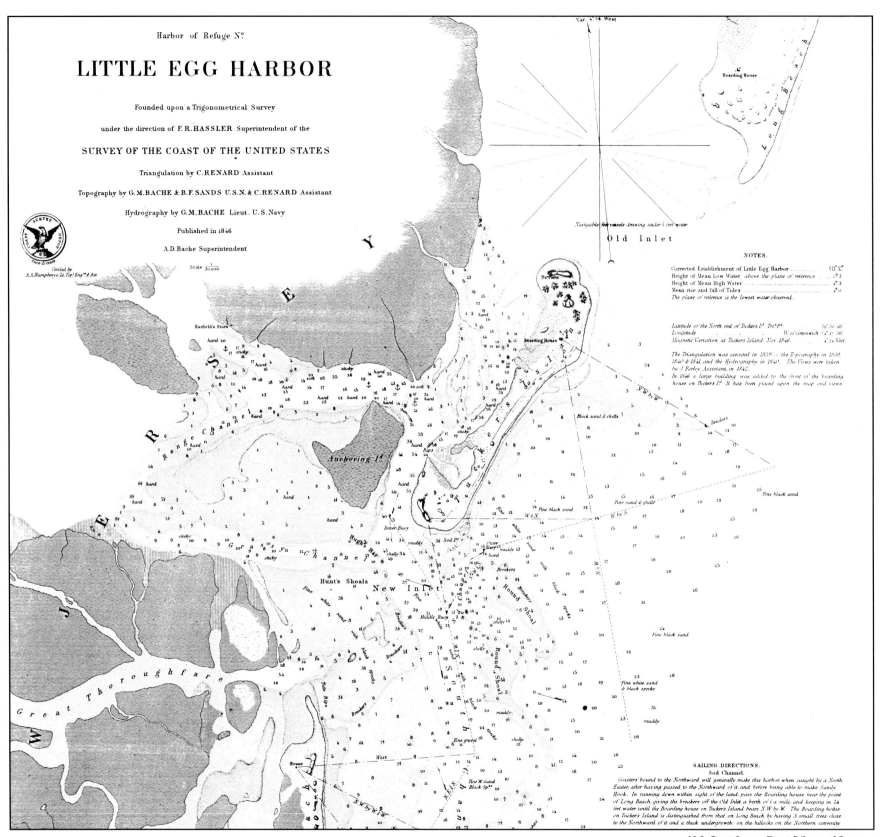

This series of maps shows the natural changes that have occurred over a period of about a century to Tucker's Island, off the southern end of Long Beach Island. In 1846, above, Tucker's was a separate island. By the turn of the century the growing southern tip of Long Beach Island surrounded Tucker's and attached to it (facing page). The following pages show a disappearing island that was home to a lighthouse (which washed into the sea in 1927), a small community, and a Coast Guard station (abandoned in the late 1930s). In the 1990s the island is resurfacing, an enduring example of the tenuous nature of barrier islands.

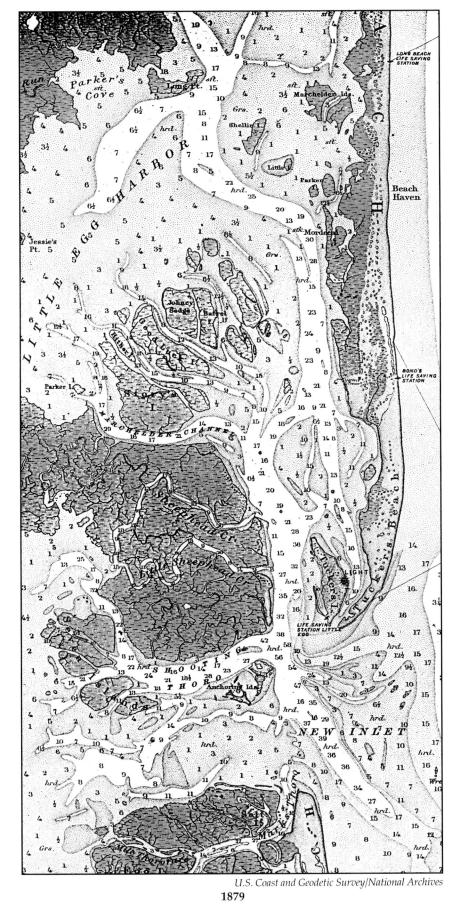

**1879**

**January 1921**

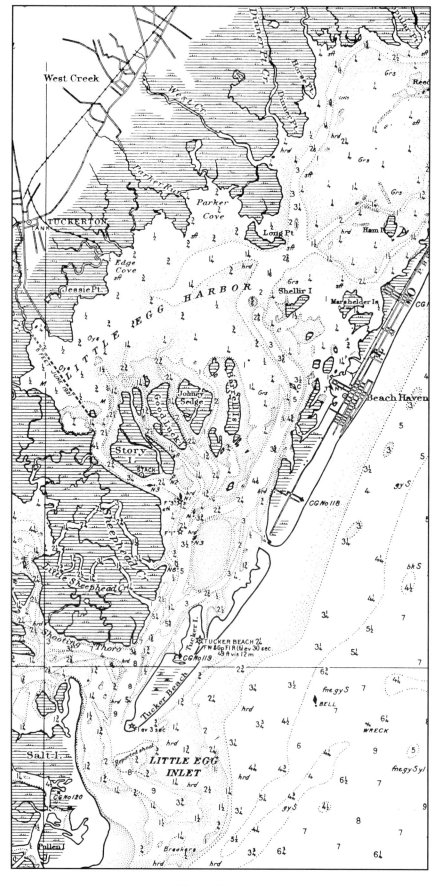

**November 1921**

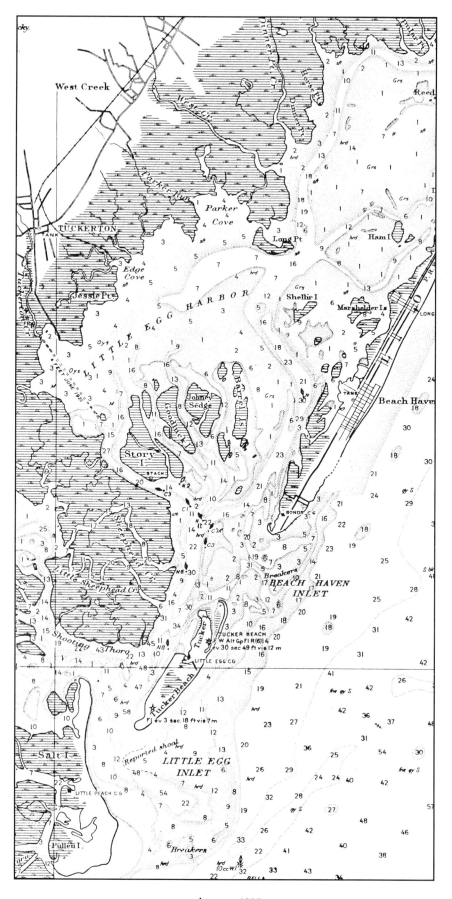

**August 1925**

**April 1935**

*U.S. Coast and Geodetic Survey/Library of Congress (all)*
**October 1954**

The *Cape May County Gazette* agreed:

> Seashore towns must not "follow the ocean" when the high water line recedes. Wildwood has resisted this temptation with the result that there was a minimum of damage there last week. Respecting King Neptune, Wildwood realizes that what comes in may go out. The fact that its beach is miraculously wider than it used to be doesn't mean that someday the ocean won't reclaim part of the strand.

The editorials ring like echoes down a long-disused corridor. Cries for beach protection had been made after the 1933 hurricane, sounded again after the 1944 hurricane, and again after every beach-eating storm or unusually high tide since. In 1957, a federal agency called the U.S. Beach Erosion Board devised a plan "for protecting every mile of New Jersey's richest natural resource," according to *New Jersey County Government*.

The "threshold of opportunity" that was finally crossed was not the one Secretary Udall had in mind. Despite all the official intentions and officious editorials, private property proved to be stronger than the prospect of catastrophes to come. The result is best described in these memoirs by Andrew Johnson, whose family's summers in Holgate came to an end in 1944:

> The house met a violent end, falling victim to the quality of its own construction. It was so tightly built that it exploded when the barometric pressure dropped. The house disappeared in a flash. The sea which flowed over the island carried off the remains, and every trace of human habitation that had accumulated around it.
>
> The meadows and dunes met a less dramatic but equally devastating end. They are now covered with rows of houses whose driveways, patios and white-pebbled yards have completely obliterated all aspects of the place's natural beauty.

Johnson does not begrudge the new residents "the enjoyment of their seaside retreats" and concedes that more people being able to enjoy the shore "is undeniably a good turn of events." Yet, he adds:

> I do regret, however, that the democratization of our coast has been achieved through its desecration. The mindless destruction of the dunes and meadows and marshes of our barrier islands could have been avoided.

> The builders of these new houses fought hard to overcome the meadows and thickets that coexisted so peacefully with the old houses. But they have tamed only the land-bound wilderness, not the sea, and their time as conquerors will be short. These matchbox houses have no more chance of standing up to the power of the sea than the *Rosa rugosa* that preceded them had of resisting the cold metal of the bulldozer.

Increased building has meant the cost of storms has risen, too. In 1954 the total storm damage nationally was estimated at $1 billion. The next year it was over $2 billion. The single northeaster of 1962 — the Great Atlantic Storm — cost $500 million and took thirty-two lives. It destroyed 1,147 buildings, inflicted major damage on 3,689 others and minor damage on 47,490 more. But the much-shorter and less-severe storm of December 1992, which swept no houses out to sea, destroyed no bridges, ripped up no roads, still managed to rack up a cost of $500 million.

*Andy Bolton/The* SandPaper

A new high was reached in 1992 when Hurricane Andrew tore $30 billion out of the Florida landscape.

One limit to building on the shore had always been the better-than-even chance of losing the place to the weather. A good indication of the risk was the fact that insurance companies refused to issue flood coverage. In 1968, the federal government took it on. Its intent was to provide protection for those who lived and worked there. Its effect was to subsidize costly vacation homes, as if to say, as one critic commented, "Go ahead, build on the shore; we've got you covered."

In the ten years before federal flood insurance, there were 186 deaths and $2.2 billion in damage from shore storms. In the following ten years, those figures jumped to 411 deaths and $4.7 billion.

Leland Stanford remembers one man who asked his advice about a particular site in Cape May:

> So I said, "Well, where you're talking about, in 1962 the tides swept right across. In fact, they deposited so much sand it was three days before we could get the road clear." I told him I had no idea how deep the water was because nobody in his right mind would even have been there during that period. I said, "Forget about it, find another location. It's a vulnerable spot."
>
> "Oh," he said, "I don't know. It's been ten years since anything's hit the coast. So I'll build there and I'll insure it and what isn't covered by insurance I'll take as a tax write-off."
>
> I looked at him and I said, "Well, that's fine for you, but what about the poor jerk that has to come out to your house, maybe to rescue your wife and kids, and risks his life in the process?" Well, he stormed out of my office like I was the worst guy in the world.

Farrell thinks a block of ruin should have been preserved after the 1962 storm, "just to remind people." Most present beach dwellers have come to the shore since 1980.

> Where there was a single-story bungalow there now stands a $1.2 million Taj Mahal. These things were put up by the hundreds. And if they can't sit on their Jacuzzi deck and look out over the water they feel they're not getting their money's worth.

"We have not always been this foolish," said Pilkey, "or this greedy." He cited the Outer Banks, where people used to build on long, narrow lots so that owners could move houses back as the shoreline ate up the beach in front of them. One house had been moved three times in the last hundred years, two hundred feet at a time, and was due again.

❝ ❝ ❝

By 1990, the population of the 364 counties that border the coastlines of the Atlantic Ocean and the Gulf of Mexico had reached 70 million. In New Jersey alone, insured property values rose by 75 percent in the 1980s, to almost $90 billion.

"Picture a 250-ton locomotive screaming toward your home... That's the force of a hurricane." So says a pamphlet the Federal Emergency Management Agency prepared, trying to educate new shore dwellers that seaside weather and inland weather are different weathers. The coastal zone of New Jersey is considered a distinct climatic area, described by David Ludlum as "a province wherein a battle between oceanic and continental influences is constantly in progress. The outstanding weather specialty of this region is the coastal storm."

A National Weather Service survey revealed that four out of five of those living in threatened areas have no experience with hurricanes. With all its modern devices, from hurricane-tracking satellites to hurricane-hunting planes, a 24-hour hurricane forecast has a margin of error of one hundred miles. Leland Stanford gives the odds of evacuating the barrier beaches of New Jersey in that time as "nil, maybe less."

A flood plain study of Cape May County shows that a storm tide of fifteen feet would cover half of it. The 1962 storm involved fourteen out of the county's sixteen municipal districts and affected all but 5,000 of its 52,000 citizens. Stanford adds that approximately half the public campsites in the state are located there. "During the season there can be 30,000 to 40,000 people there, all in light vehicles, all trying to get out at once." He also noted the increasing number of older people who are retiring in shore communities.

Or, in the words of coastal geologist Nicholas Coch, "People need to understand that inevitably there will be a very serious tragedy."

No hurricane has come ashore here since 1821. But a hurricane that passes offshore has a long fetch over which to send storm-driven water, allowing waves to build to towering proportions, and it can deliver these during its entire passage, accompanied by ripping winds and lashing rains. The damage from this kind of sustained pummeling can be greater than that from the more localized effect of a beaching monster, as the hurricane of 1944 demonstrated. Euphemistically referred to as "brush-bys" by meteorologists, these have occurred on an average of once every three years in this century. Frequency varies considerably, though, with the mid-1950s seeing three a year for two years in a row, and the 1980s only one, Hurricane Gloria.

Prime season is September, when most of the summer people have traded beach chairs for desk chairs, tans for pallors, and concerns about the weather to concerns about the market. But August is second on the hurricane hit parade. An old folk rhyme has it, "June, too soon; July, stand by; August, the worst; September, remember; October, all over" — easy to remember, perhaps, but about as useful as rubbing toads on warts. The season can start in June and last through November.

Like a living thing, a hurricane tends to follow its food supply, which is warm water, one reason why so many tropical storms hug the Gulf Stream as they travel north. But some meteorologists, noting the steady warming of all the waters of the North Atlantic in the last few years, are predicting an increasing incidence in hurricanes as well.

Those who keep track of such things say the end of the long drought in the African Sahel also helps create conditions suited to the spawning and growth of major hurricanes. Dr. William Gray of Colorado State University has found that the number of hurricanes rises as the amount of rainfall in West Africa rises. Ten times the number of intense storms ruffled the East Coast of the United States from 1943 to 1969, a time of higher-than-normal rainfall in Africa, than from 1970 to 1987, the height of the drought there. As a further insight to the complicated intermeshing of the earth's climates, he also found that the fluctuations coincided with the waxing and waning of El Niño, the mysterious, warm current in the Pacific that comes and goes like a willful teenager, and with about as much notice.

What a direct hit can mean is perhaps best illustrated in this Weather Service report of the damage inflicted by Hurricane Hazel in 1954 on North Carolina's Outer Banks:

*All traces of civilization on that portion of the waterfront were practically annihilated. Grass-covered dunes some 10 to 20 feet high behind which beach homes had been built in a continuous line five miles long simply disappeared, dunes, houses, and all. Of the 357 buildings, 352 were totally destroyed and the other five damaged.*

Some people welcome the idea. "A good leveler would get everybody's attention," said Andy Frank, who had moved from Seaside Park because it was getting "congestipated" to the Outer Banks, only to be followed by thousands of others fleeing, it would seem, one another. Apparently the enjoyment of being "by the seaside, by the beautiful sea," is diminished in direct proportion to the number of others humming the same song. Controversies over building by the sea have been complicated by fights over access to it, and those with beachfront homes consider part-time vacationers as interlopers and day-trippers as immigrants from some alien land.

Pilkey sees no loss in the loss of their sandcastles.

*Compared with the number of people who want to use the beach, the number who have built right next to it is very small, so the hell with them. There's not much good you can say about these people. They build in a very dangerous place, they are responsible for the big expenditure of flood insurance, they make access to the beach difficult for the public, and they make the beach ugly.*

He is sure that the next "big one" will result in hard regulations against what he calls the New Jerseyization of the coast. He agrees with the Chinese philosopher Lao-Tse: "The world is ruled by letting things take their course. It cannot be ruled by interfering. If you try to change it you will ruin it. If you try to hold it you will lose it." But he is not optimistic.

*A state would have to be tough indeed to compel the captains of American industry, the pillars of local society and the cream of local politics to move their houses, or let them fall into the sea, or outlaw the building of sea walls.*

With the evidence of beach-creep at their feet, however, most oceanfront owners acknowledge the fragility of the shoreline, and of the paradox that in this fragility lies its strength. One longtime resident of the Outer Banks, naturalist Jan DeBlieu, states it bluntly.

*Saying that I want a major hurricane to hit the Outer Banks is, I suppose, grasping at straws. But the environmental pressures, the overdevelopment, have to be reversed, and nothing seems to be working. The ecosystem of these islands can only support the people who were here before modern development, even if it means people like me have to leave.*

In his *Barrier Island Handbook*, Stephen Leatherman insisted:

*Only low-density and low-cost development should be allowed on migrating barrier islands. Only those who understand the risks and accept the inevitable capital losses without compensation should be granted building permits.*

One of the areas South Carolina exempted from its tough rules was a section called, appropriately enough, Folly Beach, which had been all but wiped out by Hurricane Hugo in 1989. Just north of the hurricane's eye, the area had been swept with sustained winds of 138 miles per hour, gusts up to 179 miles per hour, and a storm surge seventeen feet high. Author Bob Shacochis described what he saw there a year later:

*The houses were still shells, the town's streets ramparted with sickeningly tall mounds of rubble. People had been trapped in their houses, their furniture floating around them. Then the houses themselves had come unmoored and floated. Mile after mile, the roadside was leveed with the vestiges of apocalypse; houses piled into splintered cones of bathtubs and toilets, appliances, sofas and chairs and mattresses, carpets and drywall and shingles — everything, the frame and the skin of the low country's former self, all the mundane fixings and furnishings of life, resonating not tragedy as much as the dull hum of pathos.*

But with all their echoes of Armageddon, it is not hurricanes that pose the greatest threat to the shore, nor is it the yearly blitz of northeast storms, even giants like the one in 1962. It is the less spectacular but more constant erosion that nibbles away at the beaches. Leatherman estimates that 80 percent of the coastline is currently undergoing "significant" erosion and warns that if current rates continue, almost everything built on the East Coast beachfront will be threatened by the Atlantic before 2020.

Then there is the maybe-so, maybe-no greenhouse effect. Some scientists predict a rise in global sea level of three to six feet in the next century; others say less, some say more. It has been rising on the average of about one foot per century. A Scandanavian coastal engineer, Per Bruun, calculates that along the East Coast of the United States, the sea will move onto the land 300 to 400 times the distance it rises; even a two-foot rise would mean an incursion of 600 to 800 feet, enough to cover all the barrier beaches on the Jersey shore. Houses on pilings might survive, but access would have to be by long piers or boat.

Few who have studied the situation talk of solutions anymore, just of holding actions. Sea walls and dune walls have been rejected in many areas as too harmful to the beach and too expensive to replace each time the sea takes them out. Wide beaches and wide, more than tall, dunes seem to be the best way to dissipate the energy of storm-driven seas, and replenishment of the beaches the best way to maintain them, as well as the least costly even at $1 million per mile. Studies show that a replenished beach has a maximum life expectancy of ten years, but of course one good storm can reduce that to zero. In the 1920s, one hurricane accounted for half of the beach loss for the entire century in Florida. As an official with the Corps of Engineers said about the $65 million beach replenishment project in Jacksonville, "This project should last indefinitely, providing a major storm doesn't come by."

Groins, the low-level piles of rock the sea can wash over, seem able to maintain some consistency on beaches where they are evenly spaced. There are about 130 down the length of Long Beach Island, set every four blocks or so, and while there is variation from time to time on individual beaches, the sand that moves one way one day can move back the next when the current shifts. Jetties, however, which are built higher than mean high tide, impede this natural flow with consequences that oceanographer Willard Bascom calls "disastrous."

Charles Zaimes, courtesy Betty Panunto

**Governor Richard J. Hughes inspects Ocean City storm damage in 1962.**

Other devices designed to break the force of incoming waves are constantly being tested. One involves massive stands of plastic seaweed — dubbed "astrosurf" — to mimic the great kelp forests which help stabilize the California coast. Another is the placement of artificial reefs fashioned of huge concrete blocks that will, theoretically, cause the waves to spill their energy offshore, creating a kind of lagoon, much the way coral reefs around South Pacific atolls do. There is even a proposal to counter the rise in sea level by storing excess water in existing reservoirs such as the Caspian Sea or the Great Lakes, and building new ones in some of the vast valleys in the Canadian Rockies.

The U.S. Environmental Protection Agency, perhaps overwhelmed at the size of the problem and apparently unimpressed by any of these suggestions, has recommended "abandonment of low-lying areas in an orderly fashion."

All shore communities have evacuation plans. Most islands are limited in access to the mainland, often by a single bridge across several miles of bay and low-lying marsh. In the 1962 storm when Leland Stanford was civil defense coordinator for Cape May County, he realized there were only three roads leading off the peninsula, capable of handling about six hundred cars per hour, "and that's without any tie-ups." Knowing what a major storm could mean if summer crowds were caught in such bottlenecks, he made provisions for what he called "vertical evacuation" — putting people in high-rise structures above the flooding. Another scheme was to turn the Delaware Bay ferries into refuge centers capable of holding six thousand people. He had large signs prepared to indicate the various evacuation routes, and put all civil defense personnel in uniform, whether they were directing traffic or handing out doughnuts: "We found that the public always listened to people in uniform, whether they were firemen or the Salvation Army. If it was a nurse's aide, it was an authority figure. This might or might not be a good thing generally but it sure helps in emergencies."

So thorough were the procedures he put into effect that they were used as a model for civil defense units all over the country.

But when the disasters that breed such plans fade in the summer sunshine, civil defense officials have trouble claiming their portions of municipal, county and state budgets. Another problem is convincing people to get out in time rather than wait and see, or even wait to see. Sea Isle Mayor Vincent Lamanna said after the 1962 storm, "One storm won't chase them out, even a storm like that one." And after Hurricane Connie in 1955, the *Beachcomber* published this sentiment.

> On Long Beach Island, many people listened, read, and hurriedly packed their things and left. Island businessmen lost a huge amount of business. But the real tragedy is that many people missed one of the greatest spectacles that nature has to offer.
>
> The wind blew gusts of fresh, clean air over everything. Waves reached up on the beaches, sweeping away debris and dirt, leaving them sparkling clean and shining with new life. The thunderous waves beat against the rocks sending showers of spray and creating over and over again endless patterns, wonderful to behold and impossible to describe. It was a sight that can't be traded for anything in the world, surely just as much a part of vacation enjoyment as the sun, calm waters and lazy surf. It was something vital, alive, thrilling and awesome all at the same time.

There is no question that a major storm will hit the East Coast again. Nor is that prospect likely to discourage what might turn out to be our lemming-like rush to the sea. After all, there is no question that a major earthquake will hit California, or a major flood inundate the Mississippi delta, yet people still build on fault lines and levees.

A month after the Great Atlantic Storm of 1962, Ocean County planning consultant Eugene Oross told newspapers, "We're a tough breed and we're used to the ocean's quirks." Plans for a revived, revitalized and refinanced shore reported in the *Philadelphia Bulletin* included "hundreds of those delightful lagoon-type houses where you park your boat at your own private dock," a new generating station designed to be convertible from coal to nuclear energy, a $200 million international airport in the pinelands, a bridge across Delaware Bay from Cape May to Lewes, Delaware, and a major East Coast seaport at the mouth of the Mullica River. The airport and seaport were to be connected to New York and Washington by "that fantastic new method of transportation, the Levacar, which Ford says is in the 200 to 500 mile per hour range."

And to conquer that ancient bugaboo — changing weather — that so crimps the resort season, "large removable plastic bubbles would be raised over the beaches for winter play, a proposal that would put Frank Lloyd Wright to shame."

Lao-Tse again: "When men lack a sense of awe, there will be disaster."

# CHAPTER EIGHT

# The Storm That Eats The Jersey Shore

*I have seen tempests, when the scolding winds*
*Have rived the knotty oaks, and I have seen*
*The ambitious ocean swell and rage and foam*
*To be exalted with the threatening clouds....*
— *Shakespeare, "Julius Caesar"*

IT BEGINS IN A FLIGHT OF MOLECULES. Bits of air spiral skyward, carrying water vapor high up to where the air cools and the vapor condenses.

In the Sahel in Africa, just below the Sahara, a farmer stands in his field, shading his eyes against the sun to look at a small collection of clouds forming in the east. He nods and goes back to hacking at the earth under his hoe. It is hard work but the earth yields to him. A few years before it would not. The Sahel had weathered a long drought, almost twenty years. Now it is ending.

Rain pours onto the brick-dry earth. The farmer does not pause in his work. The clouds pass. He turns and watches the small storm move off to the west, to the sea. The sea does not need your water, he thinks. I need it here. The sun leans on him. The ground has already absorbed the rain, but the air feels light. That is good. There will be more rain, he thinks, and returns again to his work.

The farmer is right. He does not know it, but he is working under a long trench in the atmosphere through which pass waves of low pressure. Low pressure brings winds and rain. High pressure brings sunshine and clear skies. The farmer knows nothing of highs and lows. But he knows the feel of the air.

Just off the coast, near the Cape Verde Islands, a lone fisherman eyes the flat sea, looking for his living. A shadow moves beneath the surface. He holds his breath, raises his net, sets his feet firmly against the sides of his small boat. There is a ripple. He casts the net. There is a quick flurry of movement and a small explosion of pent breath. The fish flaps desperately, pulled out of its natural element into a deadly environment of air, air full of oxygen it cannot use. In its futile thrashings, it pumps this useless matter through its gills.

The bits of air disturbed by the movement and the explosion and the struggle jostle one another, pushing for position. It is a small variation of the never-ending dance that distributes their parts of oxygen, nitrogen, argon, neon, carbon dioxide and water vapor with such efficiency that their proportions in a parcel of air at the surface of the sea are the same as that of a parcel sixty-five miles up.

But heavier. A given amount of air at sea level weighs more than the same amount above the clouds. A given amount of water, on the other hand, weighs as much at the bottom of the sea as it does just beneath the surface. This is because air can be compressed; water cannot. A person standing at at the bottom of either ocean bears the weight of all the parcels above him.

The fisherman does not stagger under his burden of air. He may not be aware that he carries it, but it is of no more concern to him than the weight of the sea under his boat. He does not know, either, that the pressure that he bears is not precisely the same as that which a fisherman in the South China Sea carries on his shoulders. Pressure at sea level varies from place to place in the world and from time to time —it's 14.696 pounds per square inch along the East Coast of the United States — but it is enough of a constant to be named One Atmosphere or One G (for gravity). Scientists measure all other pressures by it, from the bottoms of mines to the tops of mountains.

Meteorologists measure pressure in inches of mercury or millibars. In 1643, Evangelista Torricelli invented the barometer, just a few years after Galileo invented the thermometer. They are still the two most basic tools of meteorology. Torricelli discovered that the weight of the atmosphere at sea level was just enough to support a column of water thirty-four feet high. He calculated that the water in the tube would fall by about one foot for every nine hundred feet of elevation.

A glass tube thirty-four feet high would be too unwieldy to haul up and down mountains. Torricelli soon found that a column of mercury about 30 inches high was the equivalent. It is this "glass" that mariners referred to in old sea logs. When the glass was dropping, it meant the atmospheric pressure was not enough to hold the mercury at the 30-inch level. Nobody knew about highs and lows then, only that a falling glass meant bad weather. Dropping below 29 inches was serious; anything below 28 inches was serious trouble. Sea level pressure on the East Coast is 29.92 inches, varying a bit with temperature.

§ § §

The fisherman boats his catch, glances at the scuds of cloud to the east and decides to head home. Slants of warm rain wet him; the sun steams him dry; the clouds dissolve, reform, move west. This he can see. What he cannot see are the molecules of air he disturbed, rolling in the sun, growing warmer. The warmth excites them to greater activity. They push at one another. Small winds snatch at them, catch them up, spill them out again. Larger winds entrain them for longer runs.

Molecules of air, rising and sinking and spinning and sliding, that's what makes weather, storms, hurricanes. Air rises when it is heated, sinks when it cools, spins because the Earth spins, slides because not every point on Earth spins at the same speed.

The heated air of the tropics rises steadily. Since warm air is less dense than cold, it creates a band of low pressure, called the equatorial trough. As it flows toward the poles, it cools. Some of it descends at about forty degrees north latitude, creating a band of high pressure. (Forty degrees north latitude slices New Jersey at about Toms River.) Most of it continues on to the polar regions where it drops down, gains weight, and begins its journey back to the tropics.

All this rising and falling air creates disequilibrium in the atmosphere. Since the forces of nature always move toward equilibrium, air shifts about to equalize things, flowing from areas of high pressure to areas of low pressure. This constant circulation of hot air rising up from the middle of the Earth and of cold air flowing down from the poles to take its place is one of the determining factors in the planet's weather.

But obviously not the only one, else we would have only winds flowing north high above Earth and south at its surface. (These wind directions would be reversed, of course, in the southern hemisphere.) That leaves a lot of winds unaccounted for.

Winds are movements of air relative to the Earth, but the rotation of the Earth puts a spin on things. A person on the equator is moving through space at about 1,000 miles per hour. (The circumference of the Earth is about 24,000 miles and any point on it makes a complete revolution every 24 hours.) At the north pole, however, the spin velocity is zero. (At Toms River, it's about 770 miles per hour.) Since air has weight, the spinning Earth drags it along, so air moving at 1,000 miles per hour as it rises from the equator is going to meet air moving a lot more slowly as it heads north. The result is something like merging traffic on the turnpike: Some speed up, some slow down, and there are inevitable collisions.

There's another result of Earth's rotation, called the Coriolis effect for the man who first figured it out. From the equator, a stone heaved toward the North Pole would not land due north but northeast because Earth's velocity changes with latitude. While the stone was moving eastward at 1,000 miles an hour, the earth under it — say Toms River if you've got a good arm — was only moving east at 770 miles an hour, so it wouldn't have

caught up with the stone yet; the stone would land east of Toms River. A stone hurled from the North Pole, however, would land to the west, again because of differing velocities. That's what happens to the winds, too: Winds coming up from the tropics or down from the arctic tend to veer to the right.

There are other things that complicate the movement of winds and thus, weather. One is the uneven distribution of land masses and open seas. Most of the land on Earth is north of the equator, most of the water south. Land and water absorb and release heat at different rates, more slowly for water in both transfers, which is why land near water is cooler in the summer and warmer in the winter.

Land also contains various features that influence the temperature and deflect winds — such as cities and forests and mountains. The sea's varying temperatures have an effect on air, too, and the sea contributes by far the majority of water vapor in the air. Mountains often regulate how much of that gets dumped as precipitation, and where; so do deserts.

Moisture is a major factor in determining weather. The amount of moisture a given piece of air can hold depends on its temperature and pressure. Warm air can hold more moisture than cold air; dense air more than lighter air. Relative humidity is the ratio of how much moisture the air does hold to how much it could hold at that temperature and pressure. A relative humidity of 25 percent means a given parcel of air is holding only one-quarter of the amount it could be holding. As the temperature or the pressure falls, the relative humidity increases until the air cannot hold the moisture, which condenses to form clouds. The point of temperature and pressure where this occurs is the dew point.

As moisture condenses, it releases the heat that had kept it in a gaseous state. This heat helps lift the air molecules higher into even cooler altitudes where more water vapor condenses. Eventually, these droplets combine into drops heavy enough to be pulled down by gravity.

Falling raindrops can evaporate again into water vapor, a phenomenon called vertigo. Radar registers precipitation, but an observer sees only a large cloud, its base clearly visible. Hanging from it like a ragged veil blown sideways by the wind is a dark mass not quite reaching the ground. It's rain, evanescing in midfall.

§ § §

A tanker laden with crude from the Mideast's oil fields makes its way across the Atlantic on a heading for Dry Tortugas at the end of the Florida Keys. The captain sees a squall ahead, like a gray broom sweeping the surface of the sea. As the rain spatters his decks, he notes a slight drop in barometric pressure registering on his "glass" — still called that, although the glass tubes of mercury were long ago replaced by aneroid barometers that work by the pressure of the air squeezing a sensitive bellows. Around him, other squalls dimple the surface of the sea.

The tanker is following a route taken by almost every sailing ship since the days of Columbus, the route of the trade winds. These blow out of the northeast in a band between ten degrees and twenty degrees above the equator. The trades got their name not from the commerce that followed this path from the Old World to the New but from a Middle English word meaning "path."

The path became, in fact, a highway, because the trades are the steadiest and most reliable of all the winds that fan the face of the Earth. They are the product of two weather makers, a midlatitude high pressure system and the Coriolis effect. The Bermuda high stretches from its namesake all the way across to the Azores. Winds move around its rim in a clockwise direction. The Coriolis effect helps low-level winds blow westward on their way to the equator. Over open water of fairly uniform temperature, with little to deflect them, they could be counted on to move a sailing ship at a predictable pace and direction.

These are the northeast trades, labeled, as all winds are, for the direction they come from. Below the equator, the trades blow from the southeast. These two trades run into each other above the equator, an encounter that might be imagined to create a zone of violent meteorological conflict — colliding winds, tossing waters, confused currents.

In fact, this area is the doldrums, a band of listless air known to becalm sailing ships for days, even weeks. In scientific terms it's called the Intertropical Convergence Zone, which shifts north and south during the year but in the summer lies at about ten degrees north latitude, just along the equatorial trough. As the trade winds near the equator, they warm and rise, thus avoiding a head-on crash but creating an unstable environment full of random encounters with uncertain outcomes. Winds blow now from this quarter, now from that. Storms form and dissolve and re-form. Sailors have always hated the doldrums for their unpredictability.

It is here that swirls of air and whiffs of cloud become hurricane seedlings.

❛ ❛ ❛

A satellite positioned over the Atlantic registers the parade of cotton balls moving eastward through the equatorial trough. A seedling that maintains its grouping of clouds for forty-eight hours gets a number and becomes a tropical disturbance. Most will dissipate. Of the hundred or so that form between June and November, an average of twenty-four will become tropical depressions. Eight will become tropical storms. Four will become hurricanes. At the National Hurricane Center in Miami, meteorologists watch the progression and wonder, which?

Among them is #89, the bunch of clouds that spilled some of its cargo on the farmer in the Sahel, that sent the fisherman heading home, that loosed squalls around the oil tanker. Like dancers auditioning for a spot in the show, each cluster struts its stuff. Any one of them, the meteorologists know, could play the part. All hold warm, moist air. All move across the sea at about 10 to 15 miles per hour, slow enough to gather up moisture but fast enough to keep from dissipating. It usually takes about a week to make the passage from Africa.

Some clouds grow quickly, rearing magnificent heads high, carrying warm, moist air thirty thousand feet into the sky, becoming thunderstorms. But the meteorologists, like Broadway impresarios, are looking for that something extra, that spin that distinguishes a star from a chorus girl.

A storm runs on the heat energy released by condensing water vapor as it rises. Air cools at the rate of 4.5 degrees Fahrenheit per one thousand feet of rise. In a mature hurricane, the temperature can go from 80 degrees at the bottom to minus 125 degrees at the top. This severe difference also adds to the updraft because heat, following another of nature's urges toward equilibrium, always flows from the warmer body to the colder.

To stay alive a storm must maintain this cycle. That means not only more air flowing in at the bottom but also a high altitude wind to carry off the exiting air at the top; otherwise the warm air collects and forms an inversion that plugs the chimney. Meteorologists call this "filling the storm," but in fact, the moist air in the column drains out the sides and the storm collapses.

At this stage, #89 is still a haphazard collection of forces operating somewhat at random. To advance to the next stage, it's got to get organized. The organizing factor is spin — winds spiraling toward the center to mold the elements into a coherent structure, each part strengthening the other until the storm needs only a stretch of warm water to sustain it, and often not even that. But first it needs spin.

To acquire that spin requires stepping out of the marching order and climbing up the latitude ladder into the ballroom of the trades, where partners are waiting to give it a whirl. The westward-moving trades impart a counter-clockwise spin. Once it gets spinning faster than 39 miles per hour it officially becomes a tropical storm, and a tropical storm really gets the attention of the watchers in Miami. A tropical storm is just one step below a hurricane.

But making the grade is tough. Given the insistent dynamics that develop almost daily during the season, hurricane watchers have always wondered why more storms don't become hurricanes. Nature prefers equilibrium — its famous balance — and a good hurricane is a good way of redistributing energy. Yet the translation rate is only 4 percent. It seems that nature has other ways of keeping its balance, less dramatic, less violent but suitable. Hurricanes serve nature the way privateers served Queen Elizabeth I: They get the job done but they're not quite respectable. And, of course, they can't be trusted.

As if to impose some sort of discipline, nature has a policeman on station, the Bermuda high. Reaching eight miles up into the atmosphere, it is big and strong and stable and it keeps the equatorial trough in place and the parade of easterly waves generally neat and even. But even this huge system wavers now and then, and when it lets down its guard, hurricanes happen.

Number 89, carrying the molecules of air it collected over Africa, the moisture it has sucked up from the Atlantic, the warmth it has steadily absorbed, breaks through the barrier. Its spinning winds surpass 39 miles per hour and continue to build. Warm, moisture-laden air rises higher and higher, shedding rain as it goes, releasing more heat which pumps it even higher. The chimney is open at the top and the cold air spills out to be carried off by high winds, eventually to sink again to the surface of the sea where it warms, gathers moisture and re-enters the cycle.

The meteorologists study their data, wish they had more. The Bermuda high appears to have taken a walk around the corner. The storm has a clear course over a warm sea with a following wind. They pin a name on it — Gabriel, the seventh of the season — and put out an advisory.

Gabriel, out of Africa, over the Atlantic, collects its winds. It is a moving force that towers fifty thousand feet, but a tower that can still be toppled. Below it, the seas churn and give up more moisture. As it grows, it expands outward. Bands of clouds spiral inward, framing successive areas of updraft. There are now several feeding channels that support the storm like flying buttresses. And somewhere out there over the equatorial Atlantic it opens its eye. Its winds cross the 74 mile-per-hour mark and it becomes Hurricane Gabriel.

The eye can be seen clearly by the satellite, seen and tracked. In Miami, the computers digest data, plot several possibilities. The watchers assess each, ponder the most likely, ask for more data.

Gabriel moves toward the Caribbean like a living thing smelling food. The dabs of islands seem hopelessly inadequate to keep it from the vast basin of warm water beyond. The storm now reaches up sixty thousand feet, to the threshold of the stratosphere. The last bits of moisture in the rising air freeze into ice crystals to form thin cirrus clouds that spread out from the top of the eye. To the satellite, the storm resembles a miniature galaxy.

The winds lash the sea until it spits back foam and spray. It is as if the storm is impatient with the simple process of evaporation alone. Gabriel has become a monster that feels its power, seeks more —insatiable, unstoppable.

But it is a monster without a mind. It cannot go where it pleases. Despite the personification that naming it has engendered, it has no will of its own. It must go where it is steered. The steering influence can be a high wind that pulls it along by its top. There are rivers of air in the atmosphere, and a storm can get caught in one like a jellyfish in the Gulf Stream. There can be a shift in pressure to form a gradient, like a slope down which it can slide.

But there is an immediate concern that absorbs the attention of the watchers in the ready room. Gabriel has paused. Still six hundred miles from landfall, it sits, turning in place. It is eerily like a field marshal surveying the battleground, deciding where to deploy, to advance, to strike. It seems to be in no hurry, for nothing on the shores that stretch before it is capable of opposing it.

And then it moves, or is moved, no longer toward the Caribbean but northward, toward Florida. The National Hurricane Center issues a hurricane alert.

Florida is used to hurricanes. Shutters go up, water is bottled, flashlight batteries are checked, canned food laid in. People gather up patio furniture and bicycles and toys. Cars are gassed up to be ready for evacuation. Radios are tuned to catch news reports.

Gabriel is a celebrity.

The storm turns again and begins to head back out to sea, a phenomenon familiar to hurricane plotters. They even have a name for it — recurvature. As a hurricane approaches the East Coast, complications arise. After sailing unopposed across open water for several days, riding a groove, feeding on the warm sea like a cow grazing in a meadow, it suddenly faces an environment not nearly as hospitable, one pocked with high and low pressures, shot through with conflicting winds, subject to wide runs of temperature.

A great current of air, part of the jet stream, can catch a hurricane and carry it off to the northeast, over cooler waters where it cannot feed. Its center, no longer a chimney, fills with clouds which empty themselves back into the sea. The hurricane becomes a scattering of squalls. Momentum keeps the winds going for a while until they subside, again, into jostling molecules of air. Its effects continue a bit longer, the great waves it raised evening out into swells that troop toward shore to delight surfers and dismay property owners. Photographers shrug, and everybody in Florida takes down the shutters and puts the flashlights back in their drawers and wonders what to do with all that canned hash.

But Gabriel is not so quickly done. In its pause it has gained greater strength. New walls of clouds spread out like buttresses. It now spans five hundred miles. Winds circle in howls. The updraft almost sucks the water out of the sea. The hurricane absorbs other storms that had followed along down the equatorial trough, taking them into itself, adding their power to its own.

A hurricane hunter plane goes up, a handful of men whose protection against this giant is a thin skin of aluminum and their skills. To gather the data Miami needs, they must go in low, from seven hundred to one hundred feet. A strong enough downdraft could knock the plane into the sea before it had time to recover, but the air deflecting off the swells acts as a cushion and the plane bounces up again.

This trip is what they call a "hairy hop." A hurricane has been estimated to produce the energy of four hundred 20-megaton hydrogen bombs in one day. If converted to electric power, it could supply all the United States' needs for six months — and it releases this amount every day for a week. Spread evenly over its realm, such fury might be manageable. But although the hurricane occupies about one million cubic miles of the atmosphere, most of its energy is compacted in the twisting bands the plane must cross.

Instruments record sustained winds of 157 miles per hour, with gusts up to 200. Winds that speed have taken a sheet of newspaper and driven it through the trunk of a tree. Passing through the fringes of the storm, the plane absorbs downdrafts that push it toward the reaching waves below, then whooshing updrafts that threaten to tumble it. The greatest danger is the torrential rain which crowds visibility up against the windows and falls on the plane like cannonballs.

And the plane bursts through the eye wall, the innermost circle of clouds, and into the eye itself, a startlingly inappropriate, awesomely beautiful, eerily serene realm of peace and grandeur.

There are scientific explanations for the eye of a hurricane. Tornadoes also have hollow cores. So does the twisting water draining out of a bathtub. Wind or water must achieve a certain speed relative to its size and weight. Once it is spinning, the Coriolis effect, which draws it tighter, is countered by centrifugal force, which wants to pull it apart. But scientific explanations seem irrelevant to those who have been inside a hurricane's eye.

It has been likened to a cathedral with sacred carvings on the walls, stately balconies protruding, even pipe organs reaching to the clear, blue dome above. It has been described as a great cavern, the shapes of the circling clouds like some fantastic formations of rock, but not solid — shifting, merging one into another, changing shape and even color. One hurricane hunter compared it to the center of a big city, a Times Square in the air where cloud towers loom, each reflecting a different piece of the sky. Another described it as being in the middle of Yankee Stadium during the World Series.

The men in the plane gaze out on this vast central room in the house of Gabriel, their duties stalled in the spectacle of it, a palace in the heavens. "You almost expected to see the gods come through the walls," one says later. But it is they who go through the walls again, into the relentless churn of the storm, taking its temperature, its pressure, recording its winds, measuring its rains, drawing its profile and sending the data back to the lab where they will be analyzed to determine Gabriel's health and, so far as is possible, its prognosis, as well as add to the knowledge that gives, each time, more insight into the anatomy of hurricanes.

As they leave the arms of Gabriel and head back to the base, they are unaware of forces that the watchers in Miami view with growing alarm. Nature's policeman, the Bermuda high, has returned to its post above the mid-Atlantic. But its partner, the high that patrols North America, has shifted in its turn, moving east. Now, lying between the two highs, is a narrow road that runs right up the East Coast, and Gabriel, like a blind man groping for a way out of a maze, has found it.

Most hurricanes never make it to the North American continent. They curve away, as if repelled by the wrong end of a meteorological magnet, and vent their awesome force instead on the forgiving sea. When they do make landfall, the havoc they wreak is like nothing else on Earth. Earthquakes have vastly more impact in the few seconds or minute or two they rend the ground. Tornadoes pack more fury into their single punches. But nothing comes close to matching a hurricane for power, because it feeds as it goes, getting larger and stronger, and the larger and stronger it gets the more it can feed. It is like some science fiction created to scare children, or an ancient myth about the beast that could not be slain.

Hurricanes do die, of course. Somewhat like dinosaurs, they die when their environment changes. They cannot adapt. They die when the sea beneath them gets too cold to supply them with moisture. They die when a massive inversion puts a lid on the chimney called the eye. They die over land, eventually. Friction slows them, mountains wound them, cold air unbalances them; they fill up or fall over or just fizzle out. These are natural causes, as seemingly random as those which form them. But there is nothing anyone has been able to do so far that can even slow down a hurricane or change its course, much less stop one.

Attempts have been made. In 1947, researchers decided to try seeding the eye wall with silver iodide crystals to make the clouds dump their rain at sea, break up, allow the heat to seep out, dissipate. Results were promising but inconclusive. In one of the experiments, the storm turned and inundated the coast of Georgia. The seeding was blamed, and the experiments were halted.

There have been proposals to anchor icebergs in the path of the storms coming across the ocean, to pump colder water up from the depths, or to spread a monomolecular layer of hexadecanol, a kind of oil, on the sea's surface to reduce evaporation. That last, it was estimated, would take a fleet of thirty C-130 cargo planes flying almost wing to wing. It was once seriously suggested that atomic bombs be detonated within the eye, but the chances of one such explosion — or a dozen — having any effect on a force equal to hundreds of thousands of such explosions seemed too remote to risk scattering radioactive fallout through a million cubic miles of atmosphere.

All that can be done, so far, is watch, and warn.

Alerts go out. All along the coast, the familiar double red-and-black flags go up. People secure their boats, take in trash cans, welcome mats, dog houses. But only a few board up their windows or store water or put matches in waterproof containers or get out the candles or do the other things the National Weather Service advises. With the exception of North Carolina's Outer Banks and, of course, Florida, few parts of the eastern seaboard have ever experienced a direct hit by a hurricane; most hurricanes pass offshore, sending a lot of wind and rain and high waves, usually no more than from a good northeaster and often a good deal less.

So when one does turn off the sea track and comes onto land in Georgia or Virginia or New Jersey, it's more like a meteor landing than a storm. There is little preparation and the area is devastated.

Gabriel is on the move, heading north.

The watchers in Miami tap their computers. Will it stay offshore? Where's the jet stream? Is it low enough to blow Gabriel's head off? How strong is the North American high? Any spot there Gabriel could breech? Is there a polar trough nearby that might cut into it? Can the prevailing westerlies wrestle it out to sea?

The hurricane has built up great momentum. No one in Miami dares sleep or could if they tried. Realization of the ground-pounding power of a hurricane charges them with the task of examining any clue about the storm's direction. The impact of some hurricanes when they hit the East Coast has been detected on seismographs in California.

These are dedicated people, working, they know, on only a fraction of the knowledge they need to give adequate and timely warning. Sound the alarm too early and be responsible for widespread evacuation, incalculable costs in time and work lost as well as the massive expenses of emergency preparation that may all prove unnecessary? Sound it too late and wonder, later, what deaths might have been avoided? They scan readouts, wish they had another satellite, send out another plane, try out scenarios on their computers, and keep their fingers close to the alarm buttons.

But it is also wildly exhilarating, the way a war can be, but without any agonizing questions of morality. The forces of nature still stir feelings that link humans directly, through some deep channel in the collective subconscious, to ancient ancestors, those who walked naked under skies that were the playing fields of the gods, who crouched beneath trees and behind rocks and inside caves as the air about them shrieked and the seas were flung about and the forests torn apart. There is still an awe that a hurricane taps like nothing else can. Churches report an upsurge in both attendance and membership after a hurricane passes.

Gabriel has picked up forward speed, from 15 to 22 miles per hour. The computers digest this, explore the ramifications among their 1s and 0s. A hurricane moving too quickly over its feedlot cannot pick up enough moisture to sustain itself. Without the rising columns of energy, it will collapse. Some become extratropical cyclones that expand, move up the coast at 50 miles an hour and deliver enough of a punch to take out Connecticut, but it's a dying blow. Whatever is pushing Gabriel is not pushing hard enough to accelerate it to obliteration; it moves with the deliberate pace of a Greek tragedy.

The central, whirling bands of wind have puckered the pliant ocean into hills that mimic the solid earth beyond. But these hills are insubstantial creations that at once seek equilibrium again, cresting, flattening, joining until they escape the winds and smooth out into long swells that run before the hurricane, heralds to announce its coming. They travel at half the speed of the winds that generated them. They will come ashore at the rate of four to six per minute, half the rate of normal waves but with far greater amplitude and force.

The satellite routinely flashes its images back to Miami. On-screen, the swirls of cirrus clouds the hurricane flings out in long, spiraling spumes could be some sort of decoration the planet is wearing, perhaps to mark its rank or to signal a change in the seasons. To the watchers, it means that Gabriel is still thriving. Successive pictures show it climbing the latitudes like a ratcheted wheel.

The hurricane has sent its outer winds against the shores of Florida, Georgia and South Carolina, its rains as far inland as the foothills of the Appalachians, its storm swells across the Outer Banks of North Carolina. But it has remained out to sea by 170 miles. The elbow of the Outer Banks, Cape Hatteras, lies directly in its path. There is no doubt: if it stays on track it will cross these thin islands —called barrier beaches in what must seem like hopeless braggadocio for a line of sand dunes which change dimensions from year to year even without hurricanes.

The alarm is sounded; a hurricane watch is announced, naming the time and place.

Some of these islands are connected to the mainland by only one bridge, some only by ferry. Some are not connected to the mainland at all but to another island. But vacation season is over, and the thousands who spread themselves over these sands in the summer have receded like the tide, leaving only the resorts' caretakers and a few late fishermen.

And a strew of cottages, thousands and thousands that weren't here the last time a hurricane scraped these islands clean. Some top the dunes, some perch on stilts, some nestle by the one road that runs the length of the archipelago. All look about as substantial as the castles children make out of Popsicle sticks on the summer beaches.

To come ashore is usually death for a hurricane, though in its death throes it deals death in turn. Over land it can find no food. The irregular landscape tears at it. It must use precious energy to overcome the friction of trees and buildings and hills. The bottom of the tower slows down, the top outruns it, and it stumbles, like a runner who has just gone from cinders to sand. Some regain their feet, in a sense, no longer hurricanes but powerful storms still that manage to keep their flailing limbs together enough for a run across country. Here any ambient low can help them. Some have even crossed the Appalachians and gone as far as Chicago, home of winds, and out onto the Great Lakes. Others have traveled along the flanks of the mountains and crossed into Canada to expire in the cold north woods, releasing their molecules, finally, far from the desert where they were recruited.

As if sensing such a fate, Gabriel does not come ashore, but swerves around Hatteras. It turns on the candy-striped lighthouse as if it were a swivel. It knocks down some of the more impudently situated beach houses, washes out a bridge, lifts a few boats from their moorings to deposit them on the highway. Then it straightens again for the farther north.

It must struggle a bit now to conserve strength. It is in danger of being overextended. It can no longer find support 250 miles out from its center. It contracts, pulls its arms in tighter. Its eye narrows. Several of its concentric bands merge.

It passes Virginia. It seems to consider an excursion into the Chesapeake for a moment, but the move is more like the feint of a running back. Miami sends warnings ahead, then pulls them back. Virginia and Maryland escape with moderate flooding in the low-lying tidewater country.

Gabriel approaches the mouth of Delaware Bay.

New Jersey does not intrude into its bordering seas the way North Carolina does. Cape May is a pendulous point, not a protuberant one like Cape Hatteras. The 127 miles from Cape May to Sandy Hook form an almost straight line with no prominent features to disturb it. Even Delaware Bay is an untroubled bowl, free of the jagged edges that make the nearby Chesapeake look as if it had been ripped into place.

To the north, New York's Long Island and the whole thrust of New England stick out, staking a claim to realms of land once smothered under weights of ice. But New Jersey lies flat and featureless, its gentle shores and nurturing wetlands and comfortable pine woods belying the fact that it is the most densely populated state in the Union. There are no huge cities here, but many small ones; no vast industries but a lot of industry; no mega-agribusiness or giga-fishing fleets, but plenty of farming and fishing.

The Jersey coast has not weathered a hurricane landfall since 1821, when its population consisted largely of sea gulls. Now homes crowd the dunes, jetties interrupt the beaches, bulkheads hem the bays. The islands no longer serve as barriers. There were a few people — those whose attention spans bridged decades, even centuries — who predicted dire dooms, booming tragedies, unimaginable consequences. They were ignored.

But hurricanes are not nature's retribution. Nature only distributes. Perhaps it is an undetected step backward by the North American high, or an unforeseen slip of the jet stream, or an unexpected dip in the polar trough. The watchers in Miami stare at their screens in fascination, frustration and with a touch of fatalism as Gabriel turns eastward. They have done all they can; they hope someone has been paying attention. The Federal Emergency Management Administration estimates it will take ten to twelve hours to evacuate the Jersey shore. Local authorities say it could be twice that.

As Gabriel moves toward the coast, the barometer at the Cape May Coast Guard Station turns steadily down. The weather recorders click and print. It is the day of the autumn equinox, also the spring tide when the sun lines up with the moon to reinforce its gravitational pull. Hurricane flags have been flying since Gabriel rounded Hatteras. The radio scans continuously for distress calls. Helicopters and cutters are on the ready line. Crews nap in full gear.

The station commander has only recently come here. His previous post was Key West. On his first tour of Delaware Bay, he was surprised at how many small boats there were. Somehow he had never pictured New Jersey as a state of sailors. Now he wondered how many of them had taken the storm warnings seriously. Did New Jersey ever get hurricanes? He recalled the one at Cedar Key in 1950 when the winds blew at 125 miles per hour for three days.

The storm surge hits, the advance guard, a high tide on a spring tide on a wind-driven swell that rises thirty feet, crest to trough, and moves with a force that can only be measured in tons. It tops the breakwater at the entrance to Delaware Bay and moves upriver. There is no traffic on the Delaware; the pilots' association had closed the river in time to clear all ships en route. The rest are moored at the refineries in Marcus Hook or anchored in the roads between Philadelphia and Camden. The surge, when it gets to them, snaps hawsers, bends anchors, cripples piers and moves one empty tanker to the middle of Petty's Island. It fills marshlands, floods farms, invades city streets.

On the seaside, along the shores of Cape May, Atlantic, Ocean and Monmouth counties, the surge feels the sea floor rise beneath it. The bottom of its roll slows but the top speeds on, tumbling over in froth and foam, riding up the slope, a line of liquid locomotives steaming over the beaches. The surge presses into the narrow inlets — Cold Spring, Hereford, Townsend's, Corson's, Great Egg Harbor, Absecon, Brigantine, Little Egg, Beach Haven, Barnegat — and creates some new ones at Harvey Cedars, Seaside Heights, South Mantoloking.

It makes Sandy Hook an island again. It pushes into the Tuckahoe River and the Mullica, buckling bridges, taking out bulkheads, undercutting roads, turning gullies into streams, streams into rivers roiling and lethal with rushing debris. It isolates every community on the shore, gives Pleasantville an ocean view, floats Lucy the Elephant from her home in Margate, returns Mystic Island to the bay, turns Toms River into Toms Marsh, Spring Lake into Spring Sea, Avon-by-the Sea into Avon-in-the Sea and Sea Bright into a memory. It gives the Shrewsbury and Navesink rivers direct outlets to the ocean, as it was in the long past. There is no part of the shore above water.

The barometer is still dropping, two inches now in two hours. The commander whistles. The hurricane flags, what's left of them, are ribbons in the wind. The anemometer is at its peak of 100 knots, 115 miles per hour. He'll know if it gets to 150 miles per hour; that's when those things tend to blow apart. He doesn't bother checking the rain gauges; the rain is coming in horizontally. He watches, rapt, as the windows bend inward.

And then comes Gabriel. Behind the storm surge, which seemed to have dumped all of the sea onto the land, comes more water, rain screaming like bullets impacted in winds now 186 miles per hour. Those who had been evacuated strain at radios in high school gyms and church auditoriums and hope they have fled far enough inland. Those who had pooh-poohed the warnings, defied the police, derided packing neighbors, know suddenly that they have never known power. There is no lesson like that borne on a 186 miles-per-hour wind — or perhaps higher. Gabriel has torn the cups from every anemometer on the coast. One is set spinning so rapidly it is found later to have fused from the heat that the friction generated.

A wind of 70 or 80 miles per hour can wrench signs from their posts, pull down dangling traffic signals, pull up shingles and scatter them like leaves. At 90 miles per hour, wires are unstrung, trees are flung to the ground, shutters are pulled off windows. Sustained winds over 100 miles per hour can roll trucks over, lift boats, move houses. At 120, a wind can loft concrete slabs, suck plate glass out of storefronts, knock down brick walls, flatten clipped grass on a golf green, pry up whole roofs, bend metal utility poles and tear up railway tracks. It also makes noises that witnesses have compared to jet engines, freight trains, rock slides and Niagara Falls.

Waves wash over the islands and into the bays behind them. The nuclear power plant at Oyster Creek shuts down because the coolant pipes have no outflow. Swells ride the high tide through the new inlets, scouring them out and depositing the sand in the Intracoastal Waterway. Rising waters jack up docks. Layers of salt are laid over acres of pineland.

The rains are beyond tropical; they are biblical. It is impossible to imagine forty days and forty nights of this. The winds are in stampede. In Cape May, the Victorian gingerbread that has so delighted generations of vacationers becomes shrapnel. In Wildwood, the Ferris wheel turns like a spinning wheel until the careening gondolas unbalance it and it shatters under strains it was never designed to handle. Stone Harbor is separated from Avalon. Sea Isle City loses the sturdy old drawbridge that was its only link to the mainland.

The century-old Deauville Inn at Strathmere, one of the last of the old-time, good-time hotels, veteran of storms and wars and Prohibition, amateur drunks and summer dances, pops its beams and gives up its seasoned timbers. The ocean in Ocean City, long denied access to the land beyond the sea wall, shrugs off the boardwalk above it and breaches the wall in twenty places.

The towns on Long Beach Island hunker behind their groins and jetties the way boys playing soldier crouch behind clumps of dune grass, as if they will provide protection. Put in to stabilize the ever-shifting sands, the rock structures prove not only useless but insignificant. Later, cranes will collect the four-ton boulders, deposited in places where dunes had been leveled to provide houses with a view of the sea. Now the view is unbroken. But the houses are gone.

Island Beach, the only stretch of barrier island not paved over, built up or bulkheaded, still in the state it was during the 1938 hurricane and the 1821 and the 1769 and how many unnoted ones before, absorbs Gabriel's fury with indifference. Nests of gulls and ospreys and piping plovers are torn apart, bayberry and holly and beach plum shredded, bluefish and fluke nurseries in the shallows of its bayside ravaged. But all these will come back. On the rest of the Jersey shore, the havoc will be reckoned in dollars. The huge increases in the amount of storm damages over the years is due to the huge amount of building that has taken place since the late forties. On Island Beach the fury is as real, but no different than it was a hundred years ago, or a thousand.

At Seaside Heights, the overhead cable cars fall to the sand early on, as if knowing they are goners and anxious to get it over with. The piers are more stubborn. The waves top them to get at the roller coasters first, stripping away underpinnings that never expected the weight on them to come sideways. The wind pries out the loose timbers and hurls them at the boardwalk until it splinters. With the surf full of debris, each swell and backwash attacks the pier pilings with a thousand weapons, until they, too, fall, adding their materials to the arsenal.

Alone on the Jersey shore, Atlantic City seems able to take on Gabriel. Under colored lights that create a glow visible twenty miles out to sea are no summer cottages, matchstick boardwalks or fishing shanties but sturdy buildings, ranked cliffs of steel and concrete firmly set.

The city sits on an island no different than the other flat sand bars that line the coast, backed by the same configuration of bay and wetland. But the men who reared the gambling palaces were no gamblers. Atlantic City had already withstood hurricanes that reduced other beach towns to splinters. Here the shore does not drop away abruptly fifty feet out but slopes slowly and gently. The lack of crashing waves has made it a favorite family resort for a century. At low tide a child can walk out to the end of the Steel Pier. The long, graded slope levels the storm surge until, by the time it reaches the beach, it is reduced to a swift but flat tide.

The rains splatter against the city's facades and run down and flood streets and seep here and there into a casino but have no real effect. The winds twist their way around angles that cut their impact, screaming, yanking planks from the wide boardwalk, stripping away tubes of neon but unable to maintain any consistency in this maze of baffles. In some places the man-made canyons boost gusts to 195 miles per hour and stop signs are hairpinned double. But mostly Gabriel can only clog the streets with the rubble it picks up from the backside of town.

The open marshes and sedge islands and shallow bays that make up the various wildlife refuges and sanctuaries for some twelve miles above Brigantine fill with water from the sea and from the sky until they are one, great, seething basin. The ever-shifting Beach Haven Inlet at the southern end of Long Beach Island no longer moves from this channel to that; it is now all channel. Long Beach Island itself is a string of short beach islands. And finally, after standing against storms and currents and the patient tides for over a century, Barnegat Lighthouse follows its predecessors into the green-demon sea as the sand beneath it turns to mush.

Above Seaside, the crowded coastal communities are swept away like quarters in a boardwalk game; the players lose. Mantoloking, Metedeconk, Manasquan — the Indian names might remind newcomers of old rules: The Indians used to strike their tents and retire deep into the woods when a storm was coming. Now Gabriel strikes all the tents.

The coast towns further north, being on the mainland, are spared the rise of bay waters at their backs, but it hardly seems to matter. Resorts set up by God-loving, God-fearing people writhe and groan under the impact of God's nature. At Asbury Park the derelict boardwalk gives up almost gladly, a glorious death after years of humiliating neglect and debilitation. The old casino, though, solidly made if shoddily maintained, almost resignedly remains in place. The elegant, Italianate houses of Deal, once walled off to the outside world, find their walls as fragile as were the mighty walls of Rome under the waves of marauding Huns.

Up to the Gateway National Recreation Area storms Gabriel, mockingly, as if it needed a gateway. Words that will be used to describe it later — smashing, shattering, devastating, devouring, ravaging, savage, astounding, appalling — are the best people can do, knowing they must all be taken together and then, somehow, intensified, magnified, heightened, broadened to convey any of the great-gulp emotions of awe and fear, wonder and terror, excitement and desperation this display of simple complex power engendered.

As Gabriel comes over the coast, it reveals its most wondrous aspect — its eye. In an instant there is no wind, no rain, no noise. The seas still act as if this is the end of the world, waters course through unfamiliar channels seeking outlets, seeking levels, but above them reigns an almost religious calm.

People react with the gratitude and wariness of freed slaves. The air seems unnaturally light. The moon, full and white as a bride, gives the churning waters an unreal look, familiar but not quite, like a negative image where the blacks and whites are reversed — the dark sea is silver and the foaming waves are black.

Most know that the air feels light because the barometric pressure is low, and that the fullness of the moon is one cause of the high waters, and that the waters themselves still run before winds that will be worse than those that went before. Winds circle through a hurricane in a counterclockwise direction. This means that as the storm itself moves north, the winds in its eastern quadrants are stronger than those in the west.

Gabriel howls. Its leading rim is already rubbing against the land. Perhaps sensing its own end, it seems to decide to go out strong rather than try to conserve its strength and drizzle away in gasping gusts and exhausted drenches. Whatever is left loose along the shore is swept and sliced away, and whatever is not yet loose is battered into rubble. Later, pictures of the whole coast will show a dreary sameness of wasted buildings, trees, boats, cars, all nearly indistinguishable in drifts of scrap and windrows of trash and wracks of ruin.

Gabriel lies on the flanks of the Appalachians, winded, wounded, spent, and dying. Its core has been pierced with cold, its access to fuel denied, its low filled in. Its buttressing bands have been torn apart. The winds that powered it reach out in all directions but find no direction. Its rains drain from the dissolving clouds in cascades that melt landscapes in one last act of transformation.

Finally the westerlies, the prevailing winds that usually convey weather systems across the continent, herd off the remaining clouds. The morning sun lights a quiet coast much different than the one on which it set.

In Miami, the weather watchers check their instruments, rub their eyes, scan the satellite feed. Along the equatorial trough other puffs and swirls march, one behind the other, like elephants in some celestial circus. The hurricane season has two months to go.

Before he ends his shift, one meteorologist makes a note: in the eastern Pacific the warm current known as El Niño seems to be stalled along the equator, allowing the submerged colder waters that flow up from the Antarctic to rise all along the western coast of South America.

The last time this happened there was drought in the Sahel.

*The story of Gabriel is fiction ... so far.*

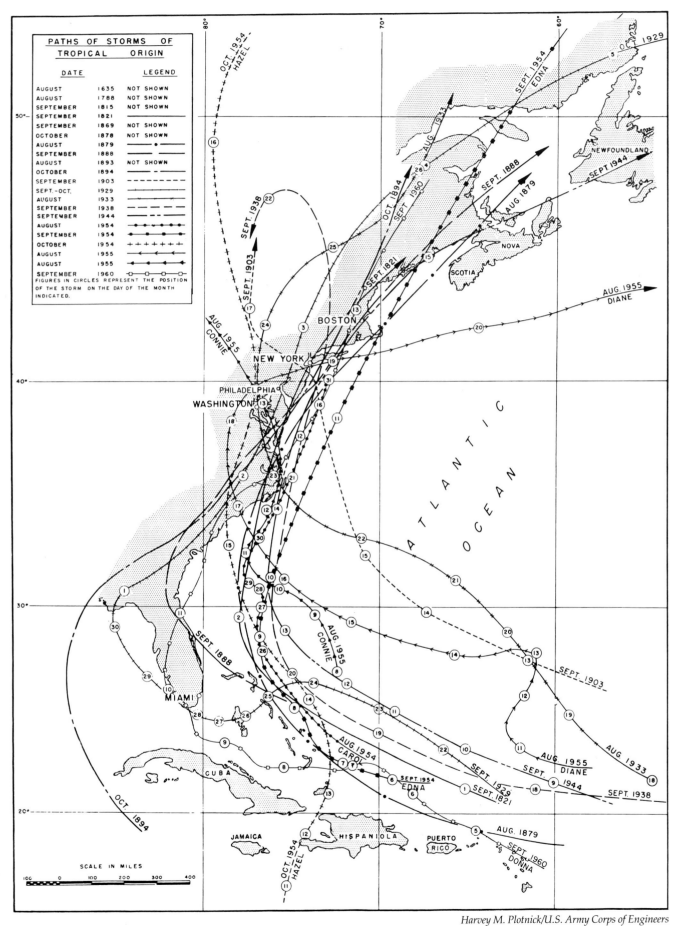

An alignment of the sun and moon, called syzygy, exerts a strong gravitational pull on the seas, and combines with a coastal storm to bring high tides and heavy surf January 2, 1987.

# Epilogue

*What fates impose, that men must needs abide;*
*It boots not to resist both wind and tide.*
— Shakespeare, "Henry IV"

THERE WILL BE MORE HURRICANES. They talk of the hundred-year storm as if it were some mythical monster that rises from the deep, like the dragons of yore that emerged from their caves every so often, breathing fire and clawing up the landscape. It will level dunes and houses, wipe the shore clean, reshape the coast and give every doomsayer his ultimate satisfaction: "I told you so." Some forecast a five-hundred-year storm that will wreak destruction just this side of Armageddon, a cataclysmic blast that swallows whole islands and relocates the Jersey shore on the far side of the Delaware River.

There will be more hurricanes. Nothing we have tried so far shows any promise, or even possibility, of halting, destroying or altering the paths of these tropical monsters. And these are storms that we can spot, measure, track, invade. What of the capricious combinations of cyclones and anticyclones, weather fronts and high altitude jet streams that suddenly surprise us with elements run amok — breezes become edged weapons, rains turned into lashes out of cloud towers seven miles high, the sea a mass of moving hills, each a battering ram with a thousand tons of force? Or the spent hurricane that can tag onto the tail end of an autumn low and, without any of the sound effects, back up the tides and flood the flat plains that comprise most of the eastern seaboard in ways that echo Noah and prefigure the dreaded greenhouse effect?

There will be more hurricanes. But the idea doesn't seem to bother most people. We swing between scientific certitude — that we can handle it — and blind luck —that it won't get me — a triumph of the human spirit, faith, hope and stubbornness ... or bone-simple stupidity.

There will be more hurricanes. And among them, a big one. Nobody knows when. People will die, damage will be in the billions, the damaged will cry for assistance, officials will call for action, editorials will preach, people will be torn between environmental and developmental urges and arguments.

It is, after all, a futile debate. Of course there will be more hurricanes. But few people will abandon the beaches and more will come. Let them have their I-told-you-sos. We nod, agree, tsk-tsk our own foolishness, and look for a still-affordable place. It isn't that we don't know the risk but that we have made that knowledge a part of our decision. All life is a risk; there's no argument there, so let the reward be worth the risk. The sea is the last great wilderness on earth.

There's something satisfyingly primitive about stripping off all but modesty's clothes to let the sun paint patterns on your skin, the sea tingle your pores. There's something reassuringly childish about running across acres of sand, poking through shell shards for a piece of original architecture. There's something basically spiritual about just gazing at a horizon behind which you know lie only other horizons, and wondering what might yet be out there, hiding in the depths of the sea, ready to crawl ashore for its turn.

It is unquestionably comforting, too, to have at hand those parts of civilization which wash down the sunsets with chilled wine and which address those of the senses that respond to the stimulation of fresh clams and flounder broiled in butter and the kind of ice cream you only think you remember from your youth because they didn't make it that good then.

Then there are those permanent midways by the sea, the boardwalks with their silly games and whoopee rides and the cheap souvenirs you end up treasuring just because they came from there.

Has anybody ever had a bad summer at the shore?

Some of those who knew the shore when it was "unspoiled" — meaning by others, not themselves, of course — bemoan and bewail the commercialization, the democratization, the liberalization that sharing it with everybody else entails.

There are empty, open beaches left in the world — the east coast of Malaysia, parts of the Pacific coast of Chile, certain islands in the Indian Ocean and the South Atlantic. But half the population of the United States now lives within fifty miles of a coast, and 40 million people are only a tankful of gas from the Jersey shore. Most of those who live at the shore depend on the visitors for their livelihood. Others would like to see them all barred. Failing that, many do rather hope for "the big one," the one that separates the purist from the tourists and the haves from the wants, for, sadly, the price of real estate has gone up so that those who "found" it originally are now losing it.

There will be more hurricanes — and, with the increased build-up, more damage. But with the new building methods there will be far less damage per board foot, and with the new forecasting tools, far fewer lost lives. There will also be more northeasters, flood tides, burying blizzards, towering, glowering thunderstorms, peltings of hail, blitzes of lightning. In between such blasting and blustering there will be subtle shifts in ocean currents, perhaps a cooling of the polar regions that will start the ancient glaciers shuffling their feet again, perhaps a global warming that will bring the surf lapping up to the foothills of the Appalachians. There may be displacements of stratospheric layers that allow radiation to leak through, shifts of the jet stream, fluctuations in the combustion of the sun, nature moving to its own beat quite indifferent to which of its children may benefit, which may suffer, and taking no more notice of any who oppose it than the tides took of King Canute, or of the sea wall at Sea Bright. The sea will not cease its assault. Sea walls and man-made dunes may repel it part of the time from part of the shore, but they cannot forever deny it the real estate it claims.

Perhaps one day that will change. Perhaps one day we will be able to contain the sea, order the tides, control the weather. Perhaps one day we can bend the winds to our bidding and send the rain to where it is needed and reserve the snow for Christmas Eve or, conversely, rear great domes over our heads, making our own weather within to our own liking.

For now, the only workable strategy seems one of cooperation, not only with nature but with one another. There must be access, there must be rules, there must be common sense and common concerns. There must, in short, be reason.

For there will be more storms.

**The Atlantic City Boardwalk, September 14, 1944**

*U.S. Weather Bureau/National Archives*

# Record Storm Tide Heights 1911-1992

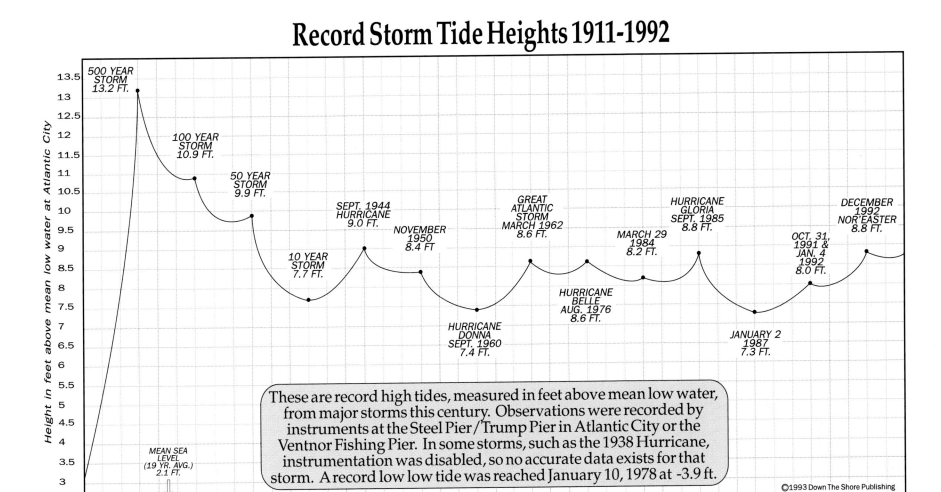

Height in feet above mean low water at Atlantic City

**500 YEAR STORM 13.2 FT.**

**100 YEAR STORM 10.9 FT.**

**50 YEAR STORM 9.9 FT.**

**10 YEAR STORM 7.7 FT.**

**SEPT. 1944 HURRICANE 9.0 FT.**

**NOVEMBER 1950 8.4 FT**

**GREAT ATLANTIC STORM MARCH 1962 8.6 FT.**

**HURRICANE DONNA SEPT. 1960 7.4 FT.**

**HURRICANE BELLE AUG. 1976 8.6 FT.**

**MARCH 29 1984 8.2 FT.**

**HURRICANE GLORIA SEPT. 1985 8.8 FT.**

**JANUARY 2 1987 7.3 FT.**

**OCT. 31, 1991 & JAN. 4 1992 8.0 FT.**

**DECEMBER 1992 NOR'EASTER 8.8 FT.**

**MEAN SEA LEVEL (19 YR. AVG.) 2.1 FT.**

MEAN LOW WATER 0.0 FT.

These are record high tides, measured in feet above mean low water, from major storms this century. Observations were recorded by instruments at the Steel Pier/Trump Pier in Atlantic City or the Ventnor Fishing Pier. In some storms, such as the 1938 Hurricane, instrumentation was disabled, so no accurate data exists for that storm. A record low low tide was reached January 10, 1978 at -3.9 ft.

©1993 Down The Shore Publishing

Based on tabulations compiled by Martin Ross, Disaster Preparedness Meteorologist, National Weather Service, from National Ocean Service, NOAA, and U.S. Coast and Geodetic Survey data ....Data for the 500, 100, 50 and 10 year storms are based on FEMA flood insurance studies for New Jersey.

# Hurricanes Within 125 Statute Miles of Atlantic City — 1893 to 1991

*Tracks of Storms — Facing Page*

| Date of Storm[1] | Storm Name[2] | At Closest Point of Approach | | |
| | | Maximum Wind (mph)[3] | Range (Miles) | Bearing (Degrees) | Forward Speed (mph) |
|---|---|---|---|---|---|
| June 17, 1893 | Unnamed | 77 | 108 | 147 | 16 |
| August 24, 1893 | Unnamed | 98 | 31 | 83 | 24 |
| August 29, 1893 | Unnamed | 81 | 100 | 323 | 29 |
| September 30, 1894 | Unnamed | 79 | 77 | 125 | 8 |
| October 10, 1894 | Unnamed | 74 | 23 | 148 | 27 |
| September 16, 1903 | Unnamed | 84 | 13 | 30 | 20 |
| September 15, 1904 | Unnamed | 75 | 22 | 40 | 54 |
| September 17, 1933 | Unnamed | 85 | 109 | 136 | 11 |
| September 8, 1934 | Unnamed | 77 | 50 | 117 | 23 |
| September 18, 1936 | Unnamed | 98 | 51 | 127 | 26 |
| September 21, 1938 | Unnamed | 101 | 83 | 71 | 51 |
| September 14, 1944 | Unnamed | 96 | 47 | 122 | 35 |
| August 14, 1953 | Barbara | 86 | 85 | 132 | 19 |
| August 31, 1954 | Carol | 98 | 63 | 98 | 35 |
| September 11, 1954 | Edna | 104 | 114 | 119 | 42 |
| August 29, 1958 | Daisy | 126 | 124 | 124 | 29 |
| September 12, 1960 | Donna | 108 | 47 | 112 | 35 |
| September 16, 1967 | Doria | 81 | 113 | 175 | 11 |
| August 10, 1976 | Belle | 98 | 43 | 107 | 26 |
| September 27, 1985 | Gloria | 99 | 26 | 154 | 44 |
| August 18, 1991 | Bob | 115 | 74 | 115 | 32 |

[1] Year, month and date that storm had maximum winds exceeding 74 miles per hour and was closest to Atlantic City.

[2] Storms were not formally named before 1950.

[3] Maximum sustained wind speed near storm center while center was within 125 statute miles of Atlantic City. This is not necessarily the wind recorded at a given site.

*from the New Jersey Hurricane Evacuation Study Technical Data Report (study managed by the Philadelphia District, Army Corps of Engineers for the New Jersey State Police Office of Emergency Management in cooperation with the National Weather Service and the Federal Emergency Management Agency)*

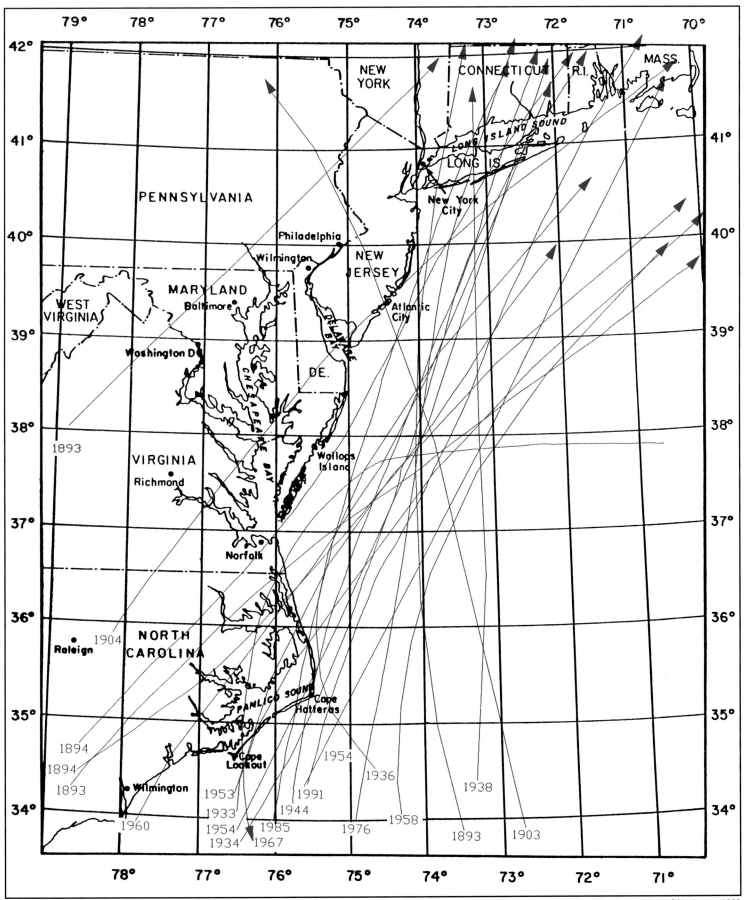

*U.S. Army Corps of Engineers, 1992*

# Hurricane and Storm Data for Atlantic City
## 1933-1962

| Date/Storm Name | Minimum Distance of Center From Atlantic City | Maximum Wind (mph) at Atlantic City | Hours Before (-) or After (+) Time of High Tide |
|---|---|---|---|
| August 1933 | 125 miles (west) | E at 76 | +4.5 |
| November 1935* | NA | NE at 66 | NA |
| September 1936 | 100 miles (east) | NE at 90 | NA |
| September 1938 | 75 miles (east) | W at 72 | +6 |
| September 1944 | 30 miles (east) | NE at 91 (gust) | High tide |
| | | N at 82 (5-minute value) | |
| November 1950* | NA | E at 72 | NA |
| October 1953* | NA | N at 29 | NA |
| November 1953* | NA | NE at 69 (gust) | NA |
| | | NE at 65 (5-minute value) | |
| August 1954 (Carol) | 50 miles (east) | NE at 57 | -3 |
| September 1954 (Edna) | 150 miles (east) | NE at 65 | -2 |
| October 1954 (Hazel) | 125 miles (west) | SE at 66 | High tide |
| | | SE at 80 (gust) | |
| August 1955 (Connie) | 125 miles (west) | S at 65 | High tide |
| August 1955 (Diane) | 65 miles (north) | SW at 49 | NA |
| October 1955 | NA | E at 60 | NA |
| September 1956 (Flossy) | NA | E at 54 | NA |
| September 1960 (Donna) | 80 miles (east) | WNW at 60 | -1 |
| | | WNW at 83 (gust) | |
| March 1962* | NA | E at 44 | NA |
| | | E at 58 (gust) | |

* Not of tropical nature

*U.S. Army Corps of Engineers*

# Bibliography

**BOOKS:**

Allen, Everett S. *A Wind to Shake the World*. Little, Brown, 1976.

Bernard, Jr., Harold W. *Weather Watch*. Walker, 1979.

Brindze, Ruth. *Hurricanes: Monster Storms From the Sea*. Atheneum, 1973.

Gentry, R. Cecil. *Experimental Program to Modify Hurricanes*. World Meteorological Organization, 1974.

Cain, Tim. *Peck's Beach: A Pictorial History of Ocean City, New Jersey*. Down The Shore Publishing, 1988.

Calder, Nigel. *Weather Machine*. Viking, 1975.

Douglas, Marjorie Stoneman. *Hurricane*. Rhinehart, 1958.

Dunn, Gordon E., and Miller, Banner I. *Atlantic Hurricanes*. Louisiana State University Press, 1960.

Helm, Thomas. *Hurricanes — Weather at Its Worst*. Dodd, Mead, 1967.

Herbert, Paul J.; Taylor, Glenn; Case, Robert A. *The Deadliest, Costliest and Most Intense United States Hurricanes of This Century (And Other Frequently Requested Hurricane Facts)*. National Oceanic and Atmospheric Administration (NOAA), 1986.

*Historical Cape May*. Rutgers University Press.

Hoel, Michael L. *Land's Edge, A Natural History of Barrier Beaches from Maine to North Carolina*. Globe Pequot Press, 1986.

Hughes, Patrick. *American Weather Stories*. NOAA, 1976.

Kotsch, Rear Admiral William J. *Weather for the Mariner*. 2d ed. Naval Institute Press, 1977.

Lloyd, John Bailey. *Eighteen Miles of History on Long Beach Island*. Down The Shore Publishing, 1986.
— *Six Miles at Sea: A Pictorial History of Long Beach Island, New Jersey*. Down The Shore Publishing, 1990.

Ludlum, David M. *Early American Hurricanes 1492-1870*. American Meteorological Society, 1963.
— *The New Jersey Weather Book*. Rutgers University Press, 1983.

Massachusetts Geodetic Survey. *Storm Tide, Hurricane of September 1938*. WPA Project, 1939.

Methot, June. *Up and Down the Beach*. Whip Publishing, 1988.

Minsinger, William Elliott. *The 1938 Hurricane*. Blue Hill Observatory, 1988.

Nash, Charles Edgar. *The Lure of Long Beach*. Long Beach Island Board of Trade, 1936.

Neumann, Charles J. *Tropical Cyclones of the North Atlantic Ocean, 1871-1986*. NOAA, 1987.

*Report of the Commissioners to Investigate the Charges Concerning the Wrecks on the Monmouth Coast*. Communicated to the Assembly, Trenton, March 20, 1846.

Snow, Edward Rowe. *Great Gales and Dire Disasters*. Dodd, Mead, 1986.

Somerville, George B. *The Lure of Long Beach, New Jersey*. Down The Shore Publishing, 1987 (Reprint; originally published 1914).

Sugg, Arnold L. *Memorable Hurricanes of the United States Since 1873*. Technical Memorandum, National Weather Service, April 1971.

Tannehill, Ivan R. *Hurricanes*. Princeton University Press, 1938.
— *Hurricanes, Their Nature and History*. Princeton University Press, 1956.
— *The Hurricane Hunters*. Dodd, Mead, 1955.

**ARTICLES:**

Brown, Andrew H. "Men Against the Hurricane." *National Geographic* (1949).

Buckley, William F. "After-storm Thoughts." *National Review* (November 15, 1985).

Clary, M. "Hurricane Gloria — Were We Overwarned?" *Weatherwise* (December 1985).

Colton, F. Barrows. "The Geography of a Hurricane." *National Geographic* (1938).

"Danger From the Tides: Perigee Syzygy." *Newsweek* (January 7, 1974).

Dolan, Robert, and Hayden, Bruce. "Templates of Change: Storm and Shoreline Hazards." *Oceanus - Woods Hole Oceanographic Institute* (1981).

Eliot, John L. "Into the Eye of David." *National Geographic* (September 1980).

"El Nino: Fewer Hurricanes." *Weatherwise* (August 1985).

Engle, Michael. "New Angle on the Weather." *Futurist* (May-June 1986).

Farrar, John. "An Account of the Violent and Destructive Storm of the 23rd of September 1815." *Memoirs of the American Academy of Arts and Sciences* (1821).

Figley, Marion. "Hurricanes Growing More Intense." *Beachcomber* (August 30, 1991).

"Fiftieth." *New Yorker* (September 19, 1988).

Frank, Neil L., and Clark, G.B. "Atlantic Tropical Systems of 1976." *Monthly Weather Review* (May 1977).

Funk, Ben. "Hurricane!" *National Geographic* (September 1980).
— "Swept Away: Danger to Coastal Communities From Hurricanes." *New York Times* (September 18, 1977).

Gentry, R. Cecil. "Disaster From the Tropics." *Natural History* (October 1973).

Gray, W.M. "Strong Association Between West African Rainfall and U.S. Landfall of Intense Hurricanes." *Science* (September 14, 1990).

Halsey, Susan D. "Hurricane A'Comin'!" *New Jersey Outdoors* (May-June 1988).

Herbert, Paul J. "Atlantic Hurricane Season of 1973." *Weatherwise* (February 1974).

Herbert, Paul J., and Taylor, Glenn. "Everything You Always Wanted to Know About Hurricanes." *Weatherwise*.
— "Hurricane Experience Levels of Coastal County Populations - Texas to Maine." *National Weather Service* (July 1975).

Hoppe, J.R. "Atlantic Hurricane Season of 1975." *Weatherwise* (February 1976).

Johnson, Andrew. "When We Took the Dunes for Granted." *New York Times* (August 12, 1990).

Kenny, Nathaniel T. "Our Changing Atlantic Coastline." *National Geographic* (1962).

Kerr, R.A. "Hurricane-Drought Link Bodes Ill for U.S. Coast." *Science* (January 12, 1990).

Kominsky, Karen J. and Halsey, Susan D. "Remembrances of Things to Come." *New Jersey Outdoors* (February 1983).

"Letter From Tuckerton." *New Jersey Mirror* (September 12, 1821).

Lindley, Daniel. "Coastal Flood Insurance." *Oceans* (May-June 1986).

Ludlum, David M. "The Great Hurricane of 1938." *Weatherwise* (August 1988).

MacDougall, G.H. "Flying Into A Hurricane." *Weatherwise* (August 1986).

MacKaye, Milton. "We're Cracking the Secrets of Weather." *Saturday Evening Post* (September 18, 1954).

McCarthy, J. "No Warning on the Beach; Northeast Coast Hurricane of 1938." *Motorboating* (September 1970).

McCarthy, Joe. "Hurricane." *American Heritage* (August 1969).

Monastersky, R. "African Rains Foretell Stronger Hurricanes." *Science News* (September 15, 1990).
— "Winter Storms in the North Atlantic Follow the Solar Cycle." *Science News* (May 14, 1988).

Pelissier, J.M.. "Hurricane Season of 1967." *Weatherwise* (February 1968).

Perdue, L.G. "Hurricane Season of 1970." *Weatherwise* (February 1971).

Pilkey, Orrin, and Evans, Mark. "Rising Seas, Shifting Shores." *Oceans* (January 1982).

Redfield, William C. "Remarks on the Prevailing Storms of the Atlantic Coast of the North American States." *American Journal of Science and the Arts* (July 1831).

Ringle, Ken. "The Gospel According to Pilkey." *Oceans* (April 1987).

"Round-Up on Hurricane Is Now Complete." *Science* (November 1944).

Sawyer, Thomas. "A New Era of Hurricanes." *Yachting* (August 1990).

Shacochis, Bob. "Written in the Big Wind." *Harper's* (September 1991).

Simpson, R.H. "Hurricanes." *Scientific American* (1954).

Simpson, R.H.; Frank, Neil L.; Johnson, H.M. "Atlantic Tropical Disturbances." *Monthly Weather Review* (April 1968).

Steefal, Larraine T. "The Season of Hurricanes." *Coast* (September 1988).

Stewart, John Q. "The Great Atlantic Coast Tides of 5-8 March 1962." *Weatherwise* (June 1962).

Strickland, Richard. "The Way of the Coast." *Oceans* (April 1987).

Sugg, Arnold L., and Perdue, L.G. "Hurricane Season of 1971." *Weatherwise* (February 1970).

Sumner, H.C. "The North Atlantic Hurricane of September 8-16, 1944." *Monthly Weather Review* (September 1944).

Waltzer, Jim. "What If It Hits?" *SandPaper* (September 13, 1991).

Whipple, A.B.C. "Storms the Angry Gods Sent Are New Science's Quarry." *Smithsonian* (September 1982).

## PUBLICATIONS:

*Atlantic Hurricane Frequencies Along the U.S. Coastline.* NOAA, 1971, Simpson, R.H., and Lawrence, Miles B.

*Five High*, U.S. Army Corps of Engineers (August 1963).

*Ocean County Sun*, "The Great March Storm, 1962."

*Life*, "1944 Hurricane" (October 2, 1944).

*Long Beach Island Development Plan* (1963).

*New Jersey County Government* (April 1962).

*The North Atlantic Hurricane of Sept. 14, 1944* (Official Report of Relief Operations of the American National Red Cross), Washington, D.C..

*Saturday Evening Post* (September 1954).

*The Siren*, New Jersey Civil Defense (Spring 1962).

*The Triangle*, New Jersey State Police (October 1944).

*Tropical Cyclones of the North Atlantic Ocean, 1871-1977*, U.S. Department of Commerce, NOAA, National Weather Service, Environmental Data Service.

## NEWSPAPERS:

Asbury Park Press, The Press (Atlantic City), Beachcomber, Beach Haven Times, Camden Courier-Post, Cape May County Gazette, Cape May Star, Long Branch Daily Record, Middletown Courier, Newark News, New York Herald Tribune, New York Times, Ocean County Courier, Ocean County Daily Observer, Ocean City Sentinel-Ledger, Ocean County Sun, Ocean Grove Times, Philadelphia Bulletin, Philadelphia Daily News, Philadelphia Inquirer, SandPaper, Trenton Times: Various issues between 1889 and 1991.

*Directory of New Jersey Newspapers, 1765-1970*, N.J. Historical Commission, Trenton (1977).

Atlantic City Daily Union (September 11, 1869).

Newark Daily Advertiser (August, September 1850).

Pennsylvania Gazette (September 14, 1769).

U.S. Gazette (Philadelphia, September 1, 1806).

## UNPUBLISHED DOCUMENTS:

Harvey Cedars Board of Commissioners, Minutes of meetings, August 19, 1944 to April 21, 1945.

Long Beach Township Commissioners, Minutes of meetings, September 15, 1944 to May 31, 1945.

National Archives, Suitland, Md. Reference Branch: Record group #26 of U.S. Coast Guard; Entry 296, Logs of vessels, stations and depots: United States Coast Guard Lifeboat Station Logs for Atlantic City, Barnegat, Bonds, Brigantine, Cape May Point, Cold Spring, Corson's Inlet, Deal, Hereford Inlet, Long Branch, Loveladies Island, Manasquan, Monmouth Beach, Ocean City, Sandy Hook, Toms River (September, 1944).

U.S. Congress, Congressional Record, Senate, Index to Proceedings and Debates of the 78th Congress, Vol. XC, 1944, page 7831. Appendix to the Congressional Record, 1944, Page A4147.

U.S. Congress, House Document No. 38, 89th Congress, 1st Session. Letter from the Secretary of the Army Transmitting a Letter from the Chief of Engineers, Department of the Army, Dated October 1, 1964, Submitting a Report, Together with Accompanying Papers and Illustrations, on an Interim Hurricane Survey of Atlantic Coast of Southern New Jersey and Delaware.

# Index